MW00614729

Ground Pounder

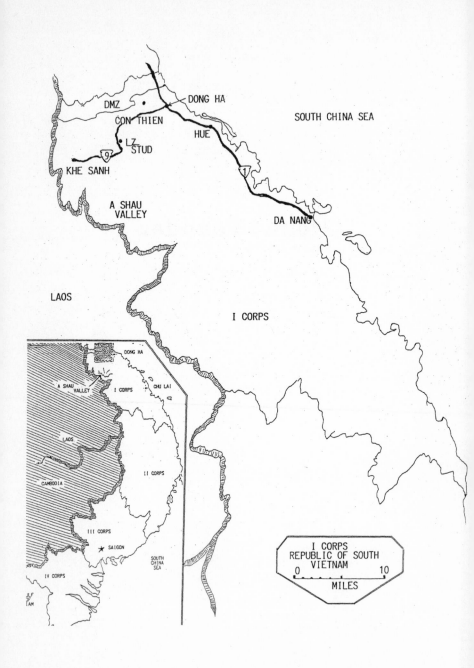

GROUND POUNDER

A MARINE'S JOURNEY
THROUGH SOUTH VIETNAM
1968–1969

GREGORY V. SHORT

Number 6 in the North Texas Military Biography and Memoir Series

University of North Texas Press

Denton, Texas

Permissions:
University of North Texas Press
1155 Union Circle #311336
Denton, TX 76203-5017

ISBN 978-1-57441-452-3

Ground Pounder: A Marine's Journey through South Vietnam, 1968–1969 is Number 6 in the North Texas Military Biography and Memoir Series.

Previously published in 2007 by AuthorHouse under the title *Arc Light: A Marine's Journey through South Vietnam*

Printed in the United States of America.

Dedicated to my brother, David,
and to my son, Jake.
And to the men and women
of America who have bravely served their country

Contents

Photos appear after page 142.

Prologue

For the last couple of years, I have been writing a book about the economic determination of human civilizations and how the people in the past have lived and fought their wars. The idea was to reveal how a society's economy affects every aspect of its culture, including its type of government, social structure, religion, and military establishment. Unfortunately, writing has never been an easy task for me. Growing up in Texas, I couldn't have cared less about getting an education. My early years had been spent playing sports and roaming the surrounding neighborhoods, while trying to avoid my two older brothers. At the time, I couldn't understand why anyone would want to sit around in an old school building and listen to a bunch of boring teachers. I was more interested in hitting a baseball or tackling a ball carrier than I was in learning how to read and write. Needless to say, my days as a student in the public school system weren't my brightest moments. Ironically though, after repeating the ninth grade and then quitting school altogether in order to join the Marine Corps in 1967, I eventually graduated from college and became a history teacher.

Of course, I would have never dreamed of picking up the pen, if it had not been for Kurt Vonnegut. Sometime during the early 1980s, I had an opportunity to hear him speak at a local university. It was an occasion that I would never forget. While sitting just behind the front row, I became completely enthralled by his presentation. It was not only what he said that affected me, but it was also how he said it. In spite of the fact that the majority of the people in the audience didn't seem to appreciate his sharp humor or his forlorn hopes for the future, I understood and related to his every word. Consciously or not, he inspired the writer in me.

Later that evening, as Mr. Vonnegut stood in the glow of the bright stage lights with his curly light-brown hair and bushy mustache, he reminded me of a modern day Mark Twain. Tall, lean, and slightly stooped at the shoulders, he came across as a man who had seen some hard times and experienced the darker side of human nature. Combined with the force of reason and his sincere humanity, he entertained us by speaking of the issues of the day with great wit and conviction. Luckily though, he also took the time to talk to us about writing. Just because a prospective writer doesn't write very well or doesn't have anything earth shattering to say wasn't at all important to him. He believed that it was absolutely essential for a person to share his or her unique experiences with the rest of the human race. In essence, Vonnegut declared, while gazing up to a wall draped with an assortment of national flags, "We need all the help we can get, when it comes to becoming more civilized."

One day, I mailed a few examples of my previous work to my brother David, who happened to live in Austin, Texas. The paper was about how and why we as a species had actually evolved from the early anthropoid apes (*Ardipithecus* or *Australopithecus*) into the modern-day *Homo sapiens-sapiens*. It was my conclusion that between the environmental changes brought about by the prevailing Ice Age and the subsequent changes brought about by our eating habits, our early ancestors were able to evolve into the mighty *Homo ergaster* (*erectus*). During the next two million years, it was this creature and the development of its nomadic economy that would eventually form the very social backbone of what we are today. To my surprise, the only comment my brother could make was, "Nobody can understand that stuff, it's way too deep for the average person." Since he is one of the most astute human beings that I have ever known, I was somewhat disappointed by his reaction.

Then sometime in 1999, he began questioning me about some of my combat experiences. During the last thirty years or so, he has rarely shown any particular interest in my early days, when I served with the United States Marines in Vietnam. While living the life of a college student during that period, he had spent most of his time attending classes, working a variety of odd jobs, and hanging out with his friends. However on this particular occasion, my stories really caught his attention, because he began asking me a lot of questions about what units I had served with and where I had seen action. Almost as an afterthought, he said; "Now, that's fascinating history, why don't you write about your combat experiences? Nobody wants to read about a bunch of damned apes."

Introduction

One of the reasons I had decided to write this book was because as a society and as a nation, I do not believe that we actually learned anything of significance from our Vietnam experience. Even today, our troops can be found patrolling distant lands and guarding foreign outposts without possessing a clear plan or a realistic objective to guide their way. Their lives and the security of this nation have been put in harm's way, all in the name of projecting our political and military influence over areas that we will never fully control and over people that we will never fully understand. By continually relying upon our military establishment as a substitute for politically and economically dealing with our foreign problems, we have failed to achieve any lasting results, except for creating a unified chorus of worldwide anti-Americanism.

If I have learned anything from my experiences in Vietnam, it's that stark military force isn't enough to overcome the brutal acts of international terrorism or the revenge-filled atrocities committed in every civil and religious conflict. By their very nature, these are political acts of desperation, which cannot be subdued by force of arms alone. Thus in telling my story, I am attempting to remind my generation and hopefully warn the future generations of the terribly high price our nation has paid in believing that we can forcibly bend the world into our own corporate image.

To my immense satisfaction, I have discovered that my mind has hidden or rejected many of my most disturbing memories about the war. Much like my adolescent years, I don't really remember the more negative experiences. Life goes on and Mother Nature tends to care for those who are always looking to the future. As any veteran will tell you, combat is a very difficult subject to accurately describe. It's almost impossible to find anyone who agrees as to what actually happened during all of the excitement. Memories fade, rumors become accepted as fact, and one's perceptions tend to change over time. In the past several years, I have read several different accounts of a particular fight in which I happened to have been a participant. Not only did these accounts differ in their content, but also they didn't coincide with what I remembered. It was as if everybody involved had experienced a totally different situation.

Throughout my story, the individual characters I will be describing were very real people. Unfortunately though, I don't really remember a lot of their names. Therefore, I will use a few aliases and nicknames for the sake of convenience. It's not that I didn't care for my fellow comrades-in-arms. It's just that I didn't go out of my way to make any long-lasting friendships while I was in Vietnam. The fear of having to watch a dear friend die in my arms was always present in my mind. Thus I tried to approach the war with a sense of emotional detachment. Over the passage of time, I believe this aloofness was very beneficial to me. After coming home and attempting to adjust to civilian life again, I didn't experience nearly the number of emotional problems that would arise in so many other returning veterans. However, it doesn't mean that I didn't have any difficulties.

During my two tours in Vietnam, I served with four different Marine units within a nineteen-month period. If it hadn't been for my desire to further my education, I would have probably signed on for another tour. Ever since I can remember, I had wanted to join the military, put on a uniform, and participate in a struggle against oppression and tyranny. Totally rejecting my peers' best efforts, I never had any desire to become a professional athlete, a hip dancer, or even a glorified rock star. Instead, I always imagined myself charging the barricades with a sword in one hand and the shield of Pericles in the other. The fact that my father was a career military man probably had a lot to do with it. Regrettably though, my parents couldn't get along, so they divorced each other before I reached my sixth birthday.

But when my brothers and I did get an opportunity to visit our father, he certainly never sat around and regaled us with all of his old war stories. While loyally serving his country for close to thirty years in the United States Air Force, he never saw a shot fired in anger. Yet in all fairness, my father did instill within his children an unswerving devotion towards serving one's country. It was not so much what he said that conveyed this idea, but rather what he represented to us. In his mind, anyone could go out and make a decent living. But what really gives meaning to a person's existence is the satisfaction of serving one's society. Thus for us, the expression of duty, honor, and country extended beyond the realm of military service. In other words, a person doesn't have to go out and become a fighter pilot or an infantryman in order to find this meaning. One can also serve his or her country by working in the fields of law enforcement, fire fighting, medicine, education, or even the media.

One of my most vivid memories of our time together was when my father took me to visit a Civil War battlefield near Fredericksburg, Virginia. Shivering in the cold wind, I was completely humbled by the thought of a group of people actually sacrificing their lives for a common cause. Being young and impressionable, I was overwhelmed with a sense of déjà vu. As we slowly walked down the rows of marbled headstones, I could swear that I heard the old soldiers' voices calling out to me, much like the Sirens had called out to Odysseus. They kept beckoning to me that there was something greater in this world than just making a living, raising a family, and paying taxes. Overall, I found the whole experience to be profoundly unsettling. As I ran my fingers across the rusty old cannons and marveled at the towering statues, it felt as though I had been there with them, sharing their hardships and aspirations.

Ever since that time, I have always admired and stood in awe of those individual servicemen and women who have dedicated their lives to the art of war. It is a profession unlike any other in the world. It requires constant dedication, hard work, and the strength of a bull just to make a go of it. Normally, a person will spend a greater part of his or her life in the military, knowing full well that they might never be called upon to utilize their professional skills. But when their nation does call, they are expected to accept the possibility of having to sacrifice their lives for the government in which they serve. Thus it takes a very special person to lead others into combat. However, it also takes a very special person to follow those leaders into the abyss of destruction.

Up to this point in my life, I had not lived a very planned or productive existence. My brothers and I had been brought up in an extremely hardworking, competitive, and live-for-today Irish environment. Considering that my mother and stepfather weren't the most educated people in the world, my brothers and I had been raised for a life of manual labor and minimum wages. Surprisingly, my oldest brother, Raymond, was the first person in our family who refused to accept this unrewarding fate. During his junior year in high school, he began working forty hours a week sacking groceries in order to save enough money to go to college. Then after he had been accepted into the University of Texas in Austin, he would continue to work in a grocery store while attending his classes.

For several years, Raymond must have worked at least eighty hours a week. His dream was to attend law school and someday to become a lawyer, so that he could go into politics and save the world from itself. Like David, my other older brother, Raymond was a very special human being. He exhibited an uncommon dignity and purpose to everything he tried to accomplish. He wasn't perfect by any stretch of the imagination, but he was resolute and dedicated in his goal of becoming something more than what was expected of him. I remember he used to sit there and look at me, and say, "If you want to shovel manure for the rest of our life, it's okay by me, Greg. But I think you're better than that."

Then in early 1967, our lives were completely turned around by the tragic death of Raymond. While sleeping in his dormitory at the University of Texas, he had been suddenly taken from us in a fire, thus ending his dreams. Not surprisingly, the shock of his death changed everyone in the family. We began to unconsciously drift apart, instead of dealing with each other's pain and sorrow. In a very real sense, I was as much a child of my brothers as I had been of my parents. Without having the opportunity to watch and learn from them, I doubt that I would have ever aspired to continue my education.

On a personal level, I did not volunteer to go to Vietnam as a gung-ho patriot or as someone who wanted to emulate John Wayne. The ambiguous idea of helping the South Vietnamese overcome their northern brothers' attempts to unify their nation had never appealed to me as a good reason to fight and die for my country. Despite our government's best efforts, the political motivation for going to Vietnam was never present in us, as it had been with the veterans in World War II. Even to the most ardent patriots, it would eventually become painfully obvious to them that the Vietnamese determination to liberate their small country from the domination of foreigners was contradictory to our beliefs in self-determination. Thus I went to war for a variety of personal reasons, none of which had anything to do with politics.

My motives for joining the Marine Corps probably had more to do with establishing my manhood and personal identity. Being brought up in the lower end of the economic spectrum, the opportunities for making a good living were rather bleak for those who didn't have any valuable skills. Similar to so many other underprivileged kids, all I wanted was a chance to prove myself and possibly earn the respect of my friends and family. And since I didn't relish the thought of continuously wandering around in a confused adolescent daze, I entered the military in order to find some meaning and direction in my life.

While serving in Vietnam, I was not a war hero in the tradition of Alvin York, Audie Murphy, David Hackworth, or even Chesty Puller. I never led any desperate bayonet charges into a hail of machine-gun fire, pulled grenade pins with my teeth, nor did I ever stand my ground and mow down rows and rows of Viet Cong. On occasion, I did some very brave things. But then sometimes, my survival instinct was much more powerful than my desire to become another casualty of war. When things did get out of control and the situation looked hopeless, I usually did the only rational thing and acted to ensure my survival. It is amazing how one can suddenly disappear into the surrounding terrain.

Like so many other Vietnam veterans returning home, I found the whole experience extremely confusing. Some of our fellow citizens treated us as heroes, while many others viewed us as being baby killers or just plain dopes. Frankly, I didn't see the other veterans or myself as being any of those things. We did what we had to do in Vietnam as a matter of necessity and survival. The unbelievably harsh circumstances were such that unless a person had actually been there, they really didn't have any right to criticize those who had experienced the ordeal. Personally holding the American servicemen and women responsible for the tragedy of Vietnam was completely off base and unfair to those who had served there. It wasn't our fault that in the final analysis we were put in an impossible situation, a situation created by forces beyond our control. Needless to say, the deep emotions that I had felt during my years in the Marine Corps would persist in me for a very long time.

It should be noted that since I have studied the history of warfare for over forty years, I have come to my own conclusions about its meaning, the way it can be successfully conducted, and its impact upon a society. Therefore, the quotations at the beginning of each chapter, which are not otherwise accredited to an author, are my own and a reflection of my acquired knowledge.

I am not writing this memoir as a historical document. It is not my intention to make it such. Instead, I am writing a personal history of the events and times as I had witnessed them. Throughout the book, I will also be sharing some of my own personal opinions and observations of those events. Since I am a veteran of the war and a trained historian, it would be remiss of me to ignore the issues. Overall, some of these viewpoints might be considered controversial. This cannot be helped, because the official version of those events is almost always incomplete and occasionally inaccurate for those seeking to understand our past. As a rule, governments rarely if ever admit their own mistakes to the citizens who had to pay the price for their lack of foresight.

Chapter One

Journey to Ixtlan

"Conflict is an essential part of the evolutionary process.
For better or for worse, it washes away the old and brings
in the new."

In the latter part of January 1968, I found myself on a bus heading towards the Norton Air Force Base located in California. Earlier that morning at Camp Pendleton, the Marine base situated just north of San Diego, we had been briefed as to what was expected of us once we reached the air base. Apparently, the officers and noncoms were somewhat concerned about the possibility of our making a break for it. All day long, they kept hovering around us like a bunch of old mother hens. However, there wasn't any need for them to have worried. After spending eight long weeks in boot camp and another six backbreaking weeks in infantry training, we weren't about to bail out now.

As new and eager U.S. Marines, the overwhelming majority of us were just kids. Although I had turned only eighteen-years-old the previous month, the other guys around me weren't much older. In fact, I would have bet that most of them had never been away from home before. Standing almost five-foot eleven, and weighing close to one-hundred-fifty pounds, I was in the best shape of my life. While possessing trimmed brown hair, deep blue eyes, and a determined chin, I probably could have passed for a Marine poster boy. Of course, I wasn't the most educated guy in the world. But I had been blessed with a lot of common sense. Looking back, the whole experience seemed like a wild adventure. We were young, ignorant, and full of spunk. We believed in our country, our leaders, and in our mission. To our way of thinking, we were invincible. We represented the best, the brightest, and the richest country in the world.

While driving through the sun-baked countryside, one could feel the excitement in the air. We talked and giggled to each other as if we were going on a high school picnic. Once we had enlisted in the Marines, we had heard a lot of war stories about Vietnam, so we weren't completely ignorant about our destination. Yet at the same time, we firmly believed that we were a part of the finest fighting organization that had ever gone to war. We considered ourselves physically fit, motivated, and sincere in our beliefs. Nothing was going to stand in our way.

As the bus weaved its way through the heavy traffic, some of us even began joking around about how we were going to quickly end this thing and go back to our homes and sweethearts. As for myself, I felt the pride swell in my chest. I was finally going to do something with my life besides serving someone else hamburgers and attending those dismal high school classes.

Then right before we reached the air base's front gate, something happened that only added to the carnival-like atmosphere. While we were waiting at a stoplight, someone in our bus yelled out, "Hey, look at the weirdo." Standing across the street on the opposite corner was an old drunken black guy. In spite of the noise from the oncoming traffic, we could hear him yelling at us in a very high feminine voice, "Now, you lovely boys be sure to come back and see me, because Old Papa Joe wants to buy every one of you dudes a cocktail."

The scene wouldn't have been so funny except for the fact that Old Joe was wearing a long green chiffon dress with white cuffs and a pair of high-heeled shoes. Parading around in a yellow wig that was shaped like a beehive, he had a cigar protruding out of his mouth in between what few teeth he had left. If I remember correctly, he was wearing a pair of sunglasses that looked like something from a Lady Gaga collection. Then smeared across his lips and into his ragged beard was a thick line of bright red lipstick. Slapping ourselves on the knees, we just laughed and laughed at this guy as he staggered around the gutter swinging his purse at the passing cars. We had never seen a real-life transvestite before. For the most part, we had come from neighborhoods where the social outcasts weren't permitted to roam the streets. Feeling somewhat uneasy, I couldn't help but wonder why someone would want to act that way. Not understanding the complexity of human nature, I always thought that guys were supposed to be guys and wearing a dress and high-heeled shoes wasn't going change that fact.

Unwittingly for many of us, weird Old Papa Joe was going to be our last vivid memory of America.

Sometime around four o'clock in the morning, our plane landed on the island of Okinawa. Before they loaded us into some more buses, we were marched over in the darkness to an Air Force mess hall for breakfast. In a Marine Corps mess hall, the enlisted men are expected to glide through the line, while the food servers slop this less than palatable food onto our metal platters. There were no special orders taken and no one could ask for seconds. Except for the officers and staff NCOs, we weren't ever fed any real fried eggs, unless it was a special occasion.

As we stood there mesmerized by the sight of sizzling sausages, piles of hot buttered pancakes, and slabs of thick bacon, the cook behind the grill looked up and asked the first Marine in line how many eggs he wanted and how did he want them cooked? Taken by surprise, the Marine stood there for a moment completely dumbfounded.

Then he meekly cleared his throat and said, "Uh, I'll take a dozen of them yellow-eyed beauties over easy." To our utter amazement, the cook began cracking open twelve eggs and then placing them onto a hot griddle without even blinking an eye. The reaction to the cook's generosity was overwhelming. Everybody in the line started surging closer to the griddle in the hopes the Air Force wouldn't run out of eggs. When the cook finally looked up at me, I couldn't resist asking for a six-egg, give-me-the-works cheese omelet.

Later, as several hundred of us were sitting around and enjoying our delicious breakfast, the mess hall was eerily quiet and subdued. What could we say? We were all thinking the same thing.

"Boy Howdy, I sure screwed up by not joining the Air Force."

While we were in Okinawa, the schedule was hectic and almost nonstop. From dawn to dusk, we were run through an assortment of medical, legal, and other administrative services in order to satisfy the government's bureaucrats. Walking from building to building, we also had an opportunity to run across several returning veterans. Most of these fellows had not seen any combat, so they felt free to fill our heads with their bizarre stories of bravery and woe. Yet the infantrymen (grunts) that we did get to meet weren't very talkative. In fact, they didn't want to deal with anybody on any level. At the time, I thought it was very unfriendly of them, because we were eager to listen to what they had to say. Confused about their behavior, I took the time to observe them for awhile. They didn't appear to me to be shell-shocked or in a daze. Instead, they seemed to be terribly pissed off about everything around them. It was only after I had served my first tour of duty in the field that I would come to understand why they were so angry and distant.

In preparation for our flight to Vietnam, we were required to attend a variety of classes on venereal diseases, drugs, and the evils of the black market. During the VD class, the naval corpsman went out of his way to scare the holy hell out of every one of us. Seemingly, the Pentagon had thought they could terrify us into not having sex with the Vietnamese women. And why they even cared about our sex lives was a mystery to me. As the corpsman continued to expound upon the risks of fornicating with the opposite sex, he began showing us pictures of swollen and diseased genitalia. Personally, I found the whole class to be somewhat perplexing and confusing. From the very first day of boot camp, we had been told by the drill instructors that homosexuality was some sort of alien disease punishable by a dishonorable discharge. Now, here they were telling us to keep our grubby hands off of the women too.

Near the end of the class, this cocky corpsman suddenly reached up to a string on the wall and yanked down a picture of a young, beautiful, naked woman. With our eyeballs almost poking out of our heads, we all leaned forward in our chairs to get a better look. Dangling underneath her rounded shoulders was a set of perfectly pointed breasts. Her pink nipples were so large and erect that they seemed to be staring back at us. From where I was sitting, she looked like an angel with the sun's rays shining against her ivory-colored skin and chestnut hair. Slowly running my eyes up her long, slender legs and into her heart-shaped buttocks, I was completely overwhelmed with a sense of homesickness. Then without any warning, the corpsman suddenly yelled out as loud as he could, "Now would any of you Marines want to screw this gal knowing your penis might fall off?"

I was so proud of us, because everyone in the class yelled back at him with a big grin, "You bet."

During our last few days in Okinawa, we kept hearing stories about how the fighting in Vietnam had greatly intensified. Unbeknown to us, the 1968 Lunar Tet Offensive had just begun. As best, as we could understand it from the sporadic news reports, it appeared as though the enemy was finally coming out into the open and confronting our troops. With over 80,000 combat troops, they had simultaneously attacked over 100 towns and cities, along with every major U.S. and

South Vietnamese installation. Lasting for almost two months, the casualties on both sides, including the civilians, would be staggering.

At the time, there was talk among the officers that we would be flown into Vietnam on a military transport, instead of using a commercial airliner. We had heard that the civilian pilots were refusing to fly us there, due to the heavy fighting. Luckily though, it wasn't true, for bright and early the next morning, the prettiest stewardesses that Pan Am had to offer were standing there at the doorway waiting to greet us.

Descending from the cold blue sky, we prepared ourselves for the adventure of our lives. I don't think any of us was truly prepared for what we would eventually experience. Peering through the small window on the plane, I was able to get my first real glimpse of Vietnam. The landscape was green, rugged, and foreboding. Amazingly, I could see a number of people working their fields and tending their water buffaloes as if the war didn't even exist. They were just going about their business, ignoring everything around them.

Then after the plane landed on the tarmac and began taxiing to the main terminal, the pilot came on the intercom and said in a smooth, ironical voice, "Welcome to the Republic of South Vietnam, gentlemen. Your bunkers will be on our left."

Since the Tet Offensive was in full swing, we were ordered to rush off of the airplane and run into a group of nearby cattle cars. The idea was to get us off of the airstrip as soon as possible, so that we could have our paperwork processed at a safer location. Since the enemy had just recently stepped up their attacks, there was a definite aura of fear surrounding the place.

Hopping down the ramp as fast as I could, my first introduction to Vietnam was the all-consuming odor of the place. After one good whiff, I began to get sick to my stomach. Growing up in Fort Worth (Cowtown), Texas, I had run across some pretty strange odors emanating from the Annual Fat Stock Show. But this was a completely different experience. It smelled like a pile of pig manure and rotten fish all rolled together into one nauseating stench. Nonetheless, a person could eventually get used to it, if they stayed in country long enough.

As we zoomed through the winding roads, I couldn't help but notice how truly filthy and primitive everything appeared. The trees, the houses, the animals, and the people all seemed to be from a different world. It was nothing like where I had been raised. There weren't any paved roads, filling stations, movie theaters, or large businesses anywhere. These folks were hard-core farmers and they were going to remain so until the end of time. I remember thinking to myself during those first few days, "What in heaven's name are we doing in this dump?"

When we arrived at the Marine transit building on the north side of the airstrip, a tall sergeant started yelling at us, "Okay, gentleman, welcome to the Third Marine Amphibious Force, South Vietnam. Yell out the last four numbers of your serial number when your name is called."

As he was calling our names out, I began to admire the colorful unit insignias painted across the plywood wall. Sitting all along the wall and under each insignia was an astute-looking clerk ready to process our paperwork. With the help of the unit insignias, I immediately recognized the 1st and 3rd Marine Divisions' process areas. Besides the different infantry regiments, there was also listed a variety of Marine air groups, engineering battalions, tank battalions, and artillery regiments. Having been trained and then classified as a mortarman (MOS-0341), I expected to be assigned to an infantry division, but one never knows while in the military. Much like any huge bureaucracy, they do the strangest things for the oddest reasons.

Within our particular Pan Am flight, the majority of us were assigned to the 1st Marine Division. To my absolute satisfaction, I had been placed into the 1st Marine Regiment, the "First of the First" as they were known in World War II. At the time, I couldn't have been happier. They had an illustrious history and I was going to become a part of it.

Then after wasting several hours standing around and waiting, we were finally led to a group of small huts next to the airstrip. The sergeant in charge told us we would be sacking out there for the night and that reveille would be at 0600 hours. Inasmuch as everything was new to us, we were too ignorant to know that we had been put in a very bad spot. The Marine transit area was located directly across the airstrip from where we kept our fighter/bombers. Thus whenever the enemy gunners fired their rockets and mortars at the jet hangars, the transit area would usually catch their short rounds. That day, we should have suspected something was awry, because the people around us were acting extremely tense.

After trying to choke down a horrible meal of stale bread, tasteless pork, and canned peas, we hit the rack several hours after dark. While lying there in the darkness, we were still excited about the events of the day, so we talked to each other for about an hour or so. Then as I was about to doze off, I was unexpectedly awakened by a crescendo of thundering explosions. Instantly rising from my cot, I could hear someone screaming and yelling, "incoming, incoming." As my mind raced through a thousand different scenarios, I was able to throw on some clothes, exit the hut, and jump into a nearby ditch with the rest of the kids. Unfortunately though, the ditch was rather small, so we ended up piling on top of each other as best as we could.

In between the igniting flares and the surrounding pandemonium, I noticed a couple of the kids had become so terrified that they began to dig into the dirt with their bare hands. It was like watching a pack of dogs burying a bone. They were throwing the dirt between their legs as it went flying through the air. Looking upward, I could see the trailing exhausts from the incoming projectiles as they whistled across the sky. Enthralled by the sights and sounds, I watched in awe as the enemy rounds exploded around the airplane hangars.

As quickly as the attack had begun, it suddenly stopped. The silence seemed strange and out of place, because it produced a false sense of well-being. Amusingly, the cessation of hostilities hadn't interfered with the diggers' enthusiasm for digging. A few of them were still burrowing away when we emerged from our hiding places to take stock of the situation. Within our own area, the damage had been slight. It seemed most of the rounds had landed on the other side of the airstrip. After brushing ourselves off, an old sergeant came by to see if we were okay. He told us that since the Tet Offensive had begun, the shelling had become a nightly affair. Then with an expression of confidence on his face, he ordered everyone, including the diggers, to go back to bed and try to get some sleep.

Settling down into our warm cots again, we felt a mixture of excitement and exhaustion. The shelling was over and we had survived our initiation to enemy fire. Although the air was thick and moist, I began to breathe easier. Life was good and I was safe. Then as I was about to fall asleep again, another salvo of rockets came screaming directly over our hut. Only this time around, I didn't even think about putting on my clothes. Similar to a herd of wide-eyed cattle, we stampeded our way right through the flimsy door and into the ditch.

Half-asleep, dirty, and tired, I sat there in my underwear underneath the flares and watched the diggers burrowing away. One of them kept mumbling to himself, "I've got to get out of here; I've got to get out of here."

During this second attack, I noticed that immediately after the shells had landed, someone on the air base had switched on this hideous sounding siren. Combined with the surrounding flares and confusion, the overall effect of the siren was chillingly Orwellian. Everybody had a good laugh about it, because it didn't make any sense to us. Why alert everyone, when the attack had already ended?

Then once we had begun to calm down again and collect our thoughts, the same old sergeant came around again to see if we were okay. Since we all seemed to be in one piece, he ordered us back to bed. Only this time, no one really slept. We just lay there in the dark with our eyes wide open and listened to the sky in eerie anticipation.

With the passing of a couple of restless hours, I started to relax a little bit. The only noise I could hear was the hum of a distant helicopter. Feeling a sense of relief, I began to drift back into my dreams. Then as I reached over to put out a cigarette butt, another barrage of rockets came whistling over our hut. After we leaped out of our cots, one of the rounds suddenly landed in our immediate area. Temporarily blinded by the unexpected flash from the explosion, we instinctively got on our hands and knees and began to crawl to the ditch. Thanks to the diggers, we were all finally able to comfortably fit into the thing. At this point, we were so tired and exhausted nothing seemed to matter anymore. Our state of mind was such that we just numbly looked at each other in disbelief.

That first night, I learned a lot about the enemy and it worried me. Their rockets and mortars hadn't really caused that much damage in terms of destroying our equipment or inducing casualties, but they did have a psychological effect upon us. It was obvious that they could hit us at any time and anywhere they so desired. Unless a person was completely deaf and immune to shrapnel, no one was really safe and no one was going to get any sleep. If I had known then what I know now, I would have joined the diggers.

When the dawn finally broke, I quickly arose from my cot and headed for mess hall. As I stepped out into the morning haze, the air was crisp and flesh. Strangely enough, the kids were still digging away. As the dirt flew every which direction, their radio was blaring out a popular song. Later while I was eating, I had to chuckle to myself. They had been digging to the tune of Martha and the Vandellas', "Nowhere to Run."

Somewhere between the incoming rockets and the lousy water, I became very ill. The symptoms were like the flu, but I had a feeling it was something different. The chills and nausea seemed to come over me in waves and then they would suddenly stop. Later that afternoon, when we were trucked to the 1st Marine Division's Headquarters situated outside of Da Nang, I was finally able to go to sick call. The naval corpsman gave me a shot and few pills, and then told me to take it easy for a few days.

At this point, I don't remember a hell of a lot, because I was almost delirious with fever. But right before we were flown to our Regimental Headquarters in Phu Bai, I remember being issued my combat gear. For my journey to the DMZ, I was given one used helmet, one very used M-16 rifle, four rusty magazines, a gas mask, and an old flak jacket with a large bull's eye drawn on the back of it. Perturbed by the lack of equipment that I had received, I asked the overweight supply sergeant when I would be getting the rest of my gear.

Sensing that I was naïve and new to the country, he responded, "What gear are you talking about, lad?"

I replied, "You know, things like canteens, battle fatigues (pants and shirts), jungle boots, field dressings, haversacks, an E-tool, a web belt, a bayonet, a rifle cleaning kit, or even a frickin' poncho."

With a huge brown cigar dangling out of his stained lips, he mumbled, "You'll get it at regiment."

As the CH-46 Sea Knight helicopter rose into the gray sky and above the clouds, several of the guys bunched up on one side of the cabin, so that they could get a better look at the coastline. Being too sick to care, I just sat there and looked at my feet. In order to avoid any enemy fire, the pilot flew us out over the ocean and then headed north to our destination. The breeze was unbelievably invigorating as it came off of the water.

Standing near the ramp, I noticed the crew chief was staring at us with malicious amusement. Unshaven with streaks of greasy dirt running up and down his flight suit, this guy looked as if he had been living in the back of the helicopter for years. He was wearing a light-blue helmet with most of the paint chipped off, a set of dark-tinted goggles, and an old pair of flight boots. Sporting a long handlebar mustache, he stood there confidently smiling at us, holding a vintage World War II grease gun (M3-A1, submachine gun). At the time, I kept wondering to myself why he had chosen to carry that particular firearm. It was a short-barreled, 45-caliber automatic weapon. I had fired pellet guns back home with greater effective range.

When we finally arrived at the 1st Marine's Regimental Headquarters in Phu Bai, I was assigned to the 2nd Battalion's Headquarters and Service Company (H&S). The word had been passed to us that there was a lot of fighting going on in Hue City, which was the capital of Thua Thien-Hue Province in the northern part of South Vietnam. Knowing that elements of the 1st Battalion 1st Marines were there, I was relieved to hear that I hadn't been assigned to them. Also, I was relieved to hear that I would be in an 81mm mortar platoon, instead of a 60mm mortar squad. From my previous training, I knew that the 60mm mortarmen were attached to the battalion's rifle companies, and thus occasionally required to go out on patrols with the infantrymen (grunts) and even help them set up ambushes. Besides, the thought of becoming a part of an 81mm crew was exciting to me. As a close support weapon, it was an extremely deadly weapon. A good assistant-gunner could discharge ten to twelve rounds of high explosives into the air before the first round had even hit the target, thus creating a powerful barrage.

While I was in the regimental area, I asked another supply sergeant if I could get some combat gear. He just looked at me as if I was crazy and said, "You'll get it at battalion." Disappointed, I began to question him about the lack of equipment. Then he finally looked up at me and said, "Look kid, you'll get all the gear you need, after your first firefight." "Gee, that makes me feel a lot better," I sarcastically responded.

Phu Bai was a large combat base surrounded by several villages and rice paddies. Filled with tents, smelly mess halls, and plywood offices, the purpose of the base was to cover the western approaches to Hue City. Much like all the other rear areas in Vietnam, it was full of personnel who didn't seem to have anything better to do than to schedule work details for anyone under the rank of sergeant. Dressed in starched uniforms and shiny boots, they lived in a completely different world than the rest of us. Rarely ever leaving their compounds, they would spend their whole tours of duty there, typing up the paper work, moving supplies to their units, or working in the headquarters section.

Upon reaching the 2nd Battalion's Headquarters, we went through the motions of signing our lives away. The Corps wanted to make sure they had all their legal bases covered in the likelihood that one of us ended up in a body bag. Out of curiosity, I asked the office clerk where our battalion happened to be located.

Glancing up from his paperwork, he said, "the hill."

I instantly replied in a quizzical manner, "the hill?"

He said, "Yep, Con Thien, the Hill of Angels, it's near the DMZ. Just walk north up Route 1 in the direction of North Vietnam. You can't miss it."

Then while I was at battalion, I asked their supply sergeant in exasperation, if I could get some combat gear. He just smiled and said, "You'll get it at your company's supply."

Once we finally arrived at our company's rear area, we were assigned to a tent and told to stow what little gear we had been given. Within my tent, there were several guys sitting around on their cots. Apparently, they were in the rear area for administrative reasons. I'll never forget the expressions on their faces when we walked through the doorway. Every one of them gazed at us with an expression of indifference. Unbeknown to us, the guys who had been in country for awhile would always look upon the new kids ("cherries") as a big pain in the backside. New guys had to be looked after and literally retrained, until they could make it on their own.

Then at that point, a burly first sergeant by the name of Knox suddenly entered the tent and began explaining to us where everything on the base was located and what was expected of us. Referred to as "Top," Knox was the type of old-breed Marine that I would come to admire and emulate for the rest of my life. These men had a look and swagger about them that spelled confidence and determination. They walked tough, talked tough, and looked tough. With his hands resting on his hips, he told us it was his third war—beginning in World War II as a private at Saipan—and that things were never as bad as they might seem. Strangely enough, he had a very comforting manner about him as he tried to ease our fears.

Following his introduction to Phu Bai, one of the kids asked him if we were going to be issued any combat gear. He just laughed and said, "You'll get it on the hill." Then he took one look at me and said, "Jesus Christ, lad, you look like death warmed over."

That evening, I still wasn't feeling very well, so I stayed in my cot. Between my high temperature and the nausea, I felt horrible. The other guys wanted to make sure that I was all right, but they were way too excited to stick around to attend to me. So as soon as Knox turned his back, they made a beeline to the Enlisted Men's Club. While they were gone, I tried to write a letter home. But in all honesty, I couldn't think of one positive thing to write about.

It must have been sometime around midnight, when the guys finally came back to the tent, roaring drunk and making all kinds of noise. As they were undressing, two of them got into a shoving match over which one of them had the prettiest girlfriend back in the States. In between the screaming and shoving, one of them finally yelled out, "My girlfriend is so pretty that she makes Marilyn Monroe look like a tramp." In response, the other guy yelled back at him, "Yea, I bet she has to sneak up on a glass of water just to get a drink."

It must have been around four o'clock in morning when I was unexpectedly awakened by the crashing sound of explosions off in the distance. Since I was too sick to move, I just lay there holding my breath and listening to the surrounding mayhem. At the time, I really didn't know if the rounds were theirs or ours, but I was determined not to spend another night in a ditch. Then out of nowhere, somebody stuck his head into our tent and yelled out in a half-drunken voice, "That's incoming, grab your gear and get your butt out on the perimeter. We're under attack." Suddenly, a rush of adrenaline surged through my body as I helplessly watched everyone scramble out the door. Instinctively reaching for my rifle, I waited there in the darkness, dreading the thought of having to fight my way out of the tent.

It didn't take long before the situation seemed to be under control. The incoming had stopped and I could hear a few people outside talking and acting up. Then just as I was about to relax a little bit, one of the intoxicated guys on the line thought he had heard something, which just happened to be a grazing water buffalo, and began firing his rifle into the nearby field. Normally, it wouldn't have been such a big deal except for the fact that his over enthusiasm had created a chain reaction. All along the perimeter, everybody started firing their rifles and chunking hand grenades as our machine gunners began spraying the area. It sounded like a full-blown battle had erupted just outside my tent.

Amidst all the yelling and firing, I suddenly heard First Sergeant Knox's voice echoing through the darkness, "Stop firing, you dumbasses, before you get somebody killed." Glancing out of the doorway, I could see his silhouette reflecting in the moonlight. Although he looked somewhat ridiculous standing there in his green underwear and his untied combat boots, he still commanded everybody's respect. Within a matter of a few minutes, he was able to organize the perimeter into some semblance of order. Knowing that Knox was out there and in charge, it didn't take long before I was able to go back to sleep.

When the morning light finally appeared through the flaps, I rolled out of my cot and got dressed. The tent was still empty, so I stumbled outside to see what was happening. Approximately thirty feet away, everybody was standing at his posts. They looked tired, ragged, and hung-over. As I cleared my eyes and surveyed the surrounding area, I saw used rifle casings, spent hand-grenade pins, and empty canteens scattered all over the ground. If one didn't know any better, it looked as if our boys had beaten back a determined enemy attack. Then peering off into the distance, I noticed a dead water buffalo was lying on its back with its feet pointed straight up in the air. At least, I think it was a water buffalo. It was so full of holes, I couldn't really tell. When I finally did approach the now fully dressed first sergeant, Knox asked me if I was feeling any better. I told him yes. Then as an afterthought I asked him, "Did we win?"

After eating a meal of powdered eggs, canned Spam, and burnt toast, a group of us were issued a few bandoleers of ammo and put on some trucks in order to guard a convoy. The Tet Offensive was heating up and the Marines in Hue had found themselves neck deep in house-to-house fighting. In spite of the fact that I felt a lot better, the idea of going there was not at all appealing. From the reports we had heard, the city had become a real bloodbath. While passing out the bandoleers, Knox explained to us that it was going to be our task to drive up Route 1 and re-supply the Marines in Hue. Only later would I learn that the French had called this particular stretch of road, "The Street Without Joy."

Route 1 was not a highway in the American sense of the word. It wasn't paved, level, or even straight. Winding through the countryside like a snake, there was never any guarantee that the bridges hadn't been blown or that the road itself was even passable. One minute, you would find yourself riding on a smooth stretch of road, and then just around the next bend, you could find yourself unexpectedly stuck at the bottom of a stream. Even in the best of times, the enemy was always blocking the road in between the cities and villages. Besides ambushing the convoys, they would place their mines in the road, and then sit back and watch the results. As we climbed into the back of a truck, I was completely unaware that I would be sharing my ride with a bunch of trigger-happy cherries. Much like everyone else in the convoy, they didn't have a clue as to what was going on around us.

The convoy itself was made up of a tracked collection of trucks, jeeps, quad-fifties (M-50), and an Army M-42 Duster (a tank-type vehicle mounting two 40mm cannons). Situated in the back of the convoy, our truck was loaded with cases of C-rations, ammo, and jerry cans full of water. Almost immediately upon leaving Phu Bai, I loaded my rifle and sat down next to the truck's railing. In a sense, it was very exciting. We had been entrusted to conduct an important mission, and every one us felt the pride of being called upon.

As we zoomed down the dusty road, the surrounding terrain was crisscrossed with small villages, thick tree lines, and smelly rice paddies. Among the crude dwellings, the livestock were mulling around and eating the straw off of the roofs. Due to the nearby fighting, most of the Vietnamese people had decided to stay out of sight. We could sense something was horribly amiss just by their absence. Then as we roared around a sharp bend in the road, lines of green tracers, which were fired by the enemy instead of the red tracers we used, flew by our heads. Instantly dropping into a firing position and lifting up our rifles, we began to return fire. But instead of using any form of fire discipline as we had been taught, we began shooting at anything that moved, including chickens, dogs, and pigs. Much like any other red-blooded American boys, quantity was more important to us than quality.

At this point, the convoy began to pick up speed, because the worst thing a vehicle can do during an ambush is to slow down or to stop. Unfortunately, this only added to our panic. During all the confusion, we would shoot to the left for awhile and then we would shoot to the right for awhile. Then we would shoot to the front for awhile and then we would turn around and shoot to the rear for awhile. When we weren't shooting into the houses, we were shooting into the parked vehicles and the vacant shops. The only thing we could hear besides the sound of our own rifles firing was our crazy driver screaming at the top of his lungs, "Let them have it, boys."

Upon reaching a bridge that spanned the Perfume River, we quickly unloaded the rations and innocently asked a bypassing lieutenant for some more ammo. To our discomfort, he seemed a little pissed at us for shooting up the place. He kept referring to us as those maniacs in the rear truck. As we were preparing to leave, the convoy commander had decided to assign a sergeant to accompany us on our return trip. Unfortunately, his presence didn't make any difference. On the way back to Phu Bai, the enemy was ready for us again. Upon entering the same bend in the road, the fire was so intense that we couldn't even raise our heads above the railing of the truck. But that didn't stop us. We just lifted our rifles over the side of the rail and blindly fired into the bypassing houses and temples. Luckily, none of our vehicles became disabled, so we were able to pass through the killing zone fairly quickly.

After my first firefight, the sensation was almost indescribable. Along with my physical exhaustion, there was a sensation of immense relief that I had survived. Glowing with pride for not letting my fellow Marines down, there was also the self-satisfaction of getting the job done. It was a mixture of pure exaltation, fatigue, and profound humility all rolled up into one gut feeling.

On the very next morning, we were introduced to a very old and proud Marine Corps institution called the "Shit Detail." Well, it's not actually an institution per se. It's more like a punishment. A shit detail can range from digging ditches, filling sandbags, burning shitters, or even carrying the dead and wounded off of a helicopter and into the hospital. It's usually a thankless but necessary task, awarded to those who are on somebody's shit list. Oddly enough, it knows no rank, color, creed, or sexual preference. Anybody can be put on some form of shit detail. On this particular occasion, we were given the opportunity to burn the battalion's shitters. Apparently, the brass was not at all pleased about our performance during the trek to Hue. Word had it that somebody in our truck had accidentally put a bullet hole through the convoy commander's helmet.

Burning shitters entailed pulling out from the stalls a cut-in-half, one-hundred-gallon drum that was brimming with human feces and urine. Between the thousands of maggots and swirling flies, the stench was beyond nauseating. Then after pouring diesel fluid all over this pool of crap, we lit the contents and watched it burn, thus creating another kind of sickening, oily smell. Once the manure had been burned to a crisp, we emptied the drums of their charred contents, poured a layer of diesel fluid into the drums, and then we placed them back into their stalls. Overall, it was very unrewarding job, in which I became unfortunately an expert.

After a few days of working senseless work details, a small group of us were informed we would be going to our unit by helicopter. The plan was to fly us to Quang Tri and then truck us up to Con Thien. Thus before the day was even over, we found ourselves in a truck and driving towards the airstrip.

As the helicopter lifted above the clouds and into the clear sky, a fresh breeze hit me in the face. With the rhythmic humming of the helicopter blades in the background, I sat there in the helicopter buried in my thoughts. I suddenly realized how truly alone I had become. One of the reasons I had joined the Marine Corps and gone to Vietnam was to escape the deep emptiness and pain I had been experiencing from Raymond's death. Without him, the world just didn't make any sense. At the same time, I also realized that yesterday is yesterday and that we can't change our past any more than we can guarantee our futures. Whether or not the Universe or God himself had already predetermined my fate, I had no idea. But I did understand one thing. In order for me to have any hopes of survival, I was going to have to become as unforgiving as my surroundings and never look back.

Chapter Two

The Hill of Angels

"The glorification of sports is a nation's first step
towards preparing its youth for war."

As a sergeant in Quang Tri explained it to me, Con Thien was the north-ernmost American outpost in South Vietnam. Situated a little over six thousand meters below the Ben Hai River, it overlooked the Demilitarized Zone (DMZ) and the southern panhandle of North Vietnam. By the end of February of 1967, the Marines had taken over responsibility of the hill from an Army Special Forces detachment. With Con Thien being the centerpiece, the idea behind our deployment there was to establish a string of outposts just below the 17th Parallel. Commonly known as McNamara's Wall, the former Secretary of Defense had envisioned this wall as a sort of technological Maginot Line. During World War II, the Maginot Line was supposed to prevent the German armies from invading France, which ended up becoming a complete and costly failure. Of course, McNamara's wall didn't work either.

Consisting of a collection of seismic and acoustic sensors for identifying troop movements, particle detectors for tracing carbon trails (campfires), heliborne "people" sniffers for testing the air for urine and sweat molecules, radio-intercept equipment, and aerial photography, it was set up to detect any and all enemy movements coming into South Vietnam. Predictably, the North Vietnamese Army (NVA) would respond to this electronic marvel by shifting their major infiltration routes through the Ho Chi Minh Trail, situated just inside of Laos. As one of their responsibilities in I Corps, the Marines would regularly rotate one of our battalions in and out of Con Thien as a matter of security. Within no time at all, the grunts would begin calling the DMZ the "Dead Marine Zone." Due to the chaos brought about by the Tet Offensive, my battalion (2/1) would serve there longer than any other Marine unit.

Con Thien was actually made up of three small, interconnected hills, the highest one being almost five hundred feet high. Compared to the soaring mountains in Vietnam, they weren't all that impressive. Yet due to the surrounding flat terrain, it was a great place for observation. Looking to the south, the artillery bases at Camp Carroll and Cam Lo were situated along Route 9. To the east, the combat bases at Gio Linh and Cua Viet were strategically located near the glittering South China Sea. Then off to the southwest was the towering mountain range overlooking the Khe Sanh Combat Base. While gazing far to the north, I always got an eerie feeling peering into the sinister-looking DMZ and beyond into North Vietnam.

Militarily, the purpose for occupying Con Thien was twofold. First, it was used as a first line of defense against the likelihood of an enemy invasion. Of course, the position itself could not have stopped a serious invasion, because there was only one Marine battalion stationed there at a time. However, it was in a good place for a unit to sound the alarm. Secondly, it was also used as a forward observation post to help interdict the northern infiltration routes. On any given day, we could call in an assortment of naval gunfire, air strikes, and artillery fire upon any suspected enemy positions or movements.

Unfortunately though, the North Vietnamese could also call on an assortment of weapons to be fired upon us. Knowing the importance of the position, the enemy constantly used the place as target practice while moving their troops into I Corps. Throughout its brief history as an American outpost, the Hill of Angels and the surrounding area would become infamous for chewing up and spitting out both Marine and NVA battalions. Among the Marines who were lucky enough to survive their time in the barrel, the DMZ would forever remain in their memories.

In the beginning, life for the grunts at Con Thien was a series of daily patrols and nightly ambushes. There hadn't been a need to construct any deep bunkers, interlocking trench lines, or huge minefields. Much like Khe Sanh and the other northern bases, everyone lived above ground and free of the constant artillery and mortar. The routine was such that we had assumed the North Vietnamese were incapable of seriously taking on the United States military establishment. With a population about as large as the state of Ohio, North Vietnam was a poor agrarian country with next to nothing in terms of industrial might and technology. We thought how in the world could they have even dreamed of challenging us?

During 1965 and 1966, there hadn't been very many major engagements with the North Vietnamese Army. While occasionally operating with the local Viet Cong (VC), the NVA units didn't possess the fire support or the logistics to engage our larger units on a full-time basis. Up to this point in the war, our primary problem had been with the local Viet Cong living in and around the populated areas. These warrior civilians, who were politically represented by the National Liberation Front (NLF), were constantly sniping, laying mines, or ambushing our patrols.

Unexpectedly though, all of this was about to change. After taking several years to build up their forces with the help of the Soviet Union and the People's Republic of China, the NVA were finally ready to make their presence felt. Beginning in April of 1967 with the "Hill Fights" northwest of Khe Sanh, which will be described later, the Marine bases along the DMZ began to light up like a Fourth of July celebration.

Right before daybreak on May 8, 1967, two battalions of NVA soldiers attacked Con Thien's perimeter with machine guns, AK-47s, and 82mm mortar barrages. The Marines had been taken completely by surprise by their sudden attack. Until then, the NVA had always used the ambush as their main tactic. The idea of them directly attacking a dug-in Marine battalion seemed unrealistic at the time. Needless to say, the issue was in extreme doubt for awhile to the consternation of the Marine commanders. Yet with the help of their supporting arms and some grim determination on the part of Alpha and Delta companies, the 1st Battalion 4th Marines were able to repel the assault at the cost of 154 American casualties. After the helicopters began to evacuate the dead and wounded Americans from the landing zone (LZ), the Marine survivors counted approximately two hundred NVA bodies strewn along the bloodstained perimeter.[1]

Then just ten days later, several Marine battalions attempted our very first deep incursion into the DMZ. In what was called *Operation Hickory*, the plan of action was for the Marines to sweep the area south of the Ben Hai River, while the South Vietnamese forces removed the civilians from all along the DMZ. From May 18–28, elements of the 4th, 9th, and 26th Marine regiments battled the NVA northwest and west of Con Thien. Using the cover of darkness, the NVA were able to re-supply and deploy their troops without any interference from our circling aircraft. At the cost of over 1,000 Marine casualties, the South Vietnamese forces were finally able to successfully relocate the noncombatants for the sole purpose of making the DMZ a free-fire zone. From then on, we were free to unleash our immense firepower into the area at a moment's notice without endangering any civilians. To many of the Marine higher-ups, the operation was a complete success. However once the civilians had been removed from the DMZ, we would also lose a great source of military intelligence.[2]

Soon afterward on May 28, the grunts in Mike and Lima companies of the 3rd Battalion, 4th Marines made contact with a heavily forti-fied NVA battalion approximately five miles southwest of Con Thien. Sitting in their concealed bunkers and deep trench lines, the NVA machine gunners had set up their defenses with interlocking fields of fire and hand detonated mines. Not until later was it discovered that they had even marked the pathways leading up to their positions. In what was to become known as the "Battle for Hill 174," the Marines were forced to go from position to position, methodically blasting the enemy out of each bunker. The enemy's camouflage had been so expertly prepared that the Marines couldn't see their positions from the ground or from the air. Using hand grenades, flamethrowers, and 3.5 rocket launchers to clear the way, our kids had to literally crawl over their wounded buddies in order to advance.[3]

In the ensuing days, the Marine companies involved would sustain 133 casualties before they were finally able to take the position. Para-doxically, as with most American operations in that region, the NVA would reoccupy the hill shortly after our units had departed the area.

Then on July 2, at the onset of *Operation Buffalo*, Bravo Company of the 1st Battalion 9th Marines would be sent out to the northeast of Con Thien into an area known as the Trace. Before the sun had even reached its zenith, the company had been overrun and forced to defend itself in small, isolated groups. In and around the old rice pad-dies and bamboo thickets, the fighting was ferocious and desperate. At the time, the Marines of Bravo Company were completely unaware that they had walked into two battalions of the 90th NVA Regiment. Running out of water and ammo, many of the stranded leathernecks had been reduced to playing dead as the enemy swept around them using their flame-throwers to flush out any Marine resistance. By mid-afternoon, the NVA gunners began pounding the nearby landing zones with their artillery and mortars in an attempt to further isolate the embattled company. For the lads of Bravo Company, they never knew what had hit them.[4]

While patrolling off to the northwest, Alpha Company was ordered to come to B Company's assistance. Then as they made their way through the hedgerows, they would also be unexpectedly blindsided by waves of camouflaged NVA. Positioned a mere thousand meters away from the Bravo survivors, the Marine commander was forced to have his troops dig in around the old rice paddies in order to save his own company. The radiomen in headquarters back at Con Thien could hear them over the intercom fighting for their very lives.[5]

In an effort to save his two companies, the Battalion Commander decided to strip his defenses at Con Thien and send one platoon from Delta Company along with four M-48 tanks to the Trace. In the meantime, Charlie Company had been alerted and was being flown to the scene from Dong Ha. Unfortunately, these forces would also end up becoming surrounded and pinned down like everybody else.[6]

Once the Marine Regimental Commander in Dong Ha realized the severity of the situation, he immediately committed parts of two other Marine battalions to the battle. For the next couple of days, enough American reinforcements had arrived that the Marines were able to blunt the NVA's onslaught and secure much of the area. Amid all of the bloodstained clothing, empty rifle casings, and scattered gear, several Marines who had belonged to Bravo Company were discovered shot through the head at close range. It appeared as if they had been coldly executed like criminals. As expected, the Marines didn't take any NVA prisoners during this engagement.[7]

Although the NVA had suffered a lot of casualties, they continued to throw their weight around. On July 7, one of their 152mm artillery rounds penetrated the 1/9's command bunker at Con Thien. Besides knocking the Battalion Commander unconscious, the blast killed fifteen of his staff members and wounded twenty-three others. In response to the enemy's escalation, the U.S. Air Force flew well over 700 B-52 missions in front of and around the hill. To many of the older Marine veterans, the fighting was reminiscent of World War II. The NVA had committed themselves in force and they weren't backing off. Thus within a twelve-day period (July 2–14), the 1st Battalion 9th Marines would suffer over 500 casualties out of approximately 800 grunts. Thereafter, the battalion was known as the "Walking Dead." As luck would have it, I ended up serving with this battalion as well.[8]

Then between July 16 and October 31, in a series of running gun battles along the DMZ called *Operation Kingfisher*, five Marine battalions engaged the NVA units during the hottest part of the year. Beginning with the encirclement of the 2nd Battalion 9th Marines just south of the DMZ, the fighting raged all around Con Thien, Dong Ha, and along Route 9 leading to Khe Sanh. In spite of the fact that the firefights were fierce and frequent, the intense heat was responsible for many of our casualties. It appeared to the Marine commanders at III MAF that the NVA were attempting to take control of the area by ambushing any of our units operating there. Standing up to our immense firepower, the NVA were able to limit the range of our patrols and thus tighten the ring around Con Thien. By September of 1967, the Marine outpost was partially cut off from its supplies and in a state of siege. Almost every other day, our convoys were being ambushed and our helicopters were being shot down. It got so bad for a while that a platoon couldn't walk a hundred meters outside of the perimeter without making contact with the enemy. As a result, the Marines suffered almost 2,000 casualties in *Operation Kingfisher* in an attempt to clear out the area and keep the road open.[9]

In response to our aggressive operations and the establishment of Con Thien as an outpost, the NVA began to frustrate our objectives by introducing their more powerful weaponry all along the DMZ. With an impressive array of Soviet-made rockets (122mm) and artillery pieces (85mm, 100mm, 130mm, and 152mm), the

NVA would, for the first time, be able to bombard Con Thien, Camp Carroll, Cam Lo, Dong Ha, Gio Linh, and the Rockpile on a continuous basis. In fact, when they had enough ammo, they could hit everyone at the same time. Thus beginning in the summer of 1967, the northern part of South Vietnam would become one big shooting gallery.[10]

My first outfit, the 2nd Battalion 1st Marines, would take over Con Thien on December 21, 1967. After replacing the 1st Battalion 1st Marines, they immediately began digging more and deeper trenches, rebuilding the battered bunkers, enlarging the surrounding minefield, and laying miles of concertina wire. The battalion's commanding officer, Lt. Col. Evan L. Parker Jr., had the engineers clear the primitive road leading into Con Thien of underbrush and then even had them pave it with gravel. Moreover, company-sized patrols were regularly sent out into the countryside as a routine procedure in order to sweep the area. Predictably, it didn't take long before the NVA introduced themselves to the Marines of 2/1.

Shortly after noon on January 22, 1968, the 2nd Battalion 1st Marines received the heaviest bombardment since they had arrived at Con Thien. Over 200 mortar and artillery rounds rained down on the outpost, killing two Marines and wounding sixteen. During the barrage, a popular black gunnery sergeant by the name of Nathaniel Weathers of Echo Company was tragically struck down by hostile fire while in the prime of his life. It was a great loss to everyone in the battalion, because he was so admired and respected as both a man and as a Marine. Meanwhile, Foxtrot and Golf Companies had made contact with the enemy not more than a couple of hundred meters from the northern perimeter. Using mortars, AK-47s, and machine guns, the NVA quickly pulled back under their covering fire. After the smoke had cleared, the 2nd Battalion's higher-ups realized what the previous battalions had learned: defending Con Thien could be a very deadly proposition.[11]

During the second week of February of 1968, I finally caught up with my battalion. Since it was the monsoon season, the weather was uncomfortably cold and wet. Upon my arrival, I noticed that everyone within the perimeter was wearing his full combat gear and carrying a rifle. Even if a person had to see a corpsman, they went to the aid station loaded for bear. The second thing that caught my attention was that everybody lived underground in bunkers. Everywhere I looked, there were piles and piles of sandbags on top of the bunkers and trench lines going all around the perimeter. I was shocked; this was not at all what I had expected to see. I had been trained to fight a low-key war around the villages and rice paddles. In my wildest dreams, I had never expected to be thrown into something that resembled a World War II battlefield. A sudden foreboding shot through my body as I realized the seriousness of the situation.

Upon entering one of the deep bunkers, I was introduced to the H & S, commander (Skipper) and the company gunnery sergeant (Gunny). The Skipper was a tall professional looking fellow from Virginia and the Gunny was a rugged-looking Hispanic from California, named Gonzales. After I sat down, the Gunny asked me if I had everything I needed. When I showed him what gear I had been issued, the Gunny hit the roof.

"How in the world can a person send somebody out into the bush [field] equipped with next to nothing?" he bellowed. The Skipper just shook his head in disgust and said to me, "We'll see if we can find you some gear and fatigues, young man."

Later that afternoon, I was escorted down to the mortar section to meet my new gun crew. Not surprisingly, they were positioned on the southern side of one of the hills, facing away from the DMZ. While I walked up to the position, I came upon one American-made 81mm mortar located inside a circular wall of interlocking sandbags. Called a parapet, the sandbags were used to form a protective barrier around the mortar. The wall was about three feet high and a couple of feet thick. However, it didn't look to me as if it offered much protection. Then situated on either side of the parapet, I could see the tops of two bunkers. Resembling a couple of garbage heaps, the roofs were covered with sandbags, steel runway matting, and anything else that could be thrown on top of them. At the time, I was told that one of the bunkers was used for storing our ammo, while the other one was our living quarters. As far as I could tell, they looked pretty sturdy.

After descending into a small stairwell, I lit a candle to get a better look at my new living quarters. The actual living space was no larger than an oversized bathroom. Luckily though, it was tall enough so that one could at least stand up straight in the thing. Then I spotted a crude desk and some homemade shelves that were situated between a set of wooden bunk beds at one end of the room. The beds were made of wood and held together with wire. Then off in one corner, there were cockroaches scampering around these small piles of rat droppings. Although this bunker was designed to house six people, there were only four kids living there when I arrived. Like everything else in Vietnam, the smell of the place reminded me of several frequently used filling station restrooms I had encountered on Route 66 to California.

My new section leader was a medium-built, brown-haired, green-eyed corporal named Chevy. He didn't seem to be very enthusiastic about his job, having only three weeks left in country. The assistant gunner was a lance corporal named Wallace. He had been in country for about three months, but to hear him tell it, he was already an accomplished veteran. Tall and skinny with sandy-colored hair and a pointed nose, he looked like the classic Californian surfer. Fortunately for us, he wasn't the brightest star in the sky, so everyone liked to tease him.

The first ammo humper was a big black kid named Washington. He was tall, heavyset, and strong as a bull. He had been in country for only two months. Back in the States, he had been attending barber college on the day he got drafted. So on occasion, he liked to set up shop at the bottom of the ammo bunker and cut everyone's hair. The only problem was that he had never been trained to cut white folks' hair. The first and only time I sat in his chair, he got so frustrated that he ended up shaving my head. The funny part about it was that he actually expected a tip.

The second ammo humper was a Hispanic kid named Perez. He had been in country for only a month. Besides proudly exhibiting a tattoo on his upper right arm, which read, "Praise the Lord and Pass the Ammo," he always had something good to say. Short with black hair and olive colored skin, he strangely reminded me of Leo Carrillo, who played Pancho in the television series, *The Cisco Kid*.

One day, I asked him what he actually believed in terms of his religious beliefs.

He looked up at me and replied, "Our Lady of Guadalupe and Vikki Carr."

As the new kid on the block, my life was going to be hard and demeaning for awhile. To my discomfort, everyone on the hill outranked me, so if there was a work detail to perform, I was going to be the man doing it. At the time, I was extremely depressed about the whole situation. My living quarters looked like something out of a World War I movie, the water tasted like chemicals, and the rats were huge and plentiful. Then making matters worse, my new crew was about as friendly as a nest of Mexican fire ants.

During the first night there, Washington and I stood watch together in the ammo bunker. As he sat there with the phone to his ear, we talked until dawn. It was a strange experience for me, because I had been born and raised in a segregated society. Growing up in Texas, I didn't have an opportunity to talk to very many Black people, much less to get to know any of them. Due to the times, I had never gone to school, to the movies, or even played sports with any Blacks. My sum knowledge of the African-American culture was based upon watching the old TV sitcom, *Amos and Andy*.

Once I remember asking my mother while we were riding on a bus back home, "Who are those chocolate people sitting in the back?"

Mom replied, "They're Negroes, dear."

Being somewhat confused by a new word I asked her, "What's a Negro?"

She said, "They are people you have no business talking to."

In all truthfulness, it wasn't until after my military experience that I was able to overcome my racially biased upbringing.

After a less than hearty C-ration breakfast of tasteless pork patties, peaches, and stale crackers, our platoon lieutenant had decided that we were in need of more sandbags. So we collected a couple of shovels and began digging away into a huge mound of dirt. While one person would hold the sandbag open, the other two would shovel dirt into it. Then once the bag had been filled, the holder would tie it shut and throw it into a pile. After filling about a hundred or so sandbags, while wearing a helmet and a flak jacket, the pain in one's back and legs would become almost unbearable.

On one occasion, as we were toiling away in the dirt, I kept hearing this strange cracking sound going through the air. It didn't seem to be very close to us, but I could definitely hear it.

Finally, I stopped shoveling and asked everyone, "What in the hell is that sound?"

As the other humpers began to giggle, Chevy replied, "That's a sniper."

I looked around for a second with my hands resting upon my shovel and said, "Well huh, aren't we supposed to hit the deck or duck or do something?"

He just chuckled and said, "Nah, this ain't nothing, just wait till the big shit comes in." Which, I might add, didn't take very long.

About two days later, while we were in the middle of burning shitters, I suddenly heard, off to the north, the eerie sounds of what appeared to be thunderclaps. Then what happened next was simply incredible. Within a span of a millisecond, the rounds from an NVA battery of 152mm artillery (Arty) came screaming into our position. By traveling faster than the speed of sound, they had already hit their targets by the time we heard them coming towards us. Generally speaking, the physical sensation they produced was like standing next to a railroad track while a freight train roared by you travelling at one hundred miles an hour. The physical force these rounds could generate was simply awesome.

As the shrapnel and debris from the explosions blew in every different direction, I propelled myself in the direction of the nearest bunker. At the time, my adrenaline was pumping so fast that I couldn't keep my feet underneath me. Every time I tried to run, my legs were moving with such speed that I would lose my balance and fall flat on my face. So instead of running, I found myself crawling to the nearest bunker. It wasn't my first experience with being physically overcome with fear, but it would be my last. I realized later that my adrenaline had almost gotten me killed, and if I expected to survive, I was going to have to control my glands.

"Damn, that was close," Wallace uttered, as he entered the bunker.

Then I remember Chevy replying, "Boys, it ain't considered close, until you can actually feel the heat from the blast."

Though we had probably run less than fifty feet, our battle fatigues were drenched in sweat and coated with red dirt. After checking ourselves for wounds, I discovered that I had lost my watch, my ring, and my cigarette lighter during my flight to safety. Strangely enough, Perez and I would spend the next hour or so looking for them without any luck. The fact that we couldn't find them was surprising, because we hadn't run very far. Afterward over a supper of oily boned chicken and bland cocoa mix, Washington reckoned my arms and legs had been moving so fast that I had probably flung the damn things into the next province.

In terms of organization, a schedule had been worked out where we would individually rotate standing watch in the ammo bunker. The ammo bunker had been installed with a landline (phone), which ran up to the Fire Direction Center (FDC), located near the Battalion Headquarters. Once the forward observers (FOs) assigned to the field companies had spotted a target and radioed the coordinates to the FDC, the FDC would then signal the person stationed inside the ammo bunker with the words, "Fire Mission." Then as he began to alert the rest of the gun crew, the FDC would begin sending us the needed information in terms of the gun's firing coordinates (elevation and deflection), along with the type and the number of rounds to be fired.

Then once the fire mission had begun, the ammo humpers would station themselves in the ammo bunker. It was our tedious job to remove each round from a plastic canister and tear off a protective beeswax wrapper. Then we would remove the required number of increments (charges) and pass them up to the A-gunner. While the gunner was setting the mortar's sights, the A-gunner would take the rounds and make sure the correct number of charges was on the round. Then after everything was ready, the A-gunner would begin dropping the rounds into the tube.

During the actual firing, the impact from the constant discharges was so powerful that the mortar's base-plate would begin to drive itself deep into the ground, thus knocking the sights off of its coordinates. It was the gunner's responsibility to constantly re-sight the gun in order to keep the rounds on target. On a typical fire mission, which could occur at any time day or night, we would fire anywhere from twenty to one hundred rounds or more. Consequently, the area around the parapet would quickly become littered with wax wrappings, canisters, and unused charges. Since the section leader and the assistant gunner were of a higher rank, we were stuck with the inglorious job of cleaning up the area after each mission.

Predictably, the inevitable truck would show up to deliver us more ammo stacked on pallets. This process entailed opening and then breaking open the wooden boxes, tearing off the plastic cover from the canisters, and then individually hauling the rounds down into the ammo bunker. Once this was done, it was also our responsibility to count the number of rounds we had stored and clean up all of the trash that was left behind.

Without a doubt, the preparation behind firing an 81mm mortar is an extremely arduous job. On the average, our gun crew was firing well over 500 rounds per week, so the work was grueling and never-ending. Since we were conducting so many fire missions, we took turns sighting and firing the gun. In this manner, everybody was trained to do everybody else's job in case someone got wounded. Then during the nighttime, we were expected to continuously fire H & I (Harassment & Interdiction) missions into the suspected enemy positions or their most likely avenues of approach.

Due to the fact that the section leader (Chevy) was exempt from getting his hands dirty, the rest of us had to do all of the work. Besides being assigned to the daily work details, unloading the ammo, firing the missions, constantly policing the area, and standing the watches (four hours a day and four hours a night per person), we probably averaged just a few hours of sleep within any given twenty-four-hour period. It didn't take long before I was walking around completely exhausted from the routine.

Since there wasn't enough water for a person to actually take a shower, we would fill our canteen cups and wash ourselves down with a wet rag. Of course, it didn't eliminate the weird body odors drifting through the bunker, but it was the best that we could do. During one memorable evening, while I was sitting at the desk and washing my feet, the bunker unexpectedly began to shake and tremble as if we were in the middle of an earthquake. As the room began moving around, the bunks started swaying and creaking. Then

I noticed the roof started shifting above our heads, as if it was about to collapse. At the time, I didn't know what to think. The walls of the bunker were literally crumbling at the seams. Then off in the distance, I could hear a series of massive explosions, which seemed to last several minutes.

Looking around at the other wide-eyed kids, I asked them, "What in the hell was that?" It wasn't until after the explosions had stopped before Wallace finally spoke up.

"That's an arc light," he responded.

Recognizing that I didn't know what he was talking about, Wallace began telling me all about our ultimate weapon in Vietnam. In so many words, he said, it was a group of three B-52 bombers, carrying twenty-seven tons of bombs apiece. Flying in close formation, they would simultaneously drop their lethal bomb loads over a concentrated area. Conservatively speaking, the U.S. Air Force could destroy an area several miles long and about a half of a mile wide in less than a minute. Chevy thought it was the greatest thing since the twist-off beer cap. He remembered that during an operation near the Rockpile, they had gone down into an underground bunker after the area had been hit by an arc light. The concussion from the bombs had been so powerful that it had literally embedded, or one could say enshrined, the unsuspecting enemy soldiers into the surrounding dirt walls of the bunker.

Over the next month or so, the NVA would hit our position almost daily. When they weren't firing their artillery rounds at us, they were usually hitting us with their mortars and rockets. Some days were worse than others, depending upon their ammo supply. The purpose behind these bombardments was to keep us pinned down in our holes, so that their patrols could move freely about the area. Even though our FOs had been stationed along the top of the hills, the incoming tended to divert their attention. It was during this time that most of our missions were directed at suspected enemy positions. But when our FOs did happen to spot a group of them, they would yell into their radio receivers, "gooks in the open" and we would hit the parapet with renewed enthusiasm. In one mission alone, our gun crew was credited with thirty-two confirmed kills.

Soon afterward, a new kid by the named of Johnson was assigned to our crew. As luck would have it, we met each other during a mortar attack. One day, a truck full of hot chow had arrived from Dong Ha. It seemed that somebody in command had decided to feed one company at a time, en masse and out in the open. As we were waiting in line, Perez brought Johnson over to me and introduced him as LSD. Inasmuch as we didn't know anything about the drug or what the letters LSD actually meant, everybody started calling him Dee. As I was about to get my chow, a couple of mortar rounds suddenly landed on the other side of the truck from us. In one quick motion, our little group leaped under a nearby water tank for cover.

Then in a semi-authentic English accent, Dee rolled over to adjust his glasses and said, "I say old chaps, friends of yours?"

After spitting some dirt out of my mouth, I replied to him, "I think it's the landlord."

Within several minutes, we crawled back out of our hiding places and formed another line. As I stood there watching the server slap gobs of instant mashed potatoes into our passing canteen cups, another salvo of rounds came whizzing right over our heads. Similar to the old Keystone Cop movies, fifty or more startled Marines began running and flying into each other in an effort to escape the barrage. Then in the middle of all this mayhem, Sergeant Major Stepanovich and Gunny Gonzales defiantly stood out in the open waving their fists towards the enemy position as they were screaming, "Give us your best shot, Charlie. You can't hit nothin' anyway." Incredibly, I had never seen anyone stand up to the incoming before. Watching these two old vintage World War II veterans was something very special. They definitely had a way about them.

Upon further inquiry, I discovered Dee enjoyed reading comic books or *Mad* magazine, while he listened to rock 'n' roll music. Over time, I became closer to him than to any other person in Vietnam. He possessed a medium build, brown eyes, and a perpetual look of aggravation upon his face. Also, he was one of the most unpredictable human beings on the face of the planet, which made him a lot of fun to be around, and how he got through Marine boot camp I'll never know. He didn't like authority, uniforms, schedules, or any type of structure operating in his life. He was the type of guy who was capable of receiving either the Congressional Medal of Honor or a stiff prison sentence. His life was a maze of contradictions, bubble gum wrappers, and sandbagging (Marine slang for evading work). However, like the overwhelming majority of Marines, he would stick by you when the going got tough.

Born in Seattle, Washington, in 1948, Dee had lived a very turbulent, if not disturbing childhood. The scuttlebutt was that as an eleven-year-old kid, his parents dropped him off at a foster home. Since he was always getting into trouble, the local school officials had labeled Dee an incorrigible delinquent. Then around his thirteenth birthday, he ran away from his foster parents and joined a circus. Working odd jobs and travelling around the country, he never really found a home until he enlisted in the Marine Corps. With a devious grin stretched across his face, his one comment about joining the Corps was, "What better place can a person get three square meals a day, a warm place to crap, and a sergeant who loves you?"

One rainy afternoon, we were unexpectedly called together for mail call. The letters and packages from home were always something we looked forward to. On this particular occasion, Wallace had received a package full of canned hams and chili, along with packaged fruits and candy bars. As we watched him inventory his goodies, it became painfully obvious to us that he had no intention of sharing his good fortune. Every time he lifted a can up in the air for inspection, someone would say something like, "Man, that sure looks mighty good."

At one point, I even tried to make a deal with him by offering him a few bucks for a can of chili. Unimpressed Wallace responded, "No way Jose." For several minutes, we sat there and looked at his canned food like a pack of hungry wolves. Finally in complete exasperation, Perez asked him, "What makes you so special?" Wallace just snickered and replied, "You're just jealous, because somebody back home loves me." Then off in a dark corner, we could hear Dee's voice echoing through the bunker, "Well now, ain't you the one."

Food was a very important subject to us, because our diets had become extremely limited to say the least. If memory serves me correctly, a case of C-rations consisted of twelve different boxes of meals. At three meals a day, it didn't take very long before a person would become totally disgusted with the lack of variety. Then adding insult to injury, the C-rations we ate were from a World War II surplus. Each box consisted of a can of meat, a can of fruit, a can of pastry, and a tiny can of peanut butter or cheese. Ranging from meatballs and beans, beef and potatoes, and ham and limas, the meals were old, congealed, and tasteless. The canned peaches and pears weren't all that bad, but the pound cake was the only pastry worth eating. Come to think of it, I don't think I ever saw anyone eat the fruitcake more than once. The fact that the instant coffee had become crystallized into a hard little brick didn't really bother anyone. But the peanut butter had a way of sticking to the roof of your mouth for days on end.

Sometime in late February, I received a very strange piece of mail. Unlike the usual letters from home, this one was stamped "Urgent United States Government." Hoping the guys in Washington, D.C. had finally realized their mistake by sending me to Vietnam, I eagerly ripped open the letter. As my fingers moved along each sentence, I couldn't believe my eyes. I just sat there stunned.

Finally, Dee broke the silence and asked, "What did you get?"

Almost misty-eyed, I glanced up at everyone in the bunker and said, "You fellows aren't going to believe this, but I've been drafted."

They couldn't believe it either. It was like the left hand of our government didn't know what the right hand was doing. It was a scary thought, which had crossed my mind on more than one occasion. Of course, the other guys believed it was a big mistake and that I should just forget about the whole thing.

However to my bizarre way of thinking, I had received an order by my federal government to report to the nearest Selective Service Office. Therefore, I reasoned, it had become my utmost responsibility to fulfill my obligations as a citizen. Marine Corps or no Marine Corps, my government had obviously wanted me in the U.S. Army. Who was I to ignore an order from our Commander-in-Chief? Obviously, I needed to go back home and report for duty. Later, when I tried to explain all this to the Company Gunny, he just looked up at me as if I was nuts and then he threw me out of his bunker.

With my head hanging low in rejection, I walked past Dee, who had been waiting for me beside the road. Then in a childlike voice, I heard him whine, "I told you it wouldn't work, you knucklehead."

Chapter Three

Yankee Station

"People will always march off to war, whenever they have been convinced of the righteousness of the cause."

As I was standing watch in the ammo bunker one early morning, Washington came down the stairs to relieve me. After a brief exchange of hellos, I handed him the inventory sheet listing every round in the bunker. "If anybody gives a damn," I said, "We have nine hundred ninety-one 81mm rounds, three boxes of M-16 ammo, and one brand new mortar." Then ironically as an afterthought, I wondered how big of a crater it would leave if the bunker happened to blow up. He said, "I don't know, man. But as long as gooks don't use any of those delayed fuses, we'll be okay."

The delayed fuse was something we all came to fear and despise. Normally fired by an NVA 130mm or a 152mm artillery piece, the round would burrow into the ground about ten feet deep before it exploded. Used as an anti-bunker shell, it wasn't much of a threat to a person standing some distance away, but it was murder on underground bunkers. One could always tell when the NVA were using delayed fuses, because you would hear a sickening thud right before the round exploded.

When I finally reached our living quarters, everybody was still asleep. So I tiptoed over to the desk and began preparing an unappetizing breakfast of mushy beans and weenies. Then as I was about to light a heat tablet, a salvo of 152mm artillery rounds came screaming into our area. Only this time, they hit so close to our bunker, the other guys didn't even have time to grab their helmets or flak jackets. In one quick motion, everyone dove under his bunk.

Evidently, our section of two mortars must have really pissed off the NVA, because they were aiming their artillery rounds right for our bunkers. With each new salvo, one could feel the ground shake and rumble as if the earth itself was in convulsions. While we were hugging the floor for everything it was worth, the sounds of the ripping explosions and flying shrapnel echoed through the thin air. Looking up at the tiny rays of light, I could see streams of sand and gravel trickling down from the bunker's ceiling. Every time I tried to speak, chunks of dirt and debris were hurled down the stairwell and into my face. Lying in the semidarkness, I felt completely helpless as the rounds continuously marched across our position. The concussions alone were beginning to rattle our insides and destroy our bunker. Between the screaming rounds and the hellish roars that followed, I didn't believe it was ever going to end. At the time, I kept thinking to myself, "Where in the hell is our Air Force?" But what really shook me up was when I could hear Wallace tenderly praying for his mom.

Trying to survive this man-made inferno of steel and fire, we instinctively balled ourselves up into a fetal position and stuck our fingers into our ears. With each powerful explosion, we looked at each other as if it was going to be our last moment on earth. The expression of absolute fear and horror I saw in their faces that morning was something I'll never forget. As the bombardment continued, I noticed there was a predictable pause of a few minutes between each salvo.

Much like the old war movies I had seen as a kid, the NVA were using that time to reload their guns. Thus between the salvos, the other guys in the bunker had time to get dressed and put on their protective gear.

After taking a quick head count, Chevy asked, "Where in the hell is Washington?"

I told him that he was standing watch in the ammo bunker.

"Well, I'd better go get him," he replied.

As we stood at the entrance together, I suggested it might be a good idea for him to wait a few more minutes—until after the next salvo had been fired. It was obvious to me that they were about to fire again. In a fit of anger, he told me to shut my mouth, because he knew what he was doing. To my utter amazement, he just stood there and waited and waited. I couldn't believe it. It was as if he had never seen any of the old war movies.

I doubt if Chevy could have timed it any better, even if he had tried. Immediately after he leaped out of the stairwell and disappeared from my sight, another salvo roared into our area. Only this time, it sounded as though the rounds had landed only a few feet away. I instantly assumed that old Chevy had bought the ranch. Then within a matter of a few seconds, he came flying back into our bunker with the look of a crazed wild man on his face. He started jabbering about how he had just begun to descend the stairs of the ammo bunker when a 152mm round crashed through the roof.

As he was describing the engulfing flames and the intense heat from the impact, I yelled at him, "Where's Washington?"

"Damned, if I know, man," he rambled, "All I saw was a wall of flames."

Temporarily stunned, I looked at the others in utter disbelief. We just knew that Washington had met his maker. Then out of the blue, Washington stumbled down the stairs. He was screaming and yelling his head off about how this dud had come through the roof with such force that it spewed flames, mortar rounds, and pieces of wood all over God's half-acre.

As we began to tend to Washington's wounds, it became obvious to us that he was badly hurt. Besides having a large hole in his ass and some facial wounds, the immense heat from the impact had burned most of the black skin right off of his arms. In the dim light, we could see it hanging there like shredded pieces of charred nylon clothing. The sweet, sickening smell of his seared flesh was so strong that it made Wallace sick to his stomach. The poor kid began puking all over the floor. Upon closer inspection, we also noticed a part of Washington's flak jacket had melted into his shoulders. Although he was in tremendous pain, he didn't complain. So we continued to bandage his wounds and consoled him as best we could.

After several minutes, Washington began to mutter over and over again, "Can you believe it, man, that son-of-a-bitch was a dud?"

While we were busy with Washington, none of us was aware that the barrage had stopped. Fortunately, as he was about to go into a state of shock, Gunny Gonzales arrived with a corpsman and a couple of stretcher-bearers. As we stepped aside, they were very impressive to watch. Within seconds, they had Washington loaded onto a stretcher and were hauling him up to the Battalion Aid Station. Then right before Gunny and his crew left, he told us to stay put, until we got further orders. With a sigh of relief, we sat down and patted each other on the backs for a job well done. Wallace was so impressed with himself that he yelled out, "Hell, we might even get a medal for this." While we laughed and kidded each other, we were completely ignorant of the fact that the adjacent ammo bunker was beginning to burn.

It must have been about thirty minutes after they had taken Washington away that the mortar rounds in our ammo bunker began to explode. At first, they began to explode individually. Every few seconds we could hear the rip of a detonating round. Then as the heat intensified, they started going off in groups of three and four. Due to the fact that these explosions were occurring about twenty feet from our bunker's entrance, I thought it might be a good idea for us to get the hell out of there. Obviously, no one wanted to take charge. So I stood up and said, "Screw this nonsense, I'm outta here. Who wants to come along?" Almost in unison, they replied, "We're with you, man." Then as calmly as possible, I explained that I wanted them to count to five, before they followed the guy in front of them out of the bunker. In this manner, we wouldn't be in a clustered group, thus presenting a smaller target for the enemy.

Dee looked up and said, "That sounds great, but where are we running to?"

After pausing for a few seconds, I responded, "Go to the dy-bunker directly up the hill."

The dy-bunker was a large, half-buried structure, located several hundred feet up the hill from our bunker. It was large enough to comfortably house fifteen people. Inside, the bunk beds were lined up all along the walls much like one would find in a regular barracks back home. The structure itself was supported by thick wooden beams and surrounded by piles and piles of sandbags. If I remember correctly, the bunker was being shared by a 106mm recoilless rifle crew and some kids from our mortar platoon. When driving into Con Thien, one couldn't miss seeing it, because of its immense size. During its construction, several people in our battalion had complained about it being too big. They believed it would only make a bigger target for the NVA gunners. But on this particular day, the bunker would be a godsend.

When I approached the entrance to our bunker, the noise from the explosions was deafening. With each new blast, I could feel the heat wave bounce off of my face. Looking down at their pale frightened expressions, I yelled, "Does everybody know what to do?" Nodding their heads in reluctant approval, I could tell that they weren't very enthusiastic about my idea. Nevertheless without even looking towards the ammo bunker, I ran through the entranceway and took off up the hill. Pumping my legs as fast as possible, I thought that I was moving at a pretty good clip. Then suddenly out of nowhere, the rest of the guys from the bunker came out running and zoomed past me as if I was standing still. Peering through the dense smoke, all I could see was the bottoms of their boots kicking up these huge clods of dirt. I remember one of them kept yelling at the others, "Get out of my way, asshole." In fact, Wallace was moving so fast that instead of running around a parked vehicle, he just leaped over the hood like a gazelle. After I finally reached the dy-bunker, we had a big laugh about how they were supposed to count to five before they followed me out.

Once we entered the dy-bunker, we found ourselves surrounded by a group of concerned Marines. After they had seen the stretcher-bearers headed towards our bunker, they wanted to know what had happened. As Wallace and Perez began regaling them with stories of their bravery, I could hear Dee off in one corner asking someone if he had an extra pack of cigarettes. Then as I was about to answer someone else's question, everybody in the bunker was suddenly blown through the air like a bunch of rag dolls. I guess the experience was akin to being blindsided by an oncoming eighteen-wheeler. The force of the concussion was so great that it slammed three of the kids against the wall and knocked them out cold.

To this day, I have no idea how many pounds of TNT were actually in the ammo bunker. But when it exploded, we thought the Russian Air Force had dropped a bomb on us. The jolt was so powerful and so unexpected that it took several minutes before we could get our bearings straight. Confused and in shock, we staggered around in the unsettled dust calling out each other's names. Later, I would swear to anybody who would listen that when the ammo bunker blew, I could actually feel my teeth shift around inside my gums.

"Come look at this, you ain't going to believe it," someone yelled from the doorway. Rushing outside the dy-bunker, we were not at all prepared for what we saw next. It looked as if we had been blown to a totally different hill. The landscape had been literally shifted around the surviving bunkers to where nothing was recognizable any longer. The roads had vanished, the nearby out-house had totally disintegrated, and several of the surrounding trench lines were almost completely filled in with dirt. Looking farther down the slope, we spotted a huge crater where our ammo bunker and parapet used to be. Shaped in a perfect cone the actual hole was about fifty feet wide and thirty feet deep. We could see hundreds of mortar rounds and pieces of mortar rounds littered all over the hill. To no one's surprise, we never found any part of our new 81mm mortar. Perez thought it was probably in orbit somewhere.

Running down the slope to check on our bunker, we discovered how fortunate we had been for leaving when we did. Still on the other hand, I was rather pissed off that we had been told to stay there in the first place. From what we could tell, the wall of our living quarters that had faced the ammo bunker had been literally pushed across the room and into the other wall, thus crushing everything in between. Unable to catch our breath, we just stood there and looked dumbfounded. Dee shook his head and finally broke the silence by saying, "Well, that takes care of our rat problem." As we began to dig into the bunker, the NVA decided to drop a few more rounds into the area. Only this time, I beat everyone else back to the dy-bunker.

After we had scrambled back to the dy-bunker for the second time, Dee and I were ordered to go back out into the sporadic NVA mortar fire and locate every mortar round that had been blown out of our ammo bunker. It was our chosen task to mark the rounds or the pieces of rounds with a stick or a sandbag, so that nobody would step on them in the dark. Thus as the sun was beginning to disappear, Dee and I could be seen running around the hill marking these deadly rounds, while we dodged the occasional incoming mortar round. If the assignment had not been so ludicrous, I would have been more enthusiastic about it, but the only question that kept creeping through my mind was why would someone in our battalion want to endanger our lives over something as stupid as this?

When I finally returned to the dy-bunker from marking the rounds, I jumped into the first available empty bunk. But before I could fall asleep, I felt a hand touch my shoulder. Rolling over, I was surprised to find Dee triumphantly holding up a set of used camouflaged utilities and a pair of honest-to-goodness, jungle boots. Considering that we were both still wearing our old, ragged stateside uniforms, we carried on over the newfound clothing like a couple of women at the mall.

Then in the middle of our glee, I suddenly asked him in a mocking voice, "Oh, by the way, old buddy, old pal, where did you happen to get this stuff?"

Looking somewhat guilty and ashamed, he replied, "I found them in a big pile just outside the Battalion Aid Station."

Raising a suspicious eyebrow, I said, "And what else?"

From what Dee revealed, it seemed that when the ammo bunker had exploded, the Battalion Commander and his radioman had been standing there watching it burn. Tragically, a huge rock had hit the young radioman in the head and killed him on the spot.

"Man, you wouldn't believe all the neat things they're taking off these poor guys," he blurted out.

Feeling my anger beginning to swell, I informed him that I did not intend to wear some unfortunate dead guy's clothing.

Then after an eerie interval of silence, Dee finally looked up and said, "Well, you can have my stuff instead. But you probably won't want it either, because it came off of a kid who had gotten shot between the eyes the other day by a sniper."

I just sat there and looked at him as though he was crazy.

Then in a moment of frightful clarity, Dee bent over and whispered to me, "If you don't want the stuff, I'll take it back. But it's the only jungle gear you're ever going to find in this hellhole."

Strangely enough, I ended up wearing those jungle boots for almost two years. In spite of the fact that they were a bit too large for my feet, I came to look upon them as my lucky charms.

I don't know when it actually occurred, but somewhere between the exploding bunker and the dumb-ass work details, I came to the inescapable conclusion that I didn't want to be a mortarman any longer. Even though my options were extremely limited, because of my training, I was still determined to find another job. Thus a few days after the big bang, I began asking around about my other career opportunities. And lo and behold, I discovered that there were always openings for forward observers (FOs).

It took some time, but after pestering the higher ups, I was eventually transferred to Hotel Company as an understudy to their 81's FO team. Naturally, I was going to miss Dee and the others, but I felt it was the best thing for me to do at the time. I don't know what it was, but something out in the bush kept calling my name. I just had to go out and see the beast for myself.

Once I had packed my gear and reported to Hotel Company, I was introduced to their FO team. The FO was a mellow black kid from Alabama named Davis. Well built and sturdy, possessing a thin mustache and arms the size of tree trunks, he hadn't been the Hotel Company's forward observer for very long. His radioman was a white fellow from Georgia. Everyone called him Georgie, because no one could pronounce his real name. Being about my size, he had brown hair, green eyes, and a huge set of ears. He also had an uncontrollable temper that made it very difficult to be around the guy.

Ordinarily, we all got along well enough, but because of our racial differences, there was always an underlying tension between us. Davis didn't trust whites and we didn't trust him. However to our surprise, we discovered that we had a lot more in common with each other than we ever had with any of our fellow Americans north of the Mason-Dixon line. The color of our skin may have been different, but our regional cultures were very similar. The overall experience was very strange and perplexing for all of us, because we had unknowingly carried our society's ills with us into the battlefield.

As I got to know Davis and Georgie, I didn't feel very relaxed around them. Unlike Dee, they just didn't have any magic or pizzazz about them. Raised in the streets of Fort Worth, I had observed that some people have a mystical way about them and some people don't. I always figured that it has more to do with a person's attitude and his innate faith in himself than anything else. From my experiences, the ones with magic tend to walk beyond the pale of life and death. They accept the consequences of their limited and uncertain life spans, and move forward towards their fate with a stout heart and a burning desire to live every moment to its utmost fullness. Instead of succumbing to their constant fears and inhibitions, they exist outside the realm of their society's narrow expectations, while rejecting the oppressive nature of its traditions and customs. Self-reliant, individualistic, and free from doubt, they arrogantly stand alone in a world shrouded with the aura of indecision and diffidence. In essence, the average person has a choice of either laughing or crying about the ebb and flow of their existence. These large souls chose to laugh and accept their fate.

In general, I believe that a person should become what they are doing and not deny the nature of his or her role. For instance, if you were going to be an infantryman, then be one. Don't try to be something else. Since we were in an insane situation, I believed that it was only natural for one to become a part of that insanity. I had always wanted to be an infantryman, so accepting the role of a grunt was easy for me. I could tolerate the filth, the rain, and the danger. As an individual, it was a large part of who I was. However, many of our kids in Vietnam couldn't shake off their middle-class attitudes and values. While stomping around the rice paddies and jungles, they acted as if they were back home with their friends on a Sunday picnic. In my mind, they weren't being a part of what was happening around them.

Instead, they were merely dreaming of being a civilian again, while acting out the role of a grunt. Tragically, the kids who denied the true nature of an infantryman usually ended up going home in a body bag.

No doubt about it, life as a forward observer was ten times better than the life of a mortarman. There weren't any work details to perform or any endless hours of pumping rounds down a tube. Unfortunately though, everyone had failed to mention the fact that the life expectancy of a forward observer, once his unit had made contact with the enemy, was about thirty seconds long. During a firefight, while everyone else was running for cover, they had to constantly expose themselves to enemy fire in order to get the coordinates and adjust the mortar rounds. In fact, it was one of the most hazardous jobs in the military.

Since Hotel Company was manning a section of the hill's perimeter, I would continue to see Dee and the others. They would be out there all day long filling sandbags and digging trenches, while I sat around and played cards with my newfound buddies. Instead of constantly busting my butt while operating the mortar, the battalion's FOs were responsible for standing watches in one of the three towers stationed atop the hills or going out on patrol with one of the company's platoons. While in the towers, it was our responsibility, along with the artillery FOs, to call in fire missions at anything that moved within the general vicinity. Of course, we were alerted beforehand when and where our patrols would be going outside the perimeter.

During my stay at Con Thien, I got a real kick out of my new assignment. Looking through a huge pair of binoculars in one of the towers, I could see into the southern part of North Vietnam and beyond. The view was both unbelievably beautiful and frightening. Still, the best part of it all was that we could blow the hell out the place without any questions being asked. All we had to do was give the FDC a set of coordinates, an azimuth (direction) to the target, and the number and the types of rounds to be fired. Then the FDC would direct one of the mortar crews to fire a white phosphorus (Willie Peter) round to our coordinates. Once we had spotted the white smoke, we would then adjust our fire to the target. Within seconds, we could see the high explosive (HEs) rounds hitting around the area. Of course, we could employ many different fire patterns, depending upon the nature of the terrain and the target. As long as we didn't abuse the system, we could call in a fire mission on any surrounding area, within a 5,000-meter radius.

I'll never forget the first time that I called in a fire mission as a forward observer during one of our patrols. To say the least, it wasn't my finest moment. Between trying to figure out our coordinates, the azimuth, and the coordinates of the target, I must have done something horribly wrong. Either I had the map upside down or I gave the wrong azimuth to the FDC, but whatever the case, I damn near got everybody killed.

As we were standing there on top of a small hill and waiting for the white phosphorus round to hit several hundred meters off to the east, the damn thing landed several yards behind us. Scrambling in every which direction, I was very lucky that no one got hurt or I would still be burning shitters for the Marine Corps.

At the beginning of the Tet Offensive in late January of 1968 and until the middle of March, the NVA continually bombarded the surrounding outposts, such as Con Thien, Dong Ha, Gio Linh, and Camp Carroll. Almost daily, our hill was hit by some form of Soviet or Chinese ordnance. It wouldn't have surprised anyone if they had started shooting self-propelled refrigerators into our perimeter, because they threw everything else at us but the kitchen sink. Probably the freakiest weapon they ever shot at us was the 122mm rocket. Unlike the incredibly fast artillery round, it seemed that the rocket projectile would take forever to hit its target. On more than one occasion, we could hear the rockets begin to scream in the direction of our hill, and instead of running for our lives, we would just meander over to the bunker, knowing full well that we had the time to safely get out of the way.

On one memorable day, while I was sitting in a tower, the NVA gunners began to traverse their mortar rounds across my former mortar section. At the time, Dee and the others were working on their new parapet. When the first round landed about one hundred meters away, the other rounds began to methodically move towards their position. From where I was sitting, it looked as if the explosions were going to march right through their parapet. Feeling completely helpless, I could see the guys lying there in the dirt waiting for the inevitable. Then just as the string of explosions was about to reach them, the last round unexpectedly veered off to the right and landed several meters up the hill. Since Dee and I were mortarmen, we knew exactly what had happened. The NVA gunner had failed to adjust the bubbles on his sights during their fire mission. Thus the last round went astray.

After the smoke had cleared, I could see Dee sticking his little, ugly head out of the parapet and looking around in absolute bewilderment. Suddenly, he glanced up and noticed that I had been nonchalantly sitting up in the tower and watching him.

With a big grin smeared across my face, I yelled down at him, "Boy, you're one lucky asshole."

Grinning back at me, he hollered, "You've got that right buddy. I could kiss that lazy gook's ass."

Being stationed up in a tower during a bombardment was a totally different experience from being in a bunker. Looking down, I could watch the rounds explode across the face of the hill as if I was one of the enemy's FOs. It was an eerie feeling, knowing what the guys in the bunkers were going through.

As forward observers, it was our job to locate the NVA's firing positions and direct our return fire. Even though the tower was literally covered with shrapnel holes, it wasn't a bad place to be stationed. However if you weren't careful, you could get your butt shot off in a

New York minute. During one memorable barrage, the artillery observer and I popped our heads up and turned our binoculars towards North Vietnam. To our dismay, we counted over two hundred muzzle flashes from the enemy's artillery pieces. They were obviously hitting everybody along the DMZ that day. Then while the artillery observer was fumbling around with his map and compass, a 152mm round thundered right by our tower. The shock wave was so powerful that it literally knocked us both to the floor.

"We've got gooks in the open," Davis suddenly yelled out to me one Saturday morning. Moving to the other side of the tower, I turned my glasses to where he was pointing. And sure enough, I could see a platoon of camouflaged NVA about three thousand meters away. They were making their way across an old rice paddy as if they didn't have a care in the world.

While the artillery FO was trying to figure out their coordinates, Davis called in a thirty-round fire mission to our FDC. It didn't take long before our mortar rounds began mushrooming around them in a hell storm of flying shrapnel and debris. In the meantime, the NVA began running to a nearby ravine. After the smoke had momentarily cleared, we could see a few of their buddies lying out there like so many piles of dirty laundry. Suddenly, a small group of them began popping out of their hiding places and running across the paddy in order to save their wounded buddies. Frantically, Davis began yelling into his receiver for the 81s to keep firing.

Then right in the middle of all this commotion, one of our M-48 tanks got into the action. With a terrific boom, their crew let loose with their 90mm gun. Although the round was off its mark, the explosion blew huge lumps of dirt and pieces of rock into every direction. As the tank crew began to reload their gun, I suddenly spotted four more NVA rushing out into the rice paddy. In one clean swoop, they threw one of their buddies onto a blanket and began carrying him back towards the ravine. For a minute, it looked as if they were going to make it. Oddly enough, I found myself almost rooting for them. Then just as they were about to disappear to safety, the tank fired again. Peering through the glasses, I watched the round rip into the ground right under the blanket, blowing them into atoms. Amidst the surrounding smoke and chaos, Davis and I would eventually count twelve NVA bodies and parts of several others.

Sometime in early March, Hotel Company was rotated out of the perimeter and moved to a place called Yankee Station. It was situated next to the road about five hundred meters south of Con Thien. Why it was even located there, I had no idea. The position itself couldn't have helped defend Con Thien in case of a major attack, nor could it have saved itself. Built on a small plateau with ravines running up and down its sides, the position had been designed as a company-sized outpost. After looking around, I could see the trenches and bunkers weren't very well developed and there wasn't much of a minefield around it. But there was one redeeming quality about living in Yankee Station. By the obvious lack of craters, it rarely received any incoming rounds. I guess the NVA didn't think the place was valuable enough for them to waste their precious ammunition on.

Because the accommodations at Yankee Station were not very plentiful, Davis, Georgie, and I were assigned to a bunker already occupied by a four-deuce (4.2-inch mortar) FO and his radio operator. They liked to call themselves artillery FOs, but they really weren't. A four-deuce was a one hundred-plus millimeter mortar. Much like the eighty-one, it was a deadly but unpredictable weapon.

Upon our arrival, we discovered our new bunker was a real dump. Not only was the room inside just three feet high and about the size of a doghouse, the roof had only one thin layer of sandbags. As a ritual, we had to crawl in and out of the place like a bunch of ants. After awhile, it got so frustrating we talked about building a new bunker as soon as possible. Unfortunately, there was a snag. We didn't get along with our new roommates very well. They liked to look down at us because of their superior education. It seems that one of them actually had a high school diploma, while the other guy's only claim to fame was that he had spent one semester at a local junior college. Considering there wasn't a high school diploma between Davis, Georgie, and me, they looked upon us as a crude and unsophisticated lot.

The four-deuce FO was a tall, brown-haired, skinny corporal named Mac. Having been from Chicago, he loved to gamble on anything and everything. In the evenings, he liked to entertain us with his stories of being a high school football hero and a real lady-killer. After listening to him for a couple of nights, we concluded that he was an awful liar.

As for his radioman, he was a slightly overweight Jewish kid from New Jersey called Chubby. He possessed dark hair, brown eyes, and a large nose. He was definitely too intelligent and educated to be out in the bush. He could sit there in the bunker and mentally calculate the dimensions of our perimeter in terms of its area. Chubby and Mac were both about twenty-one-years old with four months in country and completely nuts. After our first week together, I could tell that they had bonded with each other in a very peculiar fashion. In fact, they acted like an old and irate married couple. They argued constantly and furiously about nothing and everything. It seemed like that they had created their own unique world around them. Life to them was centered upon their solitary relationship. They slept next to each other, ate together, crapped together, and worked together. And I have no doubt that they were eventually blown away together. Even when I could get them to drop the act for a second, they still acted as if they were in the middle of a frickin' soap opera.

About once or twice a week, our FO team was expected to go out on patrol with one of the company's platoons. Usually, we would venture out in a southeasterly or southwesterly direction for several miles, before we were expected to return to Yankee Station. Nobody ever wanted to head north. However, the patrols were an education unto themselves. I was able to learn a lot about the different types of ordnance we employed. Similar to the moon, the area was literally covered with craters. A person couldn't walk ten feet without stepping into one. Thus during our treks through the countryside, I learned how to identify each crater and the weapon that made it.

One fine morning as we were patrolling an area to the southwest of Con Thien, we came upon an NVA squad right in the middle of their breakfast. The only reason we were able to surprise them was because our lieutenant had gotten us lost. Instead of coming from the northeast as they would have expected us to do, we came upon them from the south.

As soon as we made contact with them, the NVA started firing at us while they began running along a dense tree line. Within seconds of hitting the ground, Davis was on the horn trying to call in a fire mission. Then near the front of the platoon, someone began yelling for a corpsman. In the dust and confusion, I could hear the branches of the trees above me snapping from the enemy's fire. Snuggling next to a tree stump, I began to shoot at the shadowy figures. However, due to the thick underbrush, I didn't know if I was actually hitting anybody. Amazingly, I wasn't as scared as I thought I would be in my first firefight. The popguns they were using against us weren't near as impressive as being shot at by a 152mm artillery piece.

As Davis was about to give our mortar section the order to "Fire for effect," the firefight suddenly stopped. Up and down the line, we could hear the platoon sergeant yelling at us to cease-fire. I asked the guy next to me what was going on, but he just shrugged his shoulders as if he didn't know anything either. In a moment of uncertainty, I crawled over to where Davis and Georgie were lying. On the other side of a small ditch, we could hear the lieutenant and the platoon sergeant arguing about our next move. The lieutenant wanted to follow the retreating NVA into the next paddy, while the sergeant was telling him, "Over my dead body." As the sergeant tried to explain to him the potential for being lured into an ambush, the lieutenant got madder and madder. Then as they were about to come to blows, the lieutenant suddenly received a radio call from headquarters ordering us back to base. Rising to his feet, he began arguing with the company commander over the radio. In our amusement, we could tell that he wasn't winning that argument either. In a fit of anger, the young lieutenant finally threw the receiver at his radioman and ordered us back down the tree line.

It was almost a Marine Corps tradition for the staff NCOs of each platoon to help out the young lieutenants until they got their feet wet. But unfortunately, some lieutenants ignored their advice out of pure arrogance and we would end up paying the price.

From what I could tell, we must have killed several NVA soldiers. The only casualty we had received was a slightly wounded point man. Of course, I didn't know how the NVA played the game, so I thought the lieutenant had showed a lot of courage. But after acquiring some experience in the bush, I came to realize that he probably would have gotten us all killed, if it hadn't been for that stubborn platoon sergeant.

One day, I walked up to the hill to see Dee and the boys. At first, I had a little trouble finding them, because they had moved to another bunker. Finally, I came across them playing cards with their new section leader. As usual, Dee was winning everybody's money as if he had a stacked deck. After I was introduced to the new corporal, we had a wonderful time reminiscing about our ammo bunker's big bang.

Gazing down at my feet Dee said, "I see you're still wearing them old boots."

"Hell, I even sleep with them," I jokingly replied.

Halfway through their poker game, the section leader agreed to let me have a pile of sandbags and some engineer stakes. As we continued to talk, Dee began fiddling around with a hand grenade. I didn't think anything about it at the time, because everybody had hand grenades. Then out of nowhere Dee muttered, "Oops," as the grenade dropped to the ground and the spoon flew across the table. Instead of grabbing the damn thing and throwing it outside, I instantly made a beeline for the doorway. But before I had even reached the top of the stairs, I could hear the guys behind me laughing to the high heavens. Apparently, the new section leader had taught Dee how to rig the grenade harmless by unscrewing the top and removing the blasting cap.

Pointing his finger in my direction, Dee kept yelling, "Boy, did you see the look on Short's face when the spoon went flying?"

All I could do was stand there and look sheepish. Later, as we were loading the building material onto the mule, I reminded Dee that "Payback can be a real bitch."

The nearest American installation to Con Thien was an artillery base called C-2. It was approximately two or three miles to the southeast towards Dong Ha. Periodically, we would be assigned to a particular platoon in order to conduct a road sweep. Similar to riding in any convoy, it could either be an extremely dangerous trip or a really boring one. As far as I could tell, the idea behind the road sweep was to drive down the road until a vehicle had either hit a mine or until the convoy itself was ambushed. In the case of hitting a mine, the engineers would disembark from the trucks with their mine detectors and begin the tedious process of scanning the road. Then once they had cleared the area, we would continue on our merry way until we either hit another one or we made it to our destination. None of it seemed to make a lot of sense to me, but it was a thankless job that had to be done. Unfortunately though, one sneaky farmer could hold up an entire column of men and vehicles for most of a solid day.

In addition to hitting mines, the road sweep could also be ambushed at any point and at any moment. Usually, the NVA would shoot the hell out of the vehicles, just to see if we were dumb enough to stop the convoy. An unmoving convoy was one sure way of getting everybody killed or captured. But if the enemy were especially ambitious, they would mine the road and then set off an ambush once the first unlucky vehicle had gone flying through the air. In either scenario, we ended up the losers. With a little help from Chubby, we calculated it would have taken another million troops for us to have secured the roads in Vietnam. Slowly but surely, it was beginning to dawn on me that our leaders didn't really understand what the French had gone through before us. Our leaders may have read the books about the French/Indochina War, but it sure didn't seem like they had appreciated what the French had experienced.

During one particular road sweep, this new platoon lieutenant wanted to see what it was like to call in an 81mm fire mission. After stopping the vehicles on the side of the road, he picked out a tree line as a target and began figuring out the coordinates. As Davis handed him the horn (radio receiver) with one hand, I noticed that he made a cross over his chest like a Catholic priest with his other hand. Within a few minutes, the lieutenant had the mortar crew drop a white phosphorus round into a tree line about five hundred meters away from our position. It was his intention to traverse the rounds along the tree line, which ran parallel to our road. Everyone around him was excited with anticipation because watching a row of exploding HE rounds is something to behold.

Then once he thought everything was ready, he yelled into the receiver, "Fire for effect."

Looking back, I don't really know where the lieutenant went wrong in his calculations or why Davis hadn't caught the error. As we eagerly stood in the back of the truck, the rounds traversed right across our convoy like on oncoming train. Diving under the vehicles, some of us clutched our helmets and began praying to the heavens, while a few of us couldn't help but laugh. To everyone's good fortune, the only wounds anyone received were minor.

Within seconds of the accident, the white-faced lieutenant approached us and said, "Now, this didn't happen, right?"

I looked at him and replied with a smile, "We didn't see nothin', sir."

Of course, the lieutenant didn't get into any trouble, because we didn't rat him out to the higher ups. But the neat thing about the whole affair was if we ever needed anything from that lieutenant, he always went out of his way to be very helpful and cooperative.

In Vietnam, the only source of entertainment available to the grunts was the AM radio. Almost every other guy in the company carried one around in his backpack. In spite of the fact that we couldn't pick up any programs during the day due to the volume of military radio traffic, we were able to listen to the Armed Forces Radio Station in the evenings. For most of the guys, it was an extremely important pastime, because it gave us a sense of home and the world we had left behind. Unfortunately though, the programming left a lot to be desired. Sometimes we could even pick up Hanoi Hanna's station, but her music wasn't very good.

In an effort to please everyone, the Armed Forces Radio Station would play one hour of polkas, one hour of country and western, one hour of big band music, and finally one hour of what I enjoyed hearing: rock and Motown. The only problem with this format was that it didn't satisfy anybody. The overwhelming majority of the younger guys were into listening to either rock, Motown, or country music. The polkas and the big band music were for the older generation. What this meant was that out of four hours of nightly programming, there was usually only one hour of music a person could enjoy.

On many occasions, we would lie in our bunker at night and sing to each other. Usually, Davis would start us off with a fine rendition of Marvin Gaye or Sam Cooke. Then Mac and Chubby would form a duet and emulate the Righteous or Everly Brothers. Poor Georgie couldn't remember the words to any songs, so he just hummed along with each melody. As for myself, I loved the sounds of rock and soul, but I always thought a special occasion called for a special song. So after clearing my voice, I would sing Peter, Paul, and Mary's, "500 Miles." It was a real tearjerker, but everyone loved it all the same. Then for the grand finale, everybody in the bunker would round off the evening by singing in unison, "We've Got to Get Out of This Place," by the Animals.

Sometime in the latter part of March, our battalion received orders to be prepared to move out. After spending almost ninety days at Con Thien, my unit was finally going to be relieved. We could feel the excitement in the air as we began to square away our gear. Deciding what to take along or what to leave behind was a difficult decision for some. Mac and Chubby argued for hours on end over whether Mac should carry an extra poncho. The thought of living above ground again had put an extra step in our strides. There was something very unnatural and dirty about living like a mole in the ground.

The weather was beginning to change and the sun was becoming warmer with each morning. Everyone was laughing and giggling as if we were going on a picnic. There was even talk of the possibility of Hanoi and Washington meeting to negotiate a peace. But whatever the politics of the situation, we were all extremely happy about leaving Con Thien. It had an aura of death about it that I'm sure whoever had served there would never forget.

All during that week, the scuttlebutt was rampant about where we were going to be sent. One rumor had it we were going afloat, whereupon we would be stationed aboard naval vessels and employed as a reactionary force, but everyone knew that the 7th Marines had that assignment. Another rumor had it that we would be going to the Mekong Delta. But nobody believed that one either. Actually, the rumor I believed, which happened to be true, was that we were going to spearhead the operation (Pegasus) to relieve the siege at Khe Sanh.

However, it didn't turn out exactly that way, because *Operation Pegasus* had already been planned to be an Army affair. Apparently, General Westmoreland had already decided that the 1st Air Cavalry Division would spearhead the operation, while we went through the inglorious process of reopening Route 9. But I guess the strangest part about the operation was that the MACV (Military Assistance Command in Vietnam) headquarters back in Saigon had already determined that the siege was over. Military intelligence reports had been coming in for weeks that the NVA had been pulling out of the area. So it seemed as if we were going to have to go through the motions of appearing to save the combat base, all for the sake of publicity.[1]

A few days before we were supposed to move out, Chubby and I paid a little visit to my old mortar section buddies on the hill. We carried with us one empty claymore casing, a blasting cap, and a detonator wire. As we walked up towards their bunker, we could hear them inside, laughing and kidding with each other. Then after I had set up the mine several feet in front of the bunker door, I signaled Chubby and he started screaming down into the stairwell in a husky voice, "Okay, you slackers, get your butts topside ASAP, the Skipper has something to tell you shitbirds." Within seconds, Dee, Perez, and Wallace came stumbling out into the open air, cussing and moaning about being temporarily blinded by the bright sunshine. Looking around in confusion, they suddenly realized a claymore mine was aimed right at their chests. Then they unexpectedly recognized me standing several feet away, holding the switch to the mine's detonator wire. In a moment of naked horror, their eyes got as big as softballs as they started backing up towards their bunker.

"Remember me, fellahs? See if you can laugh this off," I yelled as I hit the switch.

Chapter Four

Tet

"To those who have never experienced combat, they will never truly understand the human passion for camaraderie or the pure exaltation of living another day."

General William Childs Westmoreland (Westy) had not been ill-prepared for the job of Commanding General. Nor was he at all ignorant about the many facets of guerrilla warfare and the politics involved. Smart, brave, and conscientious to a fault, he exemplified the image of what an American commander should look and act like. The rumor around Saigon was that he could impress the warts off of a frog. His command presence was so overwhelming to those who had met him that they would walk away believing in whatever he wanted them to believe. As an alumnus of West Point and the Harvard Graduate School of Business, he had been trained as the country's new type of commander. Schooled in corporate management, fiscal outlays, and bureaucratic procedures, he knew how to manage a modern army and deal with the Washington politicians as well. Although he wasn't as sophisticated as Douglas MacArthur or as outspoken as "Vinegar

Joe" Stilwell, he still possessed the qualities needed to be a successful combat commander.[1]

Under different circumstances, he might have left a legacy as one of America's finest generals, but it was not to be. The Vietnam War would have ruined any commander's reputation, including Eisenhower's, Patton's, Pershing's, or even Robert E. Lee's. Over the past couple of decades, Westmoreland has been highly criticized for the part he played during the Vietnam War. Some of the criticisms leveled against him were valid enough, but many of them have been unfair. For he, along with the rest of the American armed forces, had been put in a hopeless situation, brought about by the politics of a young nation suddenly finding itself as a world power.

Unlike the combat in World War II and in the Korean War, the U.S. ground forces in Vietnam were unable to consistently engage the enemy on any large scale. Though Westy had ordered his troops to find them, fix them, and finish them, it was all for naught. Possessing the advantages of inaccessible terrain, nearby sanctuaries, and a supportive population, the North Vietnamese weren't about to throw it all away by openly engaging us. After establishing their supply lines along the Ho Chi Minh Trail and through the Cambodian ports, their main units preferred to bide their time in the jungles. With the elements of time and space on their side, they didn't see any need to gamble everything upon the outcome of a single battle.

In essence, the enemy in Vietnam drove our commanders crazy with their penny-ante, hit-and-run delaying tactics. From the rice paddies of the Mekong Delta to the forests of the Central Highlands, they would suddenly appear out of nowhere and attack our positions, only to vanish at the first sign of reinforcements. For Westmoreland and the other American officers, it was all extremely frustrating. Here they were in the middle of a career-building war and the enemy wouldn't come out and fight.

After taking command of the American forces in 1964, Westy found himself in charge of a mere 16,000 American troops. The situation was a mess: the Army of the Republic of South Vietnam (ARVNs) was riddled with corruption, the Buddhists and college students were in rebellion, the Viet Cong controlled much of the countryside, and the government was in complete disarray. In response to this sad situation, Westy believed that the only way to help establish a strong Saigon government was to get American combat troops involved as quickly as possible. By early 1965, after the enemy had already attacked the U.S. Air Force base at Bien Hoa and the U.S Army bases at Pleiku and Qui Nhon, he was given the go ahead to deploy our first combat units.[2]

In order to protect our installations around Da Nang, the 3rd Battalion 9th Marines (3/9) would make a less than dramatic amphibious assault upon Red Beach 2 on March 8, 1965. Plowing ashore through the waves reminiscent of the bygone days when the Marines had landed on the Pacific Islands, it was the first assault in history in which a few local bureaucrats and a bunch of Catholic schoolgirls would be standing there on the beach waiting to greet the Marine officers with leis. There was even a sign held up by a couple of advisors, which read, "Welcome to the Gallant Marines." Previously arranged for the media back home, the recorded event lasted for about thirty minutes before the Marines were unceremoniously loaded onto some trucks and driven to the Da Nang airstrip.[3]

With a combination of economic assistance and rural pacification programs, it looked as if Westy had covered all of his bases. Our soldiers and Marines had begun patrolling the countryside, our civilian agencies were doling out money and technology, and our government bureaucrats were teaching the South Vietnamese officials the art of "nation building." But in addition to these many programs, Westy was also striving to eliminate the numerous restrictive rules of engagement which had burdened his command. With every new enemy action, he would press the politicians back in Washington for more troops and fewer rules. Since there were a lot of enemy attacks, it didn't take long before he was able to amass a very formidable force.

Throughout the early years, Westy never could get the green light to go into Laos, Cambodia, or North Vietnam, as he so desired. Much like Gen. Douglas MacArthur during the Korean War, he really wasn't concerned about the political and economic ramifications of widening the war, if that's what it would take to win. Following the tradition of Ulysses S. Grant, the father of American military doctrine, Westy had been trained to believe the solution to any military problem could be found in pure and simple attrition. Within the hallways of our military establishments, his ideas about how to conduct the war were not out of the ordinary. They had been rooted in our history and in our traditions. Unfortunately though, this strategy is almost completely useless when fighting a low intensity, guerrilla war.[4]

In the early hours of January 31, 1968, the combined forces of the North Vietnamese Army and their Viet Cong allies violated the annual New Year's truce and attacked almost every major city, military installation, and provincial capital in South Vietnam. Even though Westmoreland and his chief of staff Gen. William DePuy claimed that they had been previously aware of the high probability of the enemy's offensive occurring, the suddenness and the ferocity of the attacks caught the American forces completely by surprise. Within hours of the attack, Viet Cong sappers had infiltrated the American embassy in Saigon and held it for eight hours, before they were finally killed. From the northern province of Quang Tri all the way down to the Mekong Delta, the battles raged in and around the rice paddies, villages, outposts, and cities, until the enemy was officially overcome by the end of February. However, the intensity of the combat would continue to be heavy throughout the rest of the country until October.[5]

On a tactical level, the enemy had coordinated their plans for the offensive in order to have a maximum effect. The North Vietnamese committed their units to attacking Saigon and Hue City, while pinning down our forces at Khe Sanh. At the same time, the Viet Cong were attempting to capture the provincial and district capitals, along with many other cities and villages. Overall, it was the intention of the NVA leaders to break the military deadlock by encouraging the South Vietnamese citizens to rise up in revolt against their regime and that of their American allies. Since many of the peasant farmers, the students, and the Buddhist priests, along with the average ARVN soldier, were dissatisfied with their government's policies, Hanoi believed that the time was ripe for a revolution. By militarily exploiting the weakness of the ARVN, they hoped to politically drive a wedge between the South Vietnamese and U.S. governments and thus encourage the U.S. leaders to withdraw their troops.[6]

Even though the fighting was often harsh and sometimes bitter, the enemy had failed to reach their objectives. The casualties were high on both sides, and the civilians were caught in the middle as the U.S. and world media had a field day. Yet to the casual observer, it didn't appear as if the enemy had militarily accomplished anything of value. At the conclusion of the offensive, the enemy ended up back in their tunnels and sanctuaries, licking their wounds and counting their dead. Therefore to the average servicemen and women who were there and to our people back at home, the offensive just didn't make any military sense.

It was during this controversial period that many American officers and the media began to criticize Westmoreland's earlier decision to shift several of the U.S. Army's units up north to I Corps and thus expose the southern cities to an attack. In response, Westmoreland proclaimed that the enemy was only attacking the major cities in order to conceal their real intention of overrunning the Khe Sanh Combat Base. He began telling the world that he had intentionally stationed the Marines at Khe Sanh, so that he could draw the NVA out into the open and that the enemy had played right into his hands. Unfortunately, he was wrong on all counts.[7]

After three years of attempting to convince the American public and our politicians back in Washington that we were winning the war in Vietnam, the roof suddenly caved in around our military establishment. While proclaiming a great military victory over the enemy, which it certainly was, the Pentagon's chairman of the Joint Chiefs of Staff, Gen. Earle Wheeler, incredibly asked for another 206,000 American troops to be sent to Vietnam. This obvious contradiction between our military leaders' proclaimed victory and then their sudden demand for even more troops was just too much for the American people to swallow.[8]

Ironically though, the Tet Offensive was a great military victory for the American and South Vietnamese forces. Yet after several years of submitting optimistic reports, exaggerated successes, and inflated body counts, the politics of attrition had finally caught up with Westy. The American public did not see a resonating victory emanating from their television sets. Instead, they only saw our government's perceived lies and misinformation of the past.[9]

In a very real sense, the Tet Offensive was the turning point of the war. Before President Johnson announced to the nation that he wasn't going to run for president again, he called for a bombing halt and set a timetable for negotiating with Hanoi. Meanwhile, General Westmoreland was kicked upstairs and replaced by General Creighton Abrams, the American public's support for the war hit an all-time low, the U.S pacification programs in the Vietnamese countryside almost disappeared, and the direction of the war would become more defensive. Throughout the early part of war, LBJ had attempted to bribe, intimidate, and coerce the leaders of Hanoi, but it was all for naught. He never could understand or accept the Vietnamese determination to become a unified country again, without having to suffer the yoke of a foreign domination. Tragically, the Vietnam War would end his dream of further establishing a "Great American Society."

In late March of 1968, we humped to an artillery position called C-2, just south of Con Thien in preparation for the upcoming operation. When our trucks finally did arrive, a sergeant told us that we would be going to a base called LZ Vandegrift. None of us had ever heard of the place, so we sat back and tried to enjoy the ride.

On the first leg of the journey, we headed towards the Marine base at Dong Ha. From what we could see, the U.S. Army seemed to be everywhere. Strung out all along the roads and intersections, their armored vehicles were loaded down with C-ration boxes, water cans, and extra ammo. Some of the Marines in my truck resented the Army's operating in our part of the country, but I didn't mind a bit. As far as I was concerned, the more U.S. soldiers, the better I liked it. Then just as I was about to yell at one of the soldiers, we pulled onto Route 9 and started traveling in a westerly direction.

The road had already been cleared of mines, so our trucks were able to go through Cam Lo without any major problems. While on the way to the Rockpile, I was anxious to see the U.S. Army's long-barreled 175mm and their fat, 8-inch artillery pieces stationed there. From what I had been told, Westmoreland tried to move these batteries to Khe Sanh in order to support the Marines, but the convoy was ambushed in August of 1967, so they ended up at the Rockpile. Unfortunately though, none of these pieces could reach the enemy's artillery batteries that were located in Laos and pounding the combat base.[10]

As we roared down the dust-choked road, I couldn't help but notice the beauty and richness of the surrounding countryside. Acting like a bunch of kids, we hung over the edge of the trucks and pointed at the things that caught our attention. All around Con Thien and Khe Sanh, the terrain had been literally covered with bomb and shell craters to the point where it looked like the moon. Yet in between those semi-barren places, the land was full of tall, broad-leafed trees, bushy shrubs, elephant grass, and thick underbrush. It didn't really look like a jungle per se, but rather more like the thick woodlands one would find in the eastern part of the United States.

As far as the eye could see, there were huge green woodlands of trees stretching out for miles on end. Inhabited by an assortment of deer, monkeys, apes, parrots, tigers, elephants, and other animals, these domed forests were so thick with vegetation that it was almost impossible for the rain or sunshine to penetrate the leaves. One could hear the strangest sounds echoing through their dangling vines. Hence, the entire place was simply incredible in terms of the sights and sounds. Standing up in the truck, we could see the olive-colored jungles to the south and the mysterious blue, hazy mountains to the west.

Immediately south of the Rockpile, the terrain began to change. All of a sudden, we started descending into a valley surrounded by a chain of towering mountains. The sergeant in our truck stood up and began pointing towards a clearing, which was supposed to be LZ Vandegrift. Barely visible from the road, the base looked like a small brown patch of dirt amidst a sea of green vines and thick undergrowth. Looking up at the pointed peaks and rugged ridgelines of the surrounding mountains, we were impressed with the enormity of it all. It was all so picturesque and yet so depressing. For everybody knew, it would only be a matter of days before we would be humping up and down those monsters.

For the next several days, our battalion was ordered to guard the perimeter and patrol the surrounding area. The NVA soldiers were nowhere in sight, so it was a very enjoyable time for us. However once we got a chance to look around the area, it became obvious to us that this place was much more than just a typical landing zone. The Army engineers were everywhere building bunkers, trench lines, helicopter pads, and even an airstrip. Almost overnight, they had turned the place into a small city.

Finally, all the speculation was put to rest when our company commander informed us that we would be participating in *Operation*

Pegasus. He said that it was going to be our responsibility to work our way up Route 9 as the Army's 1st Air Cav swooped down into Khe Sanh and relieved the supposedly beleaguered Marines. Of course, as I stated earlier, the main NVA units had already withdrawn from the area. But at the time, none of us knew that. Nevertheless, the politics behind it all wouldn't have made any sense to us, even if we had known. The fact that we were able to live above ground again and enjoy the sunshine was all we really cared about. Hell, if the Army wanted to run the show, more power to them.

When the 1st Air Cav finally arrived, they were something to behold. Their helicopters poured out of the sky like a swarm of locusts. With an assortment of Cobra and Huey gunships, Chinooks, CH-53s, and flying cranes, it looked like every other guy in their outfit had his own aircraft. But what really freaked us out was when they started unloading their portable mess halls, generators, electric fans, and refrigerators. We had nothing compared to these guys in terms of equipment.

Then just as Mac muttered, "Damn, they brought everything but their girlfriends," several Army nurses hopped out of a helicopter with their duffel bags in hand. It was all too much for us to believe. Later, when we finally got an opportunity to talk to several of their pilots and gunners, they were appalled at how little equipment we possessed. They kept saying to us over and over again, "Man, you dudes don't have any gear." Overall, the feeling was like meeting your rich relatives for the first time. They couldn't help but look down their noses at us, as if we were their half-witted cousins. In their overconfidence, they even had the audacity to change the name of the place to LZ Stud, instead of continuing to use Vandegrift, who had been the Marine commander at Guadalcanal during World War II and a former Marine Corps Commandant to boot.

Yet through it all, we felt kind of sorry for those Army fellows. As they stood there, bragging about their new helicopters and mini-guns, they had no idea as to what they had stepped into by coming up north. The fighting in I Corps had always been a totally different affair than what our Army units had experienced in the other three Corps. Being positioned next to the mouth of the Ho Chi Minh Trail, the NVA had all the men, supplies, and weaponry they needed. Armed with an assortment of .51 caliber machine guns, 12mm and 37mm anti-aircraft guns, mortars, tanks, rockets, and heavy artillery, they were capable of standing toe to toe with any army in the world. Unlike the fighting in the delta, the highlands, or along the coast, where the enemy's supplies were extremely limited, we had been up against a well-equipped modern army. Around the DMZ, the NVA didn't spend their time burying booby traps and running around in black pajamas. Supported by a wide variety of heavy weaponry and supply depots, they had the punch to operate anywhere and at any time they so desired.

Of course, this does not mean to imply that the U.S. Army in Vietnam did not face a tough and determined foe. On the contrary, they fought against the same type of soldiers we had faced. But in terms of logistics and manpower, the enemy in the southern provinces didn't have nearly as many resources to draw upon.

Beginning in the middle of 1966, the North Vietnamese commanders had slowly begun to commit a few of their best divisions to I Corps. Thus the combat for the Marines had been more like what our troops had experienced during World War II. It wasn't some penny-ante guerrilla war that was being reported back home. On a routine basis, the NVA would stand their ground until they were damn good and ready to leave the area. Although the enemy wasn't better equipped than our soldiers, they were highly motivated, well trained, and remarkably organized. As some of the units in the 1st Air Cav and the 101st Airborne Divisions would soon discover in the A Shau Valley, and in particular, on Hamburger Hill (Dong Ap Bia), the NVA units in I Corps weren't about to disappear and hide with the sound of every approaching helicopter. It was their territory and they were going to make life very difficult for anyone who thought otherwise.[11]

In fact by 1967, it was quite common for us to call the Viet Cong soldier either "Victor Charlie" or just "Charlie," in reference to the U.S. military alphabet code. Up to this point of the war, the majority of our engagements had been with the VC around the isolated villages or hamlets. But after the Tet Offensive in early 1968, when our forces began to face the North Vietnamese Army on a regular basis, we began to honor their soldiers' bravery and tenacity by referring them as "Mr. Charles." At that time, they were the finest light infantrymen in the world.

Since we hadn't eaten a decent hot meal in over seventy days, it was very difficult for us to watch these Army guys go through their portable mess halls and enjoy their hot chow. Three times a day, they would intentionally walk past us snickering and belching like a bunch of guys coming out of a country club. Then making matters worse, the aroma from their kitchens would drift across the LZ and linger under our deprived noses.

Finally, it got so bad that some of our guys began hanging around their garbage cans in the hopes of finding a bone or two. But I could tell that was a waste of time and rather degrading to boot. Then on about the fourth day of this nightmare, we decided to take the situation into our own hands. One night, Mac and Davis shot several pop-up flares into the air and began screaming "incoming." Once the Army personnel had scrambled out of their cots and into the nearby trenches, the rest of us entered their tents and stole some of their clothing. Luckily, we didn't have to steal their whole wardrobe, just a few caps, and some Army blouses.

Later over a cup of twenty-eight-year-old instant coffee, we sat around and planned our strategy. Not to be too conspicuous, we thought it would be a good idea to infiltrate their mess hall in pairs, instead of as a group. We also promised each other that we wouldn't tell anyone else about our little scam. The last thing we wanted to see was a bunch of half-starving jarheads standing in their chow line dressed in Army uniforms. As fortune would have it, Georgie and I had picked the highest cards, so we won the right to go first. After a moment of hesitation, we donned their battle fatigues and headed straight to the mess hall. It was all so simple and sweet. Hiding under our Army baseball caps, we slipped right into their chow line as if we were just one of the boys.

While Georgie and I walked through the line, we tried to act as nonchalant as possible, but I'm not sure we fooled anybody. Our bellies started making the strangest gargling noises when they began doling out two pork chops, a scoop of mashed potatoes and gravy, a pile of green beans, and a chunk of honest-to-god vanilla ice cream. Afraid of being exposed, we grabbed our chow and headed to a table in the back of the tent. At the time, it looked like a pretty safe place to eat. There were only two Army guys sitting back there and they didn't even look up from their mess kits. They just kept eating away while minding their own business. Without even saying hello, we sat down and started digging into our food like a couple of starving convicts.

The experience was unbelievable. Over the past few months, we had forgotten what real food had tasted like. With every delicious morsel, our eyeballs would roll up to the top of our heads as if we were in pure ecstasy. In fact, Georgie got so carried away that he began stuffing pieces of buttered bread into his pockets. As I was about to tear into my second pork chop, I suddenly noticed the two Army guys at the other end of the table were also eating their food as if it was their last meal on earth. With every bite, they kept smacking their lips and making these deep-grunting noises, which sounded all too familiar.

Lifting up my cap to get a better look, I finally leaned over and asked them, "Don't I know you guys?"

As one of them tried to hide behind his napkin, the other guy abruptly looked up. But before I could recognize him, he smiled at me with a mouthful of greasy food and mumbled, "I see you're stilling wearing them damn old boots."

Instead of getting up and kicking the holy hell out of the little pricks, I calmly turned to Georgie and said, "By the way, old man, have you had the pleasure of meeting Dee and Perez yet?"

Sorry to say, it didn't take long before our little scam was exposed. It seems that one of their mess sergeants had recognized Chubby going through the line and all hell broke loose. As they were dragging his sorry ass out of the mess hall, Chubby kept hollering as he was kicking and screaming, "Hey damn it to hell, get your hands off of me. I'm an American taxpayer."

Later in the day, we were given General Order 681. It read, "As of this date, all personnel within this battalion will not cheat, borrow, trade, or steal any clothing from the U.S. Army. Furthermore, all personnel will not enter any Army facilities, unless otherwise advised."

Afterward, our Skipper would eventually make a deal with the Army's CO. It was agreed that we could enter their chow line, but only after they had already fed their own personnel. Unable to feed all of us, they could only serve us what extra chow was left over from that particular meal. It wasn't a bad deal and nobody got pissed off at the Army about it. Hence, one of my most vivid memories of Vietnam was observing about two hundred Marines standing out in the wind and rain, hoping that there was enough food left over so that the Army could feed at least the first few guys in the line.

For the next three nights, the westward sky ignited and exploded from the thundering bombs of the B-52s. In preparation for *Operation Pegasus*, the U.S. Air Force was sparing no expense. We had been informed that they had dropped over sixty arc lights into the known NVA positions. It gave us a warm feeling, knowing the enemy would be knocked around a little bit.

Inasmuch as nobody could get any sleep, we sat around in the darkness and watched the flashes soar through the darkened clouds. Everyone around me thought it was going to be a tough operation. They envisioned lots of casualties and lots of dead NVA. Of course, we hadn't been informed by our military intelligence that the NVA had backed off. Therefore, we continued to prepare for the worst.

As for myself, I still believed in our leaders and in our mission. If anyone had told me that we shouldn't even be in Vietnam, I would have laughed in his or her face. Anti-war movement or not, I could not believe that our government would steer us wrong. As a nation, our leaders may have made their mistakes in the past, but for the men in the field, our hearts were true and noble. We didn't harbor any dreams of conquering the world or oppressing a foreign people. For the most part, we just wanted to humbly serve our country and preserve our way of life by helping the South Vietnamese people establish a free society. Looking back, it had never dawned on any of us that our government was capable of deceiving its citizens (i.e. *The Pentagon Papers*). We had been taught since grade school that democratic governments weren't supposed to operate in that fashion. Yet despite the fact that President Lyndon Johnson had recently announced an end to the bombing and our willingness to negotiate with Hanoi, we still had to get up in the morning and serve our country.

Chapter Five

On the Road again

"In the past, human warfare has been based upon the acquisition of wealth through the conquering of new territories. But in modern times, it has been based upon the acquisition of wealth through the subsidizing of the armed forces."

On April Fool's Day, we began to follow the barrages of heavy artillery over a mountain and into the next valley. Since Mac and Chubby were with the four-deuces, they traveled along with the Battalion Headquarters group. At the time, I didn't realize how much I would miss their companionship until they were gone.

For our first objective, it was our job to sweep through the area west of LZ Stud, until we rendezvoused with a unit of engineers on Route 9. During this and every other major operation, everyone carried about sixty to eighty pounds of equipment apiece. At a minimum, our loads consisted of a backpack full of C-rations and personal gear, two to four canteens of water, ten to twenty magazines of M-16 ammunition, a couple of field dressings and hand grenades, a gas mask, bayonet, helmet, flak jacket, poncho, and a rifle. It was an ordeal just to walk down a flat road, much less through a humid mountainous jungle.

But in all truthfulness, I had it pretty easy compared to some of the other guys in the unit. For instance, the machine gunners and the 60mm mortarmen not only carried their own combat gear and ammunition, but their crew-served weapons as well. And how they were able to do it on a day-to-day basis was a mystery to me. Considering the intense heat, the rugged terrain, and the weight of our loads, one could see why the infantrymen in Vietnam had called themselves "Grunts." The whole experience of laboring through the bush was like being condemned to purgatory.

Compared to going on a regular patrol, conducting a major operation was always a real pain for the guys in the bush. Besides having to carry an array of combat gear, we were also expected to cut out LZs, dig nightly foxholes, and stand some form of watch at night. In no time at all, the days would drag into a week and the weeks into a couple of months. By the sheer repetition of our arduous movements in an incredibly inhospitable terrain, a unit would find itself slowly disintegrating into a shell of its former size. It was among these harsh conditions that the medevacs would begin to retrieve the sick and injured as a matter of routine. As a matter of fact, only 17 percent of the medevacs in Vietnam were from actual combat-related casualties. The majority of them were from heat, disease, accidents, and fatigue.[1]

During the first day out on *Operation Pegasus*, we made our way through a series of deep ravines, entangled embankments, and small winding streams. The vegetation was so dense we couldn't see ten feet in any direction. Sometimes, we even had to literally crawl up each other's backs in order to make it up a crest of a hill. Stopping ten minutes each hour, we would pull out our canteens and take a long swig of water. I didn't mind that the water tasted like chemicals or that it was boiling hot from the heat, but it just didn't satisfy my thirst. In no time at all, my lips would become dry and chapped to the point where it hurt just to lick them.

By midmorning, the pain in my legs had become so acute that it became a major effort just to throw one miserable foot in front of the other. Inundated with sweat, Davis and I kept looking at each other with the same "Holy shit" expression. Making matters worse, the straps from my backpack were beginning to cut through my flak jacket and dig into my shoulders like razor wire. It was all so frustrating. On two different occasions, we had to stop, cut out an LZ from the surrounding bushes, and medevac out several people for injuries.

Then early in the afternoon, just when we started to make some progress, something occurred that totally freaked everybody out. As we were making our way down a steep incline, one of guys in the 1st Platoon suddenly fell down and went into screaming convulsions. Several of the corpsmen ran over and began stripping him down to his bare skin as they poured water all over his head. Between his horrid screams and his violent thrashing around the ground, he appeared as if he had been possessed by a demon. Suffering from a heat stroke, his body had become so hot that his brain had begun to literally boil under his helmet.

After he was medevaced out, the Skipper decided to stop the march and set up a perimeter for the night on top of a small ridge. In spite of the fact that we didn't make any contact with the enemy that steamy day, we were still totally exhausted from the day's trek. Georgie was sucking air and looked like death warmed over after lugging his radio around all day. Davis was bleeding all over his arms from hacking his way through the elephant grass and drenched in salty sweat. And as for myself, I didn't look all that great either.

Then after making our way up to the ridgeline, we started looking around for a suitable spot to make camp. Almost immediately, everyone began stripping off their clothing and checking themselves for leeches. Not knowing how to get rid of a leech, I learned by watching the other guys. It didn't take long before I discovered that squirting them with a dab of insect repellant worked a lot better than using a lit cigarette. The little buggers had a tendency to burrow into your skin, if you put a fire to their ass.

Later on, as I was about to untie my boots and take a breather, Davis handed me an E-tool and pointed at the ground. Looking around in frustration, I noticed everyone around me was digging a foxhole. Reluctantly, I grabbed the shovel from his hand and started digging away. Within a few minutes, my shovel hit solid rock. So in exasperation, I slid over to another spot and began digging again. At the time, I kept thinking to myself, "Boy Howdy, I sure screwed up by not joining the Air Force."

Within an hour or so, the whole area was covered with foxholes and mounds of dirt. Then as I was about to try and take another breather, the company's XO walked by and ordered us to help the other grunts cut out another LZ. Struggling to our feet, we mumbled and cussed our way over to a small clearing and began cutting down the surrounding bushes.

During this operation, our Battalion Commander and his group headquarters were accompanying us through the bush. There must have been ten radios (PRC 25s and 77s) lying around within the immediate area. As we were clearing out the LZ, a whizzing sound came towards us out of nowhere, when suddenly a white phosphorus round landed right in the middle of where we were working. Nobody was hurt by the round itself, but it sure scared the hell out of everybody. The radiomen, officers, and staff NCOs began scrambling to their radios and screaming into the receivers, "cease fire, cease fire." Since the NVA didn't use smoke to mark their rounds, it was fairly obvious that one of our nearby companies had shot a Willie Peter round into our location in preparation for calling in a fire mission. Almost panic-stricken, many of us began sliding down the side of the mountain, knowing full well that we were about to be hit by our own artillery.

Luckily though, the fire mission was finally cancelled and we were saved from becoming another casualty of friendly fire.

Once the LZ had been prepared, we were finally able to go back to our holes. At this point, everybody was completely wasted. Between the hunger, the heat, and the fatigue, we could barely walk much less fight anybody.

Following a meal of coagulated beans and meatballs, we talked for awhile and then settled in for the night. Since I was the new kid, I was told that I would be standing radio watch from three to six in the morning. Knowing that I was only going to get five hours of sleep that night, I laid my head down upon my gas mask and closed my eyes. As I was about nod off into never-never land, the insects came out of their hiding places and began to eat me alive. In truth, it got so bad that I would eventually set up a routine to deal with the little bastards.

On a nightly basis, I would roll down my sleeves, button up my shirt, and cover my head with a soft hat. Then once I had my body completely covered with clothing, I would smear insect repellent all over my exposed hands and face in much the same manner as someone putting on skin cream. Like everyone else in the bush, I was faced with a dilemma when it came to attempting to get a night's rest. One could either be boiled alive in his clothing or let the bugs consume his flesh. Normally, I opted for the boiling.

While lying under the stars and listening to the various sounds in the jungle, I always got an eerie feeling. One just never knew what was lurking out there in the night. With every snap of a twig or movement in the bushes, the hairs on the back of my neck would begin to stand up on end. Slowly moving my hand onto my rifle, I would raise myself up and peer out beyond the perimeter, straining to see any movement within the dim shadows.

It was during these tense moments that I was always fearful the approaching enemy could hear my breathing, because, from where I was sitting, my heartbeat sounded like a freight train. On any given night, it could have been a bear, an ape, or even a battalion of NVA soldiers prowling around the bushes. A person just never knew. In between the unremitting fear of the unknown and the darkness, I doubt if anybody ever really slept while out in the bush. Most of the time, I would find myself lying there half-asleep, waiting for the inevitable. With one ear always pointed towards the perimeter, I had actually learned how to subconsciously filter out the different sounds. If something didn't sound right or was out of the ordinary, I was up and alert within a fraction of a millisecond.

On about our fourth day out, we finally reached our rendezvous point on Route 9. Up and down the road, the Marine engineers were busy rebuilding the bridges and bulldozing over the washed-out areas. Soaring over our heads, the helicopters of the 1st Air Cav were flying back and forth from Khe Sanh. There must have been hundreds of them, because they dotted the skies like flocks of geese.

After positioning ourselves next to the road, I could tell that the engineers were glad to see us. Throughout the day, we observed a huge green wave of men and machinery working their way down the road. It was all very impressive. Tanks, trucks, tractors, and jeeps were lined up for miles, waiting to move forward. In some ways, it was almost like watching a parade. We even noticed a few high-ranking officers standing around being photographed and interviewed by this female reporter. She had been strutting up and down the route trying to get her story. To say the least, she definitely attracted our attention.

Unfortunately, our Skipper didn't let us stick around long enough to really enjoy the show. For the very next morning, the order was given for our company to saddle up our gear and move out. Within a matter of a few hours, we were back in the mountains, struggling through the jungle again.

During one rainy night while I was standing radio watch, I became suddenly ill with dysentery. As my stomach began making these
strange gurgling sounds, I unexpectedly leaned over and threw up in
between two guys sleeping at my feet. Little chunks of C-rations and
a deluge of water came gushing out of my mouth and landed right
next to a poor lieutenant's head. It was the same lieutenant who had
almost gotten everybody killed by messing up the 81's fire mission
during the convoy excursion outside of Con Thien. I really don't
know where I got the bug, but I must have drunk some tainted water
somewhere and didn't know it.

In one quick swoop, he jumped up and began slinging his head
around like a wet dog. Then I heard him say, "Holy Mother of God,
what in the hell was that?" Looking around in the moonlight, he saw
me sitting there turning white as a ghost. In all truthfulness, he was
a pretty good sport about it, once he realized that I was actually ill.
After telling me to get some rest, he walked over and woke up his
radioman to take my watch.

As the sun broke over the horizon, I was so ill that it was coming
out of both ends. I had already crapped in my pants and my shirt
was covered in vomit. Earlier, a corpsman had given me a bottle of
paregoric and a handful of white pills, but they didn't seem to help.
Besides running a high fever and experiencing stomach cramps, the
muscles in my arms and legs began to ache from the dehydration. Too
weak to even lift my head, I just lay there and moaned.

Unknowingly, it had been decided by the head corpsman that
I wasn't sick enough to be medevaced out. So the Skipper came
over to where I was lying and told me that they were going to have
to leave me there. He reassured me that Echo Company would be
coming up the ridge the very next morning and that I was going
to be all right. Frankly, I was way too sick to argue with the guy.
Then as he was getting up to leave, Davis and Georgie came over
and lifted me onto a poncho. They carried me over to the top of

the crest and eased me down into a foxhole. Georgie gently laid my gear next to me and put his hand on my shoulder. Kneeling next to him, Davis reached over and handed me one of his precious canteens of water. The way they were acting, it was all so solemn and touching. They didn't actually say a prayer over my body, but the look on their faces was a mixture of concerned sympathy and it's been nice knowing you, pal.

After Hotel Company had left the vicinity, the medicine began to take effect. The aching in my stomach wasn't as severe and I actually quit crapping all over myself. In spite of the fact that my fever was still high and the chills continued to rush through my body, I was able to eat a few crackers. Most of the time, half-asleep and too weak to care, I found myself falling in and out of consciousness. As the stars appeared over my foxhole, the sky turned darker and more foreboding. Every couple of hours or so, I would wake up and take a drink of water, but I still wasn't strong enough to sit up and look around.

Then sometime around midnight, I was beginning to feel a little better about the situation when all of a sudden, I thought that I heard voices. Raising myself up on one elbow, I turned my head towards the slope. At first, the voices sounded muffled and far away. But then, as they got closer and closer to my foxhole, a cold chill shot through my spine like a bolt of lightning as I realized that they were speaking Vietnamese. Slowly easing myself back down into the foxhole, I took a deep breath and began to silently pray. Within a matter of a few seconds, a small group of NVA soldiers walked right by my position and over the ridge into the surrounding darkness.

Throughout the rest of the night, I could hear groups of NVA either talking, walking, or running past my foxhole. Sometimes, it seemed as though they were in a big hurry, while at other times, I could hear them jabbering away as if they were going on a picnic. Luckily, I was way too sick to do anything but lie there and hold my breath. On a few occasions, I thought that I heard them approaching my position, but as soon as they got within a few feet, they would suddenly turn away and utter something like, "shish!" Probably expressing the Vietnamese equivalent of "peeyew," I guess they thought that my particular hole wasn't worth inspecting, since it smelled like a cesspool.

As the sun began to rise, I was one relieved young fellow. There's no telling what would have happened if I had been well enough to do something stupid. After a hearty breakfast of stale crackers, jelly, and paregoric, I was able to stick my head above the foxhole and look around the ridge. Everything looked the same, except that I was probably several pounds thinner and more religiously inclined.

Around noon, I heard a bunch of Marines hacking and cussing their way up the slope. I had never been so happy in all my life to see a bunch of jarheads. Unsure as to how they would react to my being there, I waited until they were fairly close. Then after taking another deep breath, I suddenly stood up with my hands high up in the air as if I was surrendering to them. Somewhat startled, a young sergeant was about to raise his rifle towards me, when I yelled out, "Chieu Hoi, buddy." Chieu Hoi was the "U.S. Open Arms" program for any defecting NVA or VC soldiers. However to the average American grunt, it meant, I surrender.

After the grunts of Echo Company had carried me down the ridge and over a rugged plateau, they dropped me off at the Battalion Headquarters. Situated on Route 9, the 81's mortar section was bivouacked next to a rebuilt bridge. To my immense satisfaction, Dee and Perez were there to meet me. I still wasn't able to walk very well, but I was feeling better. Then as they were half-dragging me down the road, we happened to run across the same female reporter and her cameraman that we had seen earlier that week. She stopped us and asked if she could take our picture. Of course, there wasn't any way we were going to say no to that. So as she began telling us where to stand and how to pose, we quickly brushed ourselves off and tried to look as handsome as possible.

Standing next to a parked tank, I had my arms wrapped around Dee and Perez's shoulders while they were holding me up from behind by my web belt. It was a funny feeling standing there on Route 9 in the middle of a major operation, listening to this woman ordering us around like bellboys. Dressed in a helmet, flak jacket, and fatigues much like a regular soldier, she definitely appeared to be out of her element.

Nevertheless, after she focused her camera, she looked up and said with a big smile, "Now, say cheese." Then right before she snapped the shot, I remember muttering, "Semper fi," as Dee yelled out in a loud voice, "tits forever."

It was good to see Dee and the boys again. We had a great time together as they took turns caring for me. Strangely though, they looked a lot older than I had remembered back at Con Thien. However, this didn't mean they had grown up any. It seems that after I had left the mortar platoon, a new staff sergeant by the name of Jackson had reported to my old unit. It didn't take long before everyone realized he possessed a burning desire to make everyone's life as miserable as possible. Like so many other sergeants in the military, Jackson was a true-blue pain in the ass who showed little regard or any concern for the kids under him. Unbeknown to this hard charger, Dee had declared war upon him. As conflicts go, Jackson didn't stand a chance, but he was way too dense and full of himself to know it.

Besides sneaking around and pissing in Jackson's canteen every chance he got, Dee liked to drive the guy nuts by placing all kinds of dead snakes, swarming ants, or live insects inside his bedroll. Almost every other night, one could hear the surrounding serenity of the countryside being abruptly broken by Jackson's screams. Yet much like everything else in Vietnam, it was during the hours of darkness that people were at their most deadly. Right before our battalion went on *Operation Pegasus*, Dee got the brilliant idea to take a dump in the guy's gas mask. Showing the patience of a true hunter, Dee was able to slowly creep up on the guy while he was sleeping and unload a huge deposit of moist feces into the cavity of his mask.

While struggling through the bush the very next day, it didn't take long before the smell began radiating in every which direction. At one point, the poor sergeant began asking everyone if they smelled something odd. Perez just shook his head and said, "Nah Sarge, it must be your imagination." Then after awhile, the odor got so bad, the Skipper finally pulled him aside and asked him if he had accidentally crapped in his pants? Glaring up and down the jungle path amidst the sounds of snickering and chuckling, Jackson looked into his gas mask and exploded with anger as he yelled out. "I'll get you, whoever you are, you bastards."

Within a few days, I was feeling as good as new. The battalion had continued to move along Route 9, assisting the engineers in whatever way possible as the U.S. Army got all the headlines. Since Hotel Company was roaming around the surrounding mountains somewhere, I was forced to stay with the mortar section. The entire operation was less than eventful for us. The NVA had left the area and any contact we experienced was at a minimum.

Then out of the blue in early April, we were ordered to saddle up and move out to a nearby landing zone. The word had been passed along that we were to be airlifted to Khe Sanh by a group of Marine CH-46 Sea Knights. The idea of having to go to that hellhole wasn't very appealing to anyone. We had all heard the horror stories and read the reports. But on the other hand, the Marine commanders couldn't have picked a better battalion to go there. After surviving at Con Thien for over three months during Tet, we had become experts at trench warfare. The enemy didn't have a weapon we hadn't already dodged, nor could they have showed us anything new about being surrounded and cut off. At this point, we had become extremely proficient at digging in and taking the enemy's best shot.

During our flight into Khe Sanh, the surrounding terrain reminded us of the DMZ. As far as the eye could see, craters covered the landscape like a pox. It looked like a huge brown scourge had swept over the area, leaving behind the remains of leafless tree skeletons and exposed red dirt. Within seconds of descending into the valley, we heard a knocking sound coming from the top of the helicopter's cabin. When we turned around to get a better look, a line of bullet holes suddenly tore across the wall. In one quick motion, everyone instinctively dove to the floor and rolled up into a little ball. Realizing it was the worst thing one can do while in an aircraft, a lieutenant began walking down the aisle, lifting everyone up onto his feet. The engines were so loud that he had to literally scream into our ears before we could hear him. "Get your asses up or you'll get them shot off," he yelled. It's one thing to be shot at while you're on the ground, but it's a totally different experience to be shot at while you're in the air. Unlike the way we had been trained to hit the dirt, if a person lay down on the floor of an aircraft while being shot at, it only made him a bigger target. Thus, the best way to survive was to stand up, place your helmet under your balls, and pretend you're invisible.

When we finally did land at Khe Sanh, we had no idea what to expect. Every one of us sat there for a moment and collected our thoughts. Yet I could see the grim determination etched across the other faces around me. There was a feeling among us that although we were in one of the most contested places in South Vietnam, everything would be all right. No matter what the circumstances, we instinctively knew that the fellow sitting next to us could be counted on when things got rough. It was a feeling of belonging and comradeship that I have never felt before or since.

As a group, we grew to know and to rely upon everyone's strengths and weaknesses, much like a family. Yet unlike a normal family, the baptism of fire and blood had forged our collective bonds of kinship. Naturally, there were times when we couldn't stand being around each other. But when it came down to it, there was a mutual trust and a shared desire to live up to the other guys' standards, which transcended the hollow gestures of togetherness so common in today's modern societies. When the old veterans get misty eyed and choked up while reminiscing about their days in combat, they aren't remembering the bloodshed, the fear, or the pain. But rather, they are remembering the unspoken camaraderie of lost friends, the life-long friendships of the surviving few, and the inspiring devotion felt by everyone there. It was a sensation so profound and unmistakable that a veteran cannot easily explain it to anyone else except to another veteran.

Overall, the infantrymen in Vietnam existed in an environment of brutal heat, incessant filth, and constant danger. Being completely unaware of the outside world, we fought and died for our comrades-in-arms, the dreams of a better tomorrow, and the euphoria of a victorious return. While sharing our hardships, disappointments, and aspirations with those around us, we tried to cram a whole lifetime into every precious moment, knowing full well that it could be our last. Whether or not we survived the conflict, we would move through the history pages of nations as honored ghosts, echoing the sacrifices we had made.

Chapter Six

Six Flags Over Nothing

"No doubt, war is a tragic waste of human life and even a crime of sorts. But don't try to tell that to the grieving parents of the dead."

Similar to most distant outposts in Vietnam, the combat base at Khe Sanh started out as a Special Forces camp. Situated approximately six miles east of the Laotian border and about twelve miles south of the DMZ, it was initially set up by the Green Berets in order to monitor the enemy's movements into South Vietnam. With the help of the local Bru tribesmen, who were a primitive indigenous mountain people, these highly trained U.S. soldiers led their reconnaissance teams deep inside the dense jungles of Laos, while always on the lookout for enemy patrols and possible ambushes. From July of 1962 to August of 1966, they began to report a steady increase in the enemy's activities. The surrounding valleys and mountain trails leading into I Corps were slowly being prepared by the NVA for the eventual movement of their larger units.[1]

Beginning in September of 1966, a naval construction unit (CB-10) and a battalion of Marines (1/3) unexpectedly showed up to rebuild the old airstrip and enlarge the perimeter.[2] Within a matter of days, they had the place looking like a real military post. Realizing the implications of all this military brass snooping around their area, the Green Berets immediately packed up their gear and moved a few miles down the road near Lang Vei. It was a decision that they would eventually come to regret.[3]

Ever since the Marines had landed on the beaches of Da Nang in March of 1965, they had been busy patrolling the areas around the cities and villages situated near the coast. To the Marine commanders, the war was going to be either won or lost over which side could win over the general population. The idea of stomping around the remote mountains while looking for the NVA was not the way the Marines would have conducted the war. Possessing an impressive resume for fighting guerrillas in Haiti, Nicaragua, and the Dominican Republic, they believed the only way to defeat the enemy in South Vietnam was by establishing a group of secure enclaves all along the coast. Then once an area had been pacified and our economic and political programs had been given a chance to work, the idea was to slowly enlarge these enclaves by pushing our forces out to the next district. In this manner, our troops wouldn't have been asked to retake the same bloodstained ground over and over again.[4]

Undoubtedly, it would have taken years before these programs would have had any positive effect upon the average peasant. But in the long run, the Marines believed our casualties would have been far fewer and the fighting would have been much more to our liking.

However, the idea of fighting a defensive campaign was totally alien to the way in which the United States Army makes war. Sitting around and helping the farmers improve their lot, while waiting for the enemy to attack our positions, was unacceptable to everyone in the Pentagon who wanted to win the war as quickly as possible. So when Westy ordered the Marines to send a battalion to Khe Sanh in the latter part of 1966, the leatherneck commander, Lt. Gen. Lewis Walt, was utterly dismayed at his decision. Strategically, he never had any intention or desire to push their meager forces out into these distant outposts. Between the inaccessible terrain and the unpredictable weather, he and his staff believed a force stationed at Khe Sanh would eventually find itself cut off and surrounded, much as the French forces had found themselves at Dien Bien Phu.[5]

Once the outpost at Khe Sanh had been expanded into an actual air base, it didn't take long before the NVA would sit up and take notice. Beginning in April 24, 1967, a platoon of Marines walked right into a hornet's nest of NVA on Hill 861, only a few miles from the combat base.[6] Triggering the onset of the infamous "Hill Fights," where many of the new M-16s rifles failed to properly function, the local Marine commander rushed several companies from five different battalions to the area.[7] While not realizing that his troops were up against two NVA Regiments (18th and 95th), the fighting was unexpectedly intense and savage among the towering hilltops and vine-covered slopes.[8] Since the occupation of the surrounding hills (881 North, 881 South, and 861) were vital for the defense of the combat base, both sides began feeding more and more of their troops into the crescendo of exploding bombs and artillery fire.

Within a six-week period beginning with the Hill Fights, the Marines sustained over 600 casualties. For the Marine commanders, it was all very frustrating. They didn't even want to be at Khe Sanh, much less have to watch their scanty resources being wasted on some distant fight.[9]

In Vietnam, the situation was such that we could have never covered all of our bases, so long as the NVA troops were free to operate in the vast jungles of Laos and Cambodia. Considering that both of these neutral countries were unable and unwilling to protect their own borders, we were powerless to prevent the NVA and the VC from operating on both sides of our perimeter.

Caught between a rock and a hard place with the coming of the Tet Offensive, the Marines at Khe Sanh had found themselves in an impossible situation. With their overland route cut off since August of 1967 and their artillery incapable of reaching the enemy's guns in Laos, they weren't able to store any significant amount of ammunition due to the constant shelling. Exposed, isolated, and undermanned, the Marines had been put out in the middle of nowhere, strategically defending nothing. In spite of the fact that President Johnson would lurk the hallways of the White House in his pajamas while telling everyone that "He didn't want any goddamn Dinbinphoo," that's exactly what he thought Westy had created.[10] Thus in an effort to bail himself out of a tough situation, Westy ordered his ground units to retake the suburban areas and hamlets that had been overrun during the Tet Offensive, while at the same time, he relied upon an intensive bombing campaign called *Operation Niagara*, to support the combat base at Khe Sanh.

During *Operation Niagara*, we dropped almost as much tonnage of bombs in the area around Khe Sanh as we did in the European Theater during World War II. For over two months, the surrounding countryside was literally ablaze with American firepower. Under a torrent of bombs and re-supply parachutes, the Marines sat in their bunkers enduring the holocaust and awaiting the enemy's attack.[11]

Almost every day for two long months, the NVA was able to throw some kind of ordnance into the combat base. What this means is that every time a man stepped outside of his bunker, he was actually between the enemy's salvos. Besides living in the constant terror of having a 130mm artillery round coming through the roof of one's bunker, a person couldn't venture outside his hole in any direction without seriously taking his life into his own hands. The NVAs' unpredictable incoming artillery and mortar rounds only added to the feeling of hopelessness among our forces.

Of course, many of today's historians have pointed out that even at the height of the enemy's bombardments (1,307 rounds on Feb. 23), Khe Sanh didn't receive near as many rounds as our troops sustained during World War II at Corregidor (Philippines) or as several American outposts experienced during the Korean War. However, I have always found this observation amusing and insignificant on the part of these historians. For as any combat veteran will testify, it's not the intensity of the bombardment that eventually drives a man mad; it's the persistency of it.[12]

During the siege at Khe Sanh, the NVA would shoot their artillery from two different locations hidden along the Laotian border. India Company of the 3rd Battalion, 26th Marines was stationed atop Hill 881 South, where they were in a perfect position to observe their firing. From their exposed outpost, the Marine observers could see the rounds being fired from inside a huge rock formation called Co Roc. Located just on the other side of the Sepone River towards the southwest, Co Roc was probably one of the most heavily defended places in the world. Surrounded by heavily armed infantry and anti-aircraft units, it made a formidable barrier between Khe Sanh and the Ho Chi Minh Trail. Then about twelve to fourteen miles towards the northwest on a heading of 305 degrees, the enemy would regularly fire their rounds over the heads of the Marines stationed on Hill 861. It was easy enough for our people to figure out where the NVA's artillery rounds were coming from, but knocking out their batteries was a totally different story. Out of necessity, the NVA had dug their artillery pieces into the faces of the mountainsides, where our air forces couldn't reach them.[13]

Because my unit had experienced the same type of bombardment at Con Thien, I can personally testify as to its effectiveness. The psychological effect can be overwhelmingly demoralizing. Isolated within a restricted perimeter while living under the worst conditions imaginable, the men at Khe Sanh had to endure incredible hardships. They

never knew when or if they were going to be blown into little pieces
or overrun by hordes of enemy soldiers.

There isn't any doubt that the Marines at Khe Sanh didn't take
near the beating the French took at Dien Bien Phu.[14] But on the other
hand, the Marines were there, they stood their ground, and they were
prepared to take whatever the NVA might throw at them. In essence,
our boys performed courageously and faithfully while being stuck in
a very lousy situation. I couldn't have been prouder of them.

After we had landed just outside the main perimeter, the Skipper
directed us towards the main gate a few hundred yards away. Glancing to the south of us, there was a huge rock formation called the
Rock Quarry, where the 1st Battalion, 9th Marines (1/9) had been
stationed during the siege. As always, the "Walking Dead" had a hard
time of it. Positioned outside the western perimeter of Khe Sanh, their
small outpost had been blown to hell and back. There wasn't a blade
of grass left on the hill.

Later, we were told that during the siege their Battalion Commander had made the mistake of setting up another perimeter on a
small knoll (Hill 64) approximately 500 yards away from the quarry.
Manned by a platoon of fifty-eight Marines, the position was being
used as an early warning system in case of a major attack. Evidently, it
had never dawned on the commander or anyone else that instead of
staging a major attack through the area, the NVA would just eliminate
the platoon.

Hence, on the morning of February 8, the isolated Marine platoon
was suddenly awakened by an uproar of loud explosions and rifle fire.
Throwing sheets of canvas over the wire, the NVA had been able to
penetrate the perimeter within a matter of minutes. In some cases,
the fighting was hand to hand as the enemy worked their way from
bunker to bunker towards the top of the knoll. By the time a relief force
had been formed and sent to their rescue, it was too late. Among the

150 or so NVA bodies sprawled around the area, the rescuers found only one Marine out of the entire platoon who was unscathed. As for the others, twenty-seven Marines were found dead, twenty-six were wounded, and four were missing.

Once we had made our way into the perimeter and stationed ourselves behind the concertina wire, I was finally able to get a panoramic view of the place. Off to the west, I could see the mountaintops of Hills 861A, 861, 689, 558, and 881 South. To the north stood Hills 1015 and 950 and over to the south were Hills 552 and 471. Months before, it must have been a beautiful place with its towering green mountains and its emerald-hued valleys, but on this day, it looked like the sands of Iwo Jima. There were enormous craters and burnt-out forests as far as the eye could see. Our air forces had really torn the hell out of the place. Yet the area was so vast and filled with ravines and valleys, one wondered if they had actually hit anything of importance.

Being veterans of siege warfare, it didn't take long before we found a nice out-of-the-way bunker in which to await further orders. We had learned the hard way at Con Thien that standing around in a group could be hazardous to our health. So we tried to make ourselves as comfortable as possible, until we got the word to move out.

As bunkers go, ours was completely inadequate. Constructed with only two layers of sandbags across the roof, which wouldn't have even stopped an 82mm mortar round, we were bewildered as to why anyone would have actually lived in this death trap without having piled on more sandbags. In fact, it scared us a little bit. There could have been only two reasons why this bunker hadn't been properly constructed. Either the guys who had lived there were extremely lazy, or the incoming barrages had been so intense during the siege that they couldn't venture out into the open air long enough to repair it.

While Dee was in one corner of the bunker going through a pile of garbage, a helicopter suddenly roared overhead and landed not very far from our position. We immediately knew something was terribly wrong, because the LZ was supposed to be several hundred yards away. As we ran outside to see what was happening, we began to hear a succession of popping sounds. To our horror, a CH-46 Sea Knight had mistakenly landed in a nearby minefield. Thinking his helicopter was on fire after tripping a smoke grenade, the pilot had opened the rear door in order to let everyone out. Tragically, the popping sounds that we had heard were actually the Marines stepping on the mines as they were exiting from what they thought was a burning helicopter.

Reaching the edge of the perimeter, I could see several Marines and corpsmen running out into the minefield and rescuing the wounded boys. It was probably the bravest and most unselfish act I had ever witnessed in my entire life. Then as one of the corpsmen was attempting to carry a fellow out of the minefield, he suddenly stepped on a mine. Engulfed in flames, their bodies flew through the air like a pair of rag dolls. In the confusion, a piece of shrapnel hit the fellow standing next to me. Stunned, I didn't realize who had gotten hit, until I heard Perez's voice cutting through the hum of the helicopter blades. "Jesus Christ, I've been hit," he yelled out as he clutched his leg and began rolling around on the ground in agony. Within a matter of a few minutes, Dee and I were able to put a field bandage around his injured leg and drag him out of the way of the oncoming ambulances.

To my relief, it didn't take long before the corpsmen had everyone loaded up in the ambulances and headed to the Base's Aid Station, which was called Charlie Med. During this fiasco, we were extremely lucky that the NVA had decided not to shell us. It would have made things incredibly tough. It was only later that we heard Perez hadn't been hurt very badly. After lying around on his butt for a month and eating ice cream in the Da Nang hospital, he eventually returned to us good as new. Sadly though, we lost several good Marines and an incredibly brave naval corpsman in that deadly minefield.

But that was the way it was with the average naval corpsman and Army medic in Vietnam. Quite frankly, I never understood their motivation, because I was there to be a fighting man. While playing the part of a saint and a rescuing angel, there wasn't any doubt in my mind that they had the toughest job in Vietnam, bar none. Normally older and more educated than the rest of us, their dedication and courage under fire was something to behold. On more than one occasion, I had an opportunity to witness an already wounded corpsman caring for his injured men. Need I say more?

Later, as the sun was beginning to disappear behind the mountains, we had an opportunity to walk across the combat base and see for ourselves what the press had been reporting. The Battalion Commander had assigned us a position on the extreme eastern side of the perimeter, so we moved through the base much as we would have conducted a patrol, spread out and on alert. It didn't take long before we realized how bad things had gotten for the Marines and the other personnel stationed there. Everywhere we looked, the sandbags on the bunkers had been completely shredded with shrapnel, and the ground was literally pitted with all kinds of craters. Then off in the distance, we could see the wreckage of a C-130 cargo plane and a few burnt-out helicopter chassis. The entire place reeked of death and despair.

One fine day, when nobody was looking, Dee and I decided to go to the other side of the base. We wanted to check things out and see if we could find any food or supplies worth stealing. Before the siege, Khe Sanh had been a regular military base with a mess hall, a chapel, a base exchange, a small warehouse, and rows of tents that had been occupied by the rear area personnel. Yet all Dee and I could see was an outline of those structures, forming what had once been actual streets.

After the shelling commenced, our people had obviously moved underground into their bunkers. In a very real sense, the place had become a ghost town. Unless a helicopter was buzzing overhead, the only sound one could hear was the eerie rush of the wind. People just didn't congregate together in any form or fashion, unless they wanted to attract enemy fire. Life had become isolated and any communications between the units was done through telephones.

Later that day, Dee and I came across a huge blasted-out crater that used to be the base's ammo dump. In fact during the siege, the pictures of it being blown into the heavens by the enemy's artillery had been plastered across every newspaper in America. Then half-buried just a few yards away from the crater, we found the remains of what used to be the mess hall. Without even looking at each other, we dove to the ground and began digging with our fingers into the soft dirt in hopes of finding something to eat. Within no time at all, we dug up two one-gallon cans of food, one of asparagus and one of corn. Immediately looking around to see if anyone was going to take them away from us, we opened the cans with our P-38s (C-ration can openers) and began gorging ourselves. At the time, I wasn't a big asparagus fan. But I must admit that it tasted great.

Then out of the blue, a U.S. Army truck drove by us as we were eating away. However, it wasn't an ordinary truck. Instead of carrying troops or supplies in the back, the Army had installed a quad-fifty. Created during World War II as an anti-aircraft gun, it looked awesome. Set up on a traversing platform that could move either up or down or sideways, the gunner sat in between two sets of electrically operated fifty-caliber machine guns. Whether it was used against aircraft or ground targets, it was a very deadly weapon. The gunner could control each gun with a button, thus giving him the ability to fire his guns individually or in unison.

At Khe Sanh, the Army crew of this particular quad-fifty had become infamous among the Marines. Once they had been in a convoy headed towards LZ Stud, when the NVA made the mistake of ambushing them. These guys just pulled their truck over to the side of the road and began blowing the hell out of anything that moved, breathed, or passed gas. Needless to say, the convoy drove safely away without receiving a scratch. Amazingly, I had heard on more than one occasion that the gunner was so skilled that he could actually play on his guns the top-forty rock 'n' roll hit, "Wipeout," which had been played by The Ventures.

As Dee and I were headed back to our area, we accidentally ran across something neither one of us could believe. Amid all of the wreckage and debris created by the siege, we came upon two specially built bunkers. They weren't all that big as bunkers go, but they must have been deep. Surrounded by concertina wire and covered with sandbags, there were several antennas and microwave dishes sticking out of the roofs. Although the dishes were full of holes from the enemy's shrapnel, the bunker itself was one of the sturdiest looking structures I had ever seen. Heck, these guys even had their own electric generator buried in a nearby pit. Standing across the road was a fellow Marine, so we went over asked him about the bunkers.

He told us that they were United States Air Force bunkers, especially built by them for their communication's personnel. Besides having a direct line to the Pentagon in order to keep them informed, the installation was also used to call in B-52 strikes.

Hell, we didn't know the Air Force had any personnel at Khe Sanh.

Then he informed us that their presence was supposed to be top secret and that very few people on the base had even seen them.

As we were standing there listening to this guy, the unimaginable happened. Suddenly, an Air Force sergeant emerged from the bunker into bright sunshine. We could tell that the sun was hurting his eyes by the way he kept blinking. Dressed in a clean uniform with freshly shined boots and wearing a brand-new helmet, his skin was as white as the driven snow. In fact, he had been so well fed that he was actually overweight. There wasn't any doubt in our minds that they had all the comforts of home down there in the bunker. By his clean-shaven appearance and pearly white skin, it appeared to us that he hadn't left that bunker since the siege had begun back in January.

We just stood there for a second in total shock without saying a word.

Then I looked over at Dee and said, "Are you thinking what I am thinking?"

He responded, "Damn straight."

In one envious voice, we both mockingly yelled at the sergeant, "Boy Howdy, we sure screwed up by not joining the Air Force."

After spending a few days with my old mortar section, I was finally told to report back to Hotel Company. It was good seeing Georgie and Davis again. Though I hadn't been gone for very long, it seemed like a long time to me. From what the guys in Hotel Company had said, their operation and introduction to Khe Sanh had been a cakewalk. Hopping from hill to hill, they hadn't made any contact with the enemy since they had left me behind. Not wanting to be a party pooper, I didn't mention the minefield incident, but they could tell that something was different about my demeanor. Instead of jiving it up with them, I was more distant than I had been before. It's not that I didn't want to talk to the guys; it's just that I was beginning to feel something was terribly wrong in gruntsville.

For the next month, we found ourselves humping up and down those mountains like billy goats. The terrain was cluttered with deep bomb craters, shattered trees, and empty NVA bunkers. During the evenings, we would sit around and talk about cars, sports, movie stars, music, or even the meanings of life and God. Inevitably, the conversations would always revert to the basics of life. Without the distractions created by an affluent society's constant stream of misinformation and useless material enhancements, I came to realize that when one's life has been reduced to its most basic denominator, one's priorities become somewhat limited.

It didn't take long before living in the bush would begin to physically take its toll. Between the incessant filth and our inadequate diets, the majority of us suffered from all kinds of boils, lesions, and sores on our skin. While moving through elephant grass, it was quite common for us to cut our arms, neck, and face on the razor-sharp blades. Beginning as a small nick, the wound would very quickly fester into a pus-filled abscess within a matter of days. Called "gook sores" by the grunts, these red-circled, yellow-eyed cysts would spread all over a person's arms and hands, thus leaving a deep scar similar to a bullet wound. On occasion, they could get as large as a half-dollar, in which case, a corpsman would come over and lance it with his scalpel, spurting blood and pus all over everybody. Tender to the touch and painful to squeeze, they were the infantryman's plague.

Luckily, they didn't begin to appear on my skin until my last couple of months in the bush. But I can still recall watching the other grunts sitting around and casually talking to each other as they picked at their scabs and sores.

Without question, I was luckier than most of the kids in the bush. Throughout my first tour, I didn't get malaria, snake bitten, leeches and parasites up my butt, trench foot, or even some exotic disease. Periodically, I would come down with some type of jungle fever or get rotten crotch. But overall, I didn't suffer near the health problems that so many other grunts experienced.

For instance, after humping through the rice paddies and the moist jungles for several weeks, a grunt's feet would begin to soften up and form these huge, raw abscesses. In no time at all, the pain would become so excruciating that it was a major ordeal just for him to take a step. Yet what really turned my stomach was when a guy with rotten feet would take off his boots in a confined area like a bunker. The stench was so nauseating that it would literally knock you to the floor and make your eyes water.

Out of necessity, many of the grunts in Vietnam had to walk through the bush on what looked like a pair of spongy stubs of bloody flesh. During the course of a patrol, they would stumble around trying to keep their balance in the midst of great agony and wincing. And how they were able to do it on a day-to-day basis, I have no idea. As for myself, I was able to develop a sure-fire prevention system. On a routine basis, I made a habit of smelling my socks. If they smelled like plain old, stinky feet, then I knew they were okay. But when they began to smell as if something had crawled into my boots and died, then it became obvious that I going to have to do something about it. Almost immediately, I would wash my socks and then dry my feet over a pile of C-ration heat tablets.

But what literally ate me alive were the lousy ringworms. Due to our poor hygiene, they would spread all over my skin like wildfire, leaving an array of red rashes and deep welts. Though the rashes itched like mad and looked nasty as hell, the affliction was not nearly as bad as the cure. Once I finally got up the nerve to go see a corpsman, after a reddish rash had spread all around my ankles, waist, thighs, and into my crotch. Looking somewhat amused, he gave me a bottle of medicine and told me to dab it on the rashes at least three times a day. What the corpsman had failed to mention was that before the medicine would have any effect, the top layer of my skin had to be initially burned off in order for the medicine to reach the ringworms. In short, he had given me a bottle of acid.

To this day, I don't really think that I have ever felt such intense pain in my life. When I dabbed the stuff on my genitals, it felt as if I had dipped them into a vat of molten lava. The pain was so intense and agonizing that I dug my fingernails into my legs and screamed into the sky as loud as I could. The sensation was such that I feared I had done some irreparable damage to my sex life. Later, Georgie told me that several patrols had radioed back to our headquarters and asked about the weird howling sound they had heard echoing through the valleys. They said it reminded them of the long drawn-out screams they had heard in the old Looney Toon cartoons.

Sometime in early May, we got the order to get our gear together and be prepared to move out at sunrise. During our briefing, we were informed by the company's executive officer that there had been a huge firefight the day before and it had become our responsibility to help a Marine company recover their dead. He said that we were going to be choppered to a nearby hill and employed as a blocking force, while the other company returned to the scene and recovered their dead buddies.

After sitting there and listening for awhile, I raised my hand and asked him, "Sir, what are we supposed to be blocking?"

His eyes shot back at me like tiny darts as he replied, "Any NVA force that might try to interfere with the recovery."

At the time, I let the matter drop, but it seemed obvious to me that we weren't being used as a blocking force at all. Amidst the vast terrain, the NVA could have approached their position from almost any direction they so desired. Plainly, our company was being used as bait to attract the NVA gunners, while the other company could retrieve their dead. All I could do was sit there and feel the anger swell up inside of me. But I guess what really got my goat was that I was the only person who questioned the sanity of it all.

It was a well-known fact among our troops that the NVA loved to set up ambushes around American bodies. Knowing our obsession for retrieving them, it was an easy matter for them to increase their body count by setting up an ambush next to the old position. Usually, if a unit waited a week or two, they could recover them without any difficulty. Yet here we were, ready to run in there and possibly lose two companies of Marines, so that some guy back in headquarters could claim that we always bring back our dead. From a tactical standpoint, the idea was ludicrous. Instead of going out and ambushing the enemy around their dead bodies, we were knowingly walking into their ambushes.

Although it is a Marine Corps tradition to recover its dead, I have always thought that it was a wasteful way of doing things. If the XO had been talking about saving live Marines, then I would have been raring to go. But the idea of possibly losing a number of good kids in recovering dead bodies was completely alien to my way of thinking. That evening, I made no bones about it to anybody who would listen. I did not want anyone recovering my corpse at the cost of losing any more American lives.

Almost immediately after we ran out of the helicopter, two NVA 82mm mortar rounds hit right in the middle of our LZ. Diving to my left and rolling down into a muddy bomb crater, I unknowingly landed on top of Davis. "Good God almighty, get the hell off of me," he screamed as I crawled back up to the edge of the crater.

Amidst all the smoke and noise, people were scrambling in every which direction trying to escape the mayhem. The NVA had our position bracketed and their rounds were right on target. Then after looking around for a little bit, I noticed we had landed on a large barren knoll extending out from the side of a mountain. The enemy's mortars were set up across a small valley from us on an adjacent ridgeline. Every few minutes or so, I could hear the popping sounds from their tubes and see their rounds arc across the sky and land into our LZ.

Returning to the bottom of the crater, I informed the other guys that our lieutenant had passed the word to hold tight, until the Skipper could call in some counter-fire. Ironically, we couldn't call in our 81s, because our guns were back in Khe Sanh, which put them out of range. Thus we were stuck out there along with everybody else. Several of the guys around me began digging into the side of the crater as the helicopters continued to land and unload the rest of the company. Those Sea Knight pilots must have been living right, because every time they took off from the LZ, a couple of mortar rounds would land right where they had lifted off.

In order to secure the LZ, one of our platoons was ordered to move up the mountain to another knoll that was located above us. If the NVA had decided to occupy that position, none of us would have gotten out of there alive. As we watched the guys in the platoon making their way up the slope, the NVA adjusted their fire and began dropping their 82s among them. The explosions ripped through the formation and blew the guys in every direction.

Stumbling back down in confusion and disorder, the lead squad had been almost decimated. Then within a matter of minutes, another squad was ordered to try it again. This dreadful scenario continued as squad after squad made their way up the slope only to be blasted back down again. From down below, we could tell the platoon was taking a real beating. The survivors kept yelling at us, "Where in the hell is our damn counter-fire?" Tragically, while they were getting the crap knocked out of them, there was nothing we could do about it.

However, what really freaked us out the most was that after each new barrage, the loose equipment of those who had gotten caught in the explosions would come rolling down into our crater. In all honesty, there is nothing more frightening than watching a mangled helmet or a bloodstained canteen roll past your head. In fact, it unhinged everybody. The other guys in the crater started boring into the ground as if there was no tomorrow.

During all of this time, the Skipper was frantically trying to call in some form counter-fire upon the enemy's mortars. At first, he tried to radio for mortars, but Davis informed him that we were out of range. Then he tried to call in some artillery, but the Battalion Fire Support Center back at Khe Sanh cancelled his request, because there were helicopters in the area. Next, he tried to radio for some Cobra gunships, but they were refusing to fly near the enemy's position, because they thought that he had already called in the artillery. Then finally, after a couple of hours of confusion, he was able to get the okay to call in a couple of F-4 Phantom jets for air support.

I'm not sure what caused me to flip out, but something inside of me definitely snapped. Having to witness a slaughter that I didn't even think was worthwhile was apparently more than I could handle.

While everyone was digging away in a frenzy, I suddenly jumped out of the crater and began running around the bare knoll looking for some type of cover. Out of nowhere, a skinny lieutenant made the mistake of trying to stop me by stepping in my way. Just like a Mack truck, I ran right over him.

Amazingly, I couldn't see any one of the over hundred Marines who had landed with me. Somehow, they had all disappeared into the landscape. Then just immediately down from our knoll, I came upon a ravine full of vegetation. And sure enough, there must have around sixty Marines sitting in the shadows listening to the mortar rounds hit the LZ. As far as I could tell, the whole scene was one big nightmare. The counter-fire hadn't arrived yet, our kids were still being butchered on the slope and our casualties were mounting.

Once the F-4s finally arrived, they began strafing the area with their cannons and unloading their bombs. In no time at all, the enemy's mortars ceased firing. Slowly emerging from our hiding places, we tried to get ourselves organized again. Lieutenants were screaming at sergeants, sergeants were screaming at corporals, and corporals were screaming at everybody else. In the meanwhile, I came out of the ravine and helped the corpsmen move several of the wounded into an awaiting helicopter. They had been pretty badly torn up by shrapnel. I remember one poor kid was in tears, because he had lost most of his jaw.

Then after getting a royal ass chewing by the skinny lieutenant who had tried to stop me, I eventually made it back to the crater. Davis and Georgie had embedded themselves so deeply into the dirt that it took me a while to find them. Awkwardly, we acted as if everything was okay between us, but it wasn't. In their eyes, I had chickened out and flown the coop. And in a very real sense, they were right. But I remember wondering to myself, what was the difference between a guy running for safety or one burrowing into the ground for home?

Later that afternoon, we were ordered to accompany one of the platoons across the valley and onto the enemy's ridgeline. None of us was very enthusiastic about the idea, because we were still in a state of shock about having to watch our boys get blown away on the slope.

Nevertheless, our patrol was about halfway there when we suddenly started receiving sniper fire. For whatever the reasons, the sniper couldn't have hit the broad side of a barn with a shotgun. His rounds kept flying over our heads as if the sight on his rifle was broken. Moving between the torn trees and old foxholes, we ignored the sniper and finally made our way up an incline and towards the enemy's position. I guess the sniper finally ran out of ammo, because he abruptly quit firing once we had reached the ridgeline.

As we walked through the area, it became obvious to us that the enemy had just moved out. From what we could tell, there had been two mortar crews stationed atop the ridge. Among the burning logs and pieces of their mortars, we only found three NVA bodies. One of them was lying in the pathway as we quietly walked over him. Strangely, it was the first time that I had ever seen the enemy up close, so I stopped for a minute to get a better look.

What I observed did not make me feel any better about our situation. Unlike his southern cousins the South Vietnamese, who were small, wiry, and looked half-starved, this particular fellow was big, stout, and quite healthy looking. Possessing a set of broad shoulders and a thick neck, his arms and legs were well defined and strongly built. From his outward appearance, it appeared to me that he could have fought a major battle and then carried a load of supplies into the next night without skipping a beat. Yet there was something about the features on his face that reminded me of the photos I had seen of the Japanese prisoners captured on Tarawa during World War II. In both images, there was a look of uncompromising determination etched across their ashen faces.

Since our initial landing zone had been compromised, the Skipper decided to move us to another position for the night. The climb was long and steep as we made our way to another knoll. While we dug in as fast as possible, everyone was tense and on edge. There wasn't the usual talking and exchange of wisecracks. We had gotten our asses kicked and everybody knew it. All through the night, we were kept awake by the engine sounds of a C-47 (Goony Bird) gunship circling overhead.

Commonly referred to as "Spooky" or as "Puff the Magic Dragon," the C-47 had been renovated to carry three electric mini-guns and a flare ejector. While in action, the guns could literally tear up the size of football field in a matter of seconds. In fact, they could expend so much 7.62mm ammunition that their red tracers would form a long wavy line, resembling the breath of a fire-eating dragon coming out of the sky, hence its nickname, "Puff."

With our newfound firepower, the NVA had decided to disappear into the surrounding darkness at the sound of Puff's engines. They had achieved a tactical victory, so there wasn't any reason for them to press their luck. Even though the other company of Marines was able to recover their dead, I didn't see anyone jumping with joy. We had lost over twenty-five good people in order to uphold a Marine Corps tradition.

To no one's surprise when we returned to Khe Sanh, I was told to report back to the 81's platoon. Not only was I ashamed and humiliated, but worse of all, I also felt as if I had let my buddies down. Yet something else had transpired inside of me besides the guilt I felt. For the first time in the war, I was truly scared. Somewhere on the knoll, I had lost all faith in our leadership and in our cause. We just weren't fighting the war as I had envisioned it nor as I believed it could have been fought. It appeared as if we were intentionally walking into the enemy's ambushes so that we could call in our massive air and artillery support.

As fortune would have it, I was assigned to a different mortar section, located on the southeast corner of the combat base. I didn't really know any of the guys manning the two guns, and in all honesty, I didn't want to know them. Since the end of the siege, the incoming artillery hadn't been very heavy, but the NVA's guns were still buried inside of Laos, and periodically, they would find the time to throw a few rounds in our direction. Situated just behind the outside perimeter were our bunkers and parapets, which didn't endear us any to the grunts stationed in front of us. Besides being kept up half the night with our fire missions, they were always nervous about the possibility of a short round leaving our tubes and landing near them.

In Vietnam, mortar crews had become notorious for mistakenly firing a round with a wet charge. Normally, the ammo humpers were supposed to make sure the charges were dry before they would hand them to the A-gunner. However, when a crew was firing a couple of hundred rounds a day, it became extremely difficult to pick them all out. Due to the fuse's uneven burn, the short round could travel anywhere from a few feet to a couple of hundred yards. Making the eeriest sound imaginable as it left the tube, it sounded somewhat like an old bluegrass musician hitting a bent handsaw with a hammer. After hearing it slowly reverberating its way through the tube, everybody would run for cover, knowing full well that there was a hot round in the air. Luckily, I never witnessed anyone getting blown away by a short round. But it did occasionally happen wherever there were mortars firing.

Chapter Seven

Dear John

"In war, there is no substitute for victory, except survival."

Due to the fact that I wasn't feeling very warm and fuzzy about myself, my new platoon lieutenant had called me into his quarters for a rap session. After I sat down on a box of C-rations, he and a gung-ho staff sergeant tried to ease my fears and set my mind to rest. I remember the lieutenant said something like, "When your number is up, it's definitely up. There isn't any reason to go around worrying about it, because there's nothing you can do about it. So just do your duty and life will take care of itself."

Then with thick blood vessels sticking out of his barrel-shaped neck, the staff sergeant walked over and whispered into my ear, "You don't want to be a coward, do you, lad?"

Quickly looking up at him, I replied, "I ain't no coward Sarge, but I sure as hell ain't stupid either."

As I sat there listening to them, the sensation was one of being in the middle of a Federico Fellini movie. Between the odd shades of light coming through the bunker and the staff sergeant's surreal, distorted face, they tried to convince me to accept the senselessness of it all and ignore the gory consequences. The staff sergeant in particular kept poking his face into mine and saying things like, "I don't sweat nothing kid, because we're the toughest bastards in the valley," or "They haven't made the weapon yet that can get me."

Overall, I thought the lieutenant made a lot of sense, but my problem was much deeper than my fears. I wasn't scared because I was afraid. I was scared because I didn't trust my leaders any longer.

From my experience, there are basically three different mental phases an infantryman will go through during a war. I doubt very seriously if these phases have changed since the first land armies were initially formed several thousand years ago.

During the first phase or rather in the beginning of a person's tour of duty, the average infantryman believes he is destined to survive the pitfalls of combat. In his mind, getting killed or injured is not even a possibility. These individuals will walk around in a daze, dreaming of home, and relying upon their dumb luck to pull them through. Since they haven't yet witnessed the horrible consequences of combat, they don't seem to realize that they are in an armed conflict and that there is a trade to be learned. Due to the fact that they don't fully understand their predicament and the rules for survival, they tend to deny their surroundings and reject the notion that it might happen to them. Within their mind-set, death and injury only happen to the other fellow. Instead of taking the initiative, they will passively sit around and await further orders. Predictably, the individuals within this phase will make up the majority of the casualties in combat.

Upon entering phase two, the majority of infantrymen will experience several profound changes within their personalities and priorities. After realizing that they are in a shooting war by experiencing the death and dismemberment of those around them, they will begin to learn what it really means to be an infantryman. Almost overnight, these guys will begin to work at their trade and endeavor to kill the enemy. Instead of dreaming of home and the girls they had left behind, they will spend their time improving their deadly skills and preparing themselves for combat. Torn between the will to survive and the necessity to accomplish the mission, they will overcome their doubts and approach their job in a serious, focused manner. As long as they aren't sent on a suicide mission, it is quite common for them to survive even in the gloomiest situations. Bringing their professionalism to bear, they can make the difference between losing and winning an engagement. As combat leaders, I found that they are less likely to make the obvious mistakes and get people killed, because they will seize the initiative without taking any unwarranted chances.

And finally, if an infantryman has witnessed too much combat and the loss of several close friends, he might enter phase three. These poor fellows have come to understand that the longer a person remains in the fray, the less likely it is that he will return home. Professionalism or not, the odds of surviving firefight after firefight will keep getting smaller and smaller with every new engagement. Thus after coming to realize that it's only a matter of time before their number is up, they have come to see war in its true nature, which is "the continuous destruction and reforming of infantry units in a never-ending process of chewing up human beings and spitting them out into the hinterlands."

From what I had observed, the individuals in this last phase were in many ways similar to the guys in the first phase. In both groups, they tended to walk around in a stupor, living in a dream world. During World War II and Korea, many of the infantrymen in phase three came to possess what was called, "The Thousand-Yard Stare." Drained of all hope and the illusion of survival, they would stoically stare off into the distance, while awaiting their inevitable doom.

The main problem that I had with the lieutenant and the staff sergeant was that they had already progressed to phrase two. Considering that I was still in phase one, there was very little basis for any meaningful communication between us. While they were beginning to learn the trade of being an infantryman, I was still walking around in a daze, wondering what the hell was going on.

Ironically and tragically, just a few days after our conference, the hard-core staff sergeant was right in the middle of taking a shower when the NVA finally discovered a weapon that could get to him, a simple 82mm mortar.

Since I still wasn't feeling any better about myself, I decided to go visit Regimental Chaplain E. H. Luffman. If I remember correctly, he was a U.S. Navy Lieutenant Commander (major) and his lifestyle showed it. Buried deep beneath the ground, he actually had a refrigerator, a fan, a stove, and a real bed in his bunker. Shaking my head in disbelief, I had thought the Air Force were the only ones that had any electricity at Khe Sanh. But in all truthfulness, he was a very kindly and sincere fellow with a fatherly manner, who only wanted to help his charges. During my brief visit, we went through the Bible together as he showed me the various scriptures that might help me get through the uncertain days ahead. Then as he read from the Book of Psalms, it began to dawn on me that whoever had written those particular passages almost two thousand years ago had definitely possessed an innate understanding of the fear and dread of being killed. Almost every other verse seemed to be implying the same thing: "Bless me O Lord, for thy enemies are about to feed my testicles to the lions."

At the time, I didn't really find anything helpful in the scriptures in terms of inspirational motivation or emotional skills. But I did discover that the act of sharing or confiding with another person is very comforting, when you suspect that life as you know it is about to come to an abrupt halt. Although I have never really related to the various institutions of Christianity, I have learned that silent prayer helps during times of crisis and inner turmoil. For better or for worse, it gives one peace of mind believing that there is something else more meaningful beyond this flash of madness that we happen to call consciousness. Before I left his bunker that morning, he gave me a little

Bible, which I still possess to this day. He inscribed it, E. H. Luffman, Matt. 28:20.

One day, as I was sitting in my bunker pointing a rifle at my right foot and contemplating pulling the trigger, Dee suddenly walked in through the doorway. With a huge grin stretched across his face, he sat down on the cot next to mine and said, "You're not thinking of messing up one of them boots are you?"

After lowering my rifle and raising myself up on my elbow, I replied, "Actually old man, I was thinking of cutting my military career a little short. I keep having the strangest sensation that my life is worth a lot more than what I have been led to believe by our sergeants."

Instantly jumping up to our feet and slapping each other on the back, we couldn't help but have a good laugh about it. Why fight it? We knew our lives weren't worth spit, when it comes to the bureaucracies of the world. Depressed or not, it was good to see Dee again. He looked thinner and crazier than ever. Although I was hardly thrilled about my present situation, we had an opportunity to share a few laughs about the absurdity of life and its supposed meaning.

Before Dee left the bunker that day and returned to his section, he took the time to tell me an amusing story. It seems that his section leader by the name of Macklin had received an unexpected letter from his wife of ten years. Under the oak trees in Tennessee, they had married each other while they were both still quite young and naive. Producing two beautiful daughters and a fat baby boy, he had gone to Vietnam believing he had a wonderful marriage.

Then without any warning, his world came tumbling down around him in a landslide of tears and gut-wrenching regrets. Harboring several doubts, she had broken down and mailed him a Dear John letter. Over the next few days, he became so depressed and apathetic that everyone around him began taking turns watching over him.

In Vietnam, it had become quite common for a Dear John recipient to go over the deep end and do something really stupid. We had heard more than one horror story about how a grief-stricken husband would blindly stand up and then stoically walk out into a minefield, never to return. In fact, it became so common during the war that a group of soldiers in Da Nang had decided to create a Dear John Award for the best letter of the month. During their spare time, they would collect and grade the wives' letters in terms of originality, clarity, and cold-bloodedness. Then once a winner had been selected, they would send the heartless little woman a first-place ribbon and a certificate of unsurpassed cruelty.

But instead of sitting back and becoming mired in his own self-pity, Macklin decided to take a novel approach and strike back at his unsuspecting ex-wife. It must have been the very next morning, when he decided to get out of his sleeping roll and retrieve his wife's letter from the garbage dump. Then after nonchalantly strolling out to the crapper, he pulled down his pants to relieve himself and subsequently wiped his butt with her letter. At the very next mail call, he stuffed the semi-brown stained letter into an envelope and mailed it back to her.

I was giggling till my sides hurt, and then Dee said, "Hey man, it gets better," as he continued his story.

It seems that about three weeks later, Macklin received a letter full of threats from his ex-father-in-law. Full of anger and bitterness, the letter described how the father-in-law was going to kick his Marine ass once he had returned home. Of course, threatening the life of a combat veteran isn't a very intelligent thing to do. Yet being somewhat surprised by her father's temerity, Macklin sat down and thought about it for awhile. Then without saying a word, he abruptly got up and went to the crapper again. At which point, he wiped his butt with his father-in-law's letter and then cheerfully mailed it back to him, too.

On the morning of May 19, which happened to be Ho Chi Minh's birthday, I awoke with a splitting headache and the taste of FD & C yellow No. 5 in my mouth. The night before, we had strained several bottles of Mennen's after-shave lotion through some C-ration bread in an effort to make a few after-dinner cocktails. They weren't very tasty, but there was enough alcohol in them to get a small buzz.

As the sun was beginning to rise, one of our convoys had fired up their engines and was preparing to leave the perimeter. Consisting of an assortment of tanks, trucks, and other vehicles, they had been ordered to go all the way to Camp Carroll in order to pick up some supplies. For security, our Battalion Commander had assigned one of the platoons from Foxtrot Company to ride along with them. From what I understood, the grunts had been told that they would get an opportunity to go swimming, once they had reached their final destination. Half-dressed and half-asleep, they piled into the trucks completely unaware that they would be running into a large unit of NVA just outside the main gate.[1]

It must have been around seven o'clock in the morning, when the alarm was given to grab our gear and man the guns. Unbeknown to anyone, we would still be firing away fifteen hours later. Scrambling down into the ammo bunker, another fellow and I began tearing open the rounds and hauling them up to the parapet. Upon hearing the coordinates for the first fire mission, it was obvious that something was horribly amiss. The Fire Direction Center had given us a range of less than 700 meters away. I doubt that we had ever fired a mission that close before, but what really caught our attention was when we were ordered to fire fifty rounds of HE. That was a lot of rounds for just one mission.

Taking a minute to fasten my chinstrap, I yelled at the A-gunner, "What in the hell is going on?"

"Damned if I know," he replied as he began to literally throw the rounds into the tube.

In all of the excitement, the pace became incredibly intense. As we struggled back and forth from the ammo bunker, our A-gunner kept screaming at us to bring him more ammo. The urgency in his voice sent chills down my spine. Then just as we were in the middle of firing our second mission, the NVA began lobbing their artillery and mortar shells all around our position. As the incoming rounds blew dirt and debris into the air, the ground underneath our feet began to shudder with every impact. Luckily though, we were located behind a small knoll and out of the enemy's line of sight, so they couldn't quite get the range. Still, we must have been giving them all kinds of hell, because the NVA eventually moved several snipers close to our perimeter and began spraying the area. Ignoring the crack of their rifles and the incoming barrages, we just kept pumping the rounds into the sky as if there was no tomorrow.

It was at this point that the platoon of grunts manning the perimeter in front of us was ordered out of their bunkers in order to go to their rescue. The word was passed that our convoy had encountered a large enemy formation not far from the access road leading into Khe Sanh and that they needed all the help they could get. Of course, we didn't feel very good about having to watch our grunts leave. If the enemy had decided to attack our perimeter, none of us would have gotten out of there alive.

Sometime around noon, a truck showed up out of nowhere and a couple of guys began to dump several crates of 81mm ammo next to our parapet. Hoping to avoid the incoming rounds and the small-arms fire, we crawled along the ground and tried to break down the ammo as fast as possible. During one infrequent pause, I looked up just in time to see one of our F-4 Phantoms drop its bombs upon the enemy's position. In an inferno of fire, smoke, and sparks, the explosions ripped through the air with a thundering roar. Captivated by their incredible destructiveness, I sat there for a minute in complete awe. Suddenly, the shock wave from the blast came streaking across the sky, until it hit me in the face like a strong gale.

Before long, the constant firing of our mortars had become so backbreaking that we began to rotate our posts. After working as the ammo humper, I was moved into the A-gunner's position for several missions, and then I became the gunner for awhile. As the person responsible for setting the sights, I was told on more than one occasion to double-check my coordinates, because our rounds were being dropped only fifty yards away from Foxtrot's position.

All that day, we kept firing our mortars until our base plates had disappeared into the ground and the tubes had turned a glowing red from the heat. In order to keep them cool and operating, it was standard operating procedure for the A-gunners to constantly pour water upon them so that they wouldn't warp. However, it didn't take long before we had emptied our water cans and were forced to take other measures. Standing in a semi-cycle, we unzipped our pants and began pissing on the tube. As I stood there smiling and watching everyone getting sick from the odor of searing piss and cordite, a big glob of C-rations and Mennen's after-shave lotion suddenly came rushing up my esophagus and into my mouth. But instead of vomiting, along with everybody else, I had become so angry from the whole ordeal that I just closed my watery eyes and swallowed the tiny chunks back down into my throat.

Later that afternoon, the pain in my ears had become unbearable, so I tried plugging them up with cigarette butts. But it didn't seem to help. Every time I dropped another round into the tube, it felt as if my head was being hit with a sledgehammer. Exhausted and numb, we began to go through the motions like a bunch of zombies. I remember everyone was staggering around like dizzy drunks because of our fatigue. Up to this point, I don't think we even talked to each other any longer. Our battle fatigues had become shredded from crawling around on the ground, and our hands were dripping with blood from ripping open the mortar casings. Between the enemy's sniper fire, the incoming rounds, and the constant fire missions, I was beginning to doubt if it was ever going to end. On more than one occasion, I could hear someone muttering to himself, "Screw this damn war and everybody in it."

As the sun began to set behind the mountains, we continued to fire into the night. Although the firefight was over and the convoy's casualties had been evacuated from the area, someone kept calling in the fire missions. From what I could tell, it seemed that we were the only ones firing. The only thing we could hear was the blast from our own guns. Then all of a sudden, we noticed a huge wall of ammo casings, wooded crates, wax coverings, and unused charges had accumulated around our parapet to the point where we couldn't see our aiming sticks any longer.

Using flashlights to see through the darkness, I had to literally crawl out onto the pile of garbage in order to clear a path to our sights. Meanwhile, the others kept breaking open the ammo casings, while the gunner just sat there and pathetically stared at the dirt. Then finally, the order was given to cease fire. But instead of returning to our bunkers, we just lay there in our parapets and fell asleep next to our guns.

To this day, I have no idea as to how many rounds we actually fired. If I had to guess, I would say it must have been a couple of thousand rounds per gun. Overall, the experience was akin to running a marathon without wearing any shoes. We were completely exhausted and emotionally drained. Yet later from what we had been told by the Foxtrot Company's forward observer, our 81s must have blown away of a lot of NVA soldiers. He said that if it hadn't been for our constant firing, the convoy would have been wiped off the face of the earth. To our surprise, several survivors from Foxtrot Company even took the time to come by and personally thank us for our efforts. As a group, we couldn't have been prouder. The thought of actually making a difference in a desperate firefight was very gratifying.

Almost immediately following the engagement, the actions of Foxtrot's officers would come under a lot of criticism from the survivors. Apparently, we had lost a lot of good men and quite a few vehicles.

From what several survivors had told us, the engineers stationed at the front of the convoy were right in the middle of checking the road for land mines, when all of a sudden they began to receive sniper fire. But instead of staying with the convoy and continuing down the road, which would have been the prudent thing to do, the platoon lieutenant had decided to stop the convoy and deploy his unit in order to go after the snipers.

It was a rash decision, probably based upon our overall intelligence's assessment that the NVA had abandoned the area. Needless to say, after climbing down from their trucks, the platoon didn't get fifty meters into a nearby field before they were hit by a wall of exploding chicoms (hand grenades), AK-47 rifle fire, and RPG rockets. Within a matter of minutes, the platoon of Marines was isolated and the convoy was pinned down. Nobody knew exactly what was happening at the time, because it wasn't what one could call a typical ambush. It appeared to the survivors that Foxtrot had surprised the enemy more than they had surprised us.

As the company commander and the rest of Foxtrot began arriving on the scene from Khe Sanh, the NVA proceeded to overrun the stranded platoon. Moving from crater to crater, the enemy worked their way around and through the wounded Marines. Several of the platoon's survivors said afterward that they could have reached out and touched the NVA as they rushed past their position.

It was at this point of the fight that one of our M-48 tanks suddenly pulled out into the field and began cutting loose with their 90mm cannon and machine guns. Caught out in the open, several squads of NVA were immediately blown into atoms by a torrent of firepower. However, after the enemy had recovered from the shock, they quickly moved some reinforcements into position and blew the tank into a mass of flames with their B-40 rockets. Hidden by the smoke of the burning tank, the NVA continued to rush the convoy. But before they could make any headway, our 81s slammed across the enemy's front elements, creating a wall of shrapnel and flying debris. Bleeding and out of ammo, one of the wounded Marine sergeants approached the company commander about calling in some air support. Later he told the individuals in my gun crew that the Skipper replied, "We're Marines, we don't need any help."

For the greater part of the morning, Foxtrot's Skipper seemed to be completely unaware of the size of the unit he was up against. Believing they had run into a company of NVA at most, he assumed that Foxtrot Company could handle the situation. Then as his casualties began to mount and the NVA's fire intensified, it must have occurred to him that the situation was far more severe than he had originally thought. Unfortunately, we will never know how he would have responded to the crisis. A short time later, he was killed while directing his men's fire. Amidst all of the confusion and lack of information, the situation looked bleak for Foxtrot and the stranded convoy. Several precious hours had passed before a lone sergeant began requesting air strikes and pleading for more reinforcements. The higher ups had already ordered Golf Company into the air.

Right before reinforcements reached the area, the survivors said that there were about ten Marines left from the isolated platoon. Huddled in a deep bomb crater and unable to call in a medevac, they continued to throw their grenades and unload their rifles into the advancing enemy. Finally, after using up all of their ammo, it appeared to them that they were about to be overrun. They were all wounded, out of water and incapable of running for it, as the enemy closed in around their small group.

Then out of nowhere, a fellow Marine miraculously drove his truck out into the field next to their crater. Coolly jumping out of his cab while under enemy fire, he loaded the wounded survivors into the back of his vehicle without any concern for his own safety. Then in one quick motion, he jumped back into the driver's seat, threw the gear shift knob into reverse, and drove everyone out of there. To the wounded men in the crater, it was the bravest thing they had ever witnessed. They thought the guy should have received the Medal of Honor for saving their lives under such hazardous circumstances. Unfortunately, no one ever learned his name.

After elements of Golf Company arrived and added their support to the fray, the NVA began to withdraw into the surrounding hills. Besides losing the majority of the convoy's thirty vehicles and tanks to enemy fire, Foxtrot Company had been completely decimated as a fighting unit. In what was later described as a small and insignificant ambush by the media, they suffered over fifty casualties out of an already undermanned company of ninety or so kids.

Once the fighting was over, Golf Company was able to capture several of the enemy soldiers. The story they told our intelligence people was very chilling. Now whether or nor it was true is anybody's guess, but we believed it. Our 81s wouldn't have had to fire several thousand rounds for over a fifteen-hour period at a mere company of NVA. From what the prisoners told the interrogators, they had been part of a regiment that intended to overrun the combat base for Ho Chi Minh's birthday. But instead of hitting the base at dawn as they had planned, they found themselves behind schedule. As the sun was coming up, the NVA officers debated among themselves as to whether or not to cross the access road in open daylight and continue the attack. Ironically, they had planned to attack Khe Sanh's perimeter at the exact location of our mortar positions.

Since the political ramifications of temporarily overrunning the Khe Sanh Combat Base on Ho Chi Minh's birthday would have been immense, considering Westmoreland had proclaimed the area secure, the NVA commander decided to go for it and ordered his unit to push on. However just as their forward elements were beginning to cross the road, our convoy ran right into them and completely upset their plans.

Along with the timing of the attack, the NVA's intelligence gathering couldn't have been better. Manned by one undersized company (Foxtrot), they could have cut through our base's perimeter like a knife through hot butter. At the time, our headquarters had several battalions out scouring the countryside, so there weren't a hell of a lot of people around to stop them. And if the NVA had gotten into our trench lines, they could have literally worked their way around the whole perimeter.

Looking back, only by the Grace of God did I live to see another day. If the enemy had been on schedule, we would have been history. Considering the NVA possessed the element of surprise and a very sizable force to implement their plan, I doubt very seriously that we could have put up much of a fight. Furthermore, if they had been able to temporarily overrun the place, it could have altered the direction of the war. The political backlash of losing Khe Sanh, after our troops had heroically withstood the seventy-seven-day siege during the Tet Offensive, would have ended a lot of political and military careers back in Washington D. C. And quite possibly, it could have accelerated our eventual withdrawal.

To those of us at Khe Sanh, the atmosphere was very strange and frustrating. The siege was supposed to have been over on April 14, after several Marine units had retaken Hill 881 North. At least that's what the newspapers were printing. Yet the 1st Battalion, 9th Marines had suffered horrific casualties on April 16 and 17 near Hill 689 and here we were in the middle of May getting our butts thumped just outside the main gate. The siege may have been over to the big shots in Washington, but the fighting certainly wasn't.[2]

Over the next several weeks as part of *Operation Scotland II*, our battalion would be sent back out into the bush looking for the NVA. Instead of operating in the direction of Laos, we found ourselves bouncing from position to position in an area east of the combat base. The weather was rainy and somewhat chilly for that time of year, so we spent most of our days huddled under our ponchos and waiting for the next fire mission.

On one memorable day, a pair of C-123s came flying towards us as we were cleaning our mortars. They caught our attention, because they were flying way too low for cargo planes. Then just as they were about to pass over our position, a thick white vapor began spewing out from under their wings and floated to the ground. At the time, we had no idea that they were spraying us with a defoliant (Agent Orange). We had been told the Air Force was killing insects and that the spray was harmless to humans.

Of course, it wasn't until years later that the truth about Agent Orange was revealed. Looking back, the whole idea behind using defoliants seemed to me to be somewhat shortsighted. Unless of course, we were prepared to literally defoliate the whole friggin' country, the theater of operation was just too vast to believe spraying would have made a significant difference. In spite of the fact that the vegetation obviously helped conceal the NVA movements, it also helped to conceal ours. Nonetheless, the greatest problem facing our troops in Vietnam wasn't the vegetation. So long as the enemy continued to live underground and operate at night, all the spraying in the world wasn't going to expose them to our immense firepower. In the long run, all it did was destroy the countryside and poison a lot of people.

While standing underneath the vaporous sky, I'll never forget watching our platoon lieutenant wiping the droplets off of his clothing and saying, "How bad can it be? It's American made."

It was sometime around the end of May, when we heard a helicopter flying in the direction of our LZ. No one paid much attention to it, because they were always flying in and out of the place. But what we didn't realize was that this particular helicopter was special. It had been sent to us by mistake, but we weren't complaining. As we were about to sit down and eat our lunch, we were told to drop everything and report to the company's headquarters. It seems that the chopper had dropped off a load of sodas and beer at the wrong LZ. In all the excitement, I fought my way to the front of the line. Being from Texas, I had been taught that beer drinking was a way of life. I could stand doing without a lot of things in the bush, but periodically guzzling down about a half-dozen cold ones wasn't one of them.

Yet what happened next was very indicative of the Vietnam experience. After we had been issued two sodas and two beers apiece, I stood there in the rain and wondered what in the world was I going to do with my sodas. No one but a crazy person I thought would want to trade his beers for sodas. As a beverage, beer was refreshing, rich in flavor, and great tasting. Everybody back home knew that drinking a few beers was God's gift to working people, whereas drinking bland-tasting soda pops would only give them acne and bad teeth. Thus to my amazement, I didn't take ten steps before some kid covered with zits approached me and asked if I would be willing to trade my sodas for his beers. Without hesitation, I made the trade and then looked for a place to drink them in peace. In spite of the fact that they were hot, they were still the best-tasting beers I ever drank.

One night as I was watching the stars and talking to the other kids in my section, we were unexpectedly entertained with the best light show on earth. Off in the distance, Puff had been prowling up and down Route 9 looking for targets. We couldn't actually see the C-47, but we could hear the unmistakable hum of its engines echoing through the thin air.

Then all of a sudden out of the darkness, a trail of white tracers from a Russian 37mm M-1939, anti-aircraft (pom-pom) gun began soaring up into the evening sky. Just as someone yelled, "Jesus Christ look at that," the streaking shells reached a certain altitude and began exploding into an array of fiery blue gasses and hot shrapnel. Stunned by the unfolding spectacle before us, we stood there for a minute with our mouths wide open. Most of us had never seen a pom-pom gun in action before.

In response to this challenge, Puff began circling around the sky, dropping its glimmering flares to the ground in search of the enemy's gun. Then a solid red line of tracers from Puff's guns arced across the sky and into the surrounding terrain. With every ten-second burst, the mini-guns were spraying an area as large as two football fields. Almost immediately, the enemy's anti-aircraft crew retaliated by unleashing another barrage of exploding shells. The sparkling white flashes from their 37mm shells must have hit fairly close to the Puff, because we could see the silhouette of the plane from the explosions. Then as soon as their shell flashes had disappeared into small clouds of white smoke, Puff would let go with another stream of red tracers. Amazingly, this colorful exchange lasted for another twenty minutes or so, before the darkness finally reclaimed the night. To this day, I have no idea which one of them had actually won the fight, but it was something I'll never forget.

Sadly, there was another incident during this operation that I wouldn't soon forget. One day, while we were in middle of a fire mission, the order was suddenly given to cease-fire. Utilizing just three of our six guns, the mission hadn't been extremely urgent as missions go. We had been routinely dropping our 81s along a ridgeline in preparation for our approaching grunts. So it wasn't as if we had rushed through the procedure.

Mournfully, it appeared that one of our guns had mistakenly traversed its rounds across one of our companies, thus killing and wounding several Marines. Whether or not it was our gun that made the mistake, I had no idea. All of us in the mortar platoon accepted the responsibility for the tragedy with deep regret. There wasn't a kid in our unit who didn't feel a deep remorse and sadness over the incident. Someone had really screwed up and a couple of Americans had paid for it.

But on a personal level, I felt extremely angry and frustrated about the entire affair. Unlike many U.S. Army units, we had never been sent to a rear area, where a unit was supposed to be periodically rested and regrouped. For the Marine grunts, ours was a twenty-four-hour-a-day, seven days a week, thirteen-month-tour war. After constantly being inundated with work details during the day, standing endless watches during the night, and forever being bounced around from place to place, I was surprised we were even able to function, much less stay awake at our post.

After returning to Khe Sanh, things began to heat up again for the combat base. As ill fortune would have it, Foxtrot Company was on another convoy, when they ran into another ambush. Only this time, they were hit much farther down the road, so we weren't able to support them with our guns.

Incredibly within a three-week period, the company had sustained almost 70 percent casualties. But that's the way it was in Vietnam. Every battalion had its hard luck company and every regiment had its hard-luck battalion. For the 2nd Battalion, 1st Marines, it was Foxtrot Company. They were always getting knocked around. As Foxtrot's casualties began to arrive that day, my mortar section happened to be on a work detail to meet them. Knowing that we had been involved in the accidental death of a couple of Marines, the higher ups had decided that we should spend a day or two as stretcher-bearers at the Charlie Med, the Battalion Aid Station. Some of the other guys in my section thought we were getting a raw deal, but I didn't complain. I guess our Battalion Commander wanted us to get a close-up view of what high explosives could do to a human body.

Buried underneath the red dirt at Khe Sanh, the aid station bunker was designed as a makeshift operating room. Filled with crude benches, dirty cots, and homemade shelves, the medical staff worked around the clock in an effort to save lives. Due to the station's proximity to the battlefield, a wounded Marine or soldier could receive immediate medical care without having to wait until he was flown to Da Nang or Phu Bai. During emergency surgery, it was the doctors' responsibility to patch up the casualties in preparation for their flight to a real hospital. If a kid happened to be in critical condition, he stood a far greater chance of surviving once he had reached the aid station. The doctors could stabilize his wounds and then send him on to a better facility.

Luckily, I was never wounded, so I didn't really experience the medical side of Vietnam. However from what I had observed and from what I had been told by many other servicemen, our medical personnel (doctors, corpsmen, nurses, etc.) in Vietnam did a tremendous job under the most trying conditions. Much like the 1970s sitcom *MASH*, when it came time for them to do their jobs, they performed miracles.

Without question, the day I spent as a stretcher-bearer was one of the most unforgettable days of my life. Working in teams of two, it was our job to unload the wounded from the helicopters and carry them down into the operating room. Then once the doctors had finished operating on them, we would carry them out into an adjacent bunker to await the arrival of the next helicopter. Between the loading and the offloading of the casualties, things could get very confusing. As one line of stretcher-bearers would be coming into the aircraft, another line would be coming out.

On one particular occasion, as we were leaving the bunker, I could tell the guy we were carrying was about to expire. He was thrashing about on the stretcher with blood spurting out of his nose and onto his chest. So instead of putting him in the helicopter, we took it upon ourselves to return him to the operating room. When the doctor spotted us coming back down the stairs, he got really pissed off and started yelling at us to get him back on a helicopter, because there was nothing more he could do for the kid. Regrettably, the boy died before we could even get him back up the stairs.

After running back and forth with several litter cases, my arms and legs began to ache from the exertion. The pain had become so severe that I couldn't hold onto the stretcher very well. The pace was unrelenting and constant. We were expected to carry these poor guys in and out of the operating room and into the helicopters as fast as possible. Thus it didn't take long before I was overwhelmed with a sense of utter futility. Yet the most haunting aspect about the whole ordeal was when we could hear the wounded and dying crying out for their mothers and loved ones. Their begging and weeping for their lives sent cold chills down my spine and into my very soul. After awhile, it got so disheartening that I began to plug my ears with cigarette butts whenever I had to go back down into the operating room.

Sometime around noon, the NVA began to shell the area in order to scare off the helicopters. During one of these barrages, my partner and I had just left the bunker carrying a guy who had been shot through the legs, when all of a sudden, the shells began to land all around us. Instinctively, we flung ourselves, wounded guy, stretcher, and all into a nearby trench. Luckily, our patient was too doped up to feel anything. Then just as I was about to light a cigarette, the most unusual thing occurred. Out of the blue, a brigadier general of all people came flying into the trench next to us. It was the first and only time I had ever seen a general officer in the field. He was tall, middle-aged, and distinguished looking. In fact, he reminded me of a bank executive or a CEO. I remember gazing up at this huge silver star attached to his helmet and thinking to myself, "Boy Howdy, I bet he's making a helluva a lot more money than the mere $140.00 bucks a month (including combat pay) that the Corps is paying me."

As the mortar rounds continued to pepper the airstrip, the general looked down at us and in a paternal manner asked, "How are you lads doing?"

After wiping the sweat off of my face, I replied, "Not bad, sir, we're just hanging out here, hopin' for the best."

Then after glancing down at the wounded guy for a moment, he asked us, "Is he going to make it?"

The other stretcher-bearer cleared his throat and replied in an un-alarmed manner, "Well, sir, if we don't get shot to hell on the way to the chopper, he'll be all right."

Before we were able to return to our mortar section, our last duty of the day was to go down into another large bunker and prepare our dead for transportation. Unbeknown to us, the corpsmen had been stashing them in a bunker right next to the aid station. Some of these poor fellows had been killed on the field of battle, while several of them had perished on the operating table. When we reluctantly entered the bunker, there were seventeen bodies lined up on the floor in two neat rows. Instantly repelled by the rancid odor and the sound of a thousand buzzing flies, none of us was very enthusiastic about carrying out our task. Before we placed the bodies, or what was left of them, into a body bag, a corpsman had to tag the bodies with their names and ID numbers. Then once they had been tagged and readied for transportation, we had to carry them out to the waiting helicopters. Throughout the whole experience, I doubt if anyone said a word to each other. We just stoically went about our business with a feeling of deep sorrow and loss.

"You cheatin' no good bastard," Dee yelled out with a grin to the guy sitting across the table from us.

"I didn't cheat," the guy responded, "You just don't know how to play poker."

Earlier, Dee had convinced me to accompany him to the western part of the perimeter in order to play poker with a bunch of artillery-men in their makeshift bunker. He had heard the games were for high stakes and that they weren't very good players. Naturally, I had quit playing poker a long time ago. I was never lucky in cards or lucky in love for that matter. And it always bothered me to give up my hard-earned money to someone who just happened to be dealt the best hand. When it comes down to it, skill doesn't mean that much in poker, unless one is dealt the best cards. A person can only bluff so often, before he has to either show up or give up.

But on this occasion, it appeared as if they were getting the better of Dee. Every time, he would throw down a straight, someone would throw down a flush. Then, someone would have three of a kind, while he would have two of a kind. I could tell that he was becoming more and more frustrated with every lousy hand. His cheeks were beginning to turn red as little beads of sweat rolled down his face.

Then out nowhere, Dee was unexpectedly saved from losing all of his money. As another hand was being dealt out, we suddenly heard a huge crash followed by a loud thud somewhere close by. For a split second, the ground began to shift underneath our feet as we scrambled outside the door.

To our utter amazement, sitting on top of the bunker next to ours was a small aircraft. As far as we tell from the crumbled up wreckage, it looked like an L-19-01 Bird Dog. Used as a Forward Air Controller, it was the pilots' job to fly these little planes above the most hazardous territories in Vietnam and call in air strikes upon any enemy installations or troop movements. Without question, it was an extremely tough assignment.

As we began looking for the pilot amid all the wreckage, a piece of debris suddenly flew up in the air. Popping his head up, the pilot nonchalantly crawled out from under this twisted ball of metal and began dusting himself off. Thankful that he wasn't hurt, we crowded around him for an explanation as to what had happened.

With an expression of relief etched across his face, he finally said, "The damn thing just ran out of gas."

Once the excitement was over, the artillerymen returned to their bunker to finish their game. But Dee and I just stood there for a minute with the pilot, staring at the wreckage. With his hand resting on top of his holstered .45 caliber pistol, the pilot kept whispering to himself, "Man, I sure loved that airplane."

Then right in the middle of repeating himself again, a big chunk of metal unexpectedly rolled off of the top of the bunker and came to rest at our feet.

In a very dry voice, Dee looked at the pilot and said, "Well, sir, you might want to go ahead and shoot the frickin' thing and put it out of its misery."

Just a few days later in early June, as I was attempting to swallow a mouthful of greasy turkey loaf, the company clerk entered our bunker and asked us if anyone wanted to go on R&R (rest and relaxation) to Hawaii. Since no one said anything, I cleared my voice and raised my hand. Most of the guys wanted to wait until their tours were almost over before they went on one, so they didn't show any interest. At the time, I had a feeling that I had better seize the opportunity while I could. Not only had I heard that Hawaii was an incredibly beautiful and exotic place to visit, but I also wanted to take this opportunity to see my mother again.

After the death of my oldest brother, we had drifted further apart and there were still some issues between us. While trying to raise three strapping young boys, holding down a full-time job, and playing housewife to a husband, I was amazed she even knew my name. Through no fault of her own, she always seemed like was some distant stranger to me, zooming around the house trying to accomplish a hundred different tasks. Knowing my time in Vietnam had been terribly hard on her, I thought it would be a good idea for us to see each other again. I wanted to tell her that I loved her and that there were no hard feelings. In essence, I wanted to tell her goodbye.

To say I was excited about my first R&R would have been an understatement. As I was flying back to the rear area on a CH-53 helicopter, I couldn't stay in my seat. My orders had been cut and I was going to spend seven heavenly days and nights in good-old Honolulu, a land rich in beer, females, soft beds, and real food. The thought of getting away from the slaughterhouse for a few days was a thrill in itself. For an entire glorious week, no one was going to tell me when to eat, when to sleep, what to think, or where I could relieve myself.

Then after my helicopter landed in Phu Bai, I was abruptly thrown back into reality. Almost immediately, these rear area commandos started in with their incessant harassment. It was as if they had nothing better to do and that they had been waiting there specifically for my return. Within minutes of checking into headquarters, I was put to work burning shitters, policing the area, and standing guard duty. Although I was twenty-five pounds underweight, covered with ringworms, inundated with grime, and emotionally in shock from my four-month ordeal, these rear area people acted as if they couldn't have cared less about us.

From what I had heard later, the idea behind the harassment was to make life so miserable for the grunts in the rear area that they would want to return to the bush. And I must admit that I certainly wanted to get the hell out of there after enduring a few days of their pettiness. However, harassing people who intended to return to the bush was no way to run an outfit. We needed rest, nourishment, and time to ourselves, and not some fellow with a chip on his shoulder making our lives even more miserable. To this day, whenever I dream about my Vietnam experiences, I rarely visualize myself fighting the NVA or reliving the horrors of combat. Instead, I'm usually trying to avoid the rear area commandos.

On the night before I was to fly to Da Nang, I went to the Enlisted Men's Club to have a few beers. After finding an empty seat, I nestled down next to five other guys and began to introduce myself. Three of them had just gotten into country and acted as if they were full of themselves. They kept boasting about how they were going to put a hurtin' on the NVA. One of them in particular kept predicting about how he was going to become America's foremost Cong killer. From what I understood, the three of them were from the same hometown, and oddly enough, assigned to the same 106 recoilless rifle section.

Calling themselves the "Studs from L.A.," it was their intention to single-handedly win the war and get back to the beaches of Southern California as fast as possible. Not being one to ruin a good party, I didn't say anything. If I had learned anything in Vietnam, it was that delusions are what people live by.

The fourth guy sitting at our table was returning from home to begin his second tour of duty. The idea of signing up again seemed crazy to me, so I made an effort to strike up a conversation with him. But before I could ask him any questions, the fifth guy in our small group kept interrupting everybody as if he didn't have a care in the world. With one arm in a sling, a brace around his neck, and bandages wrapped all around his head and chest, he looked as if he had just crawled out of a hospital bed. Displaying a huge grin and a twinkle in his eye, he just sat there with a beer in one hand and a stupid look on his face. Then whenever he burst out laughing, droplets of blood would ooze through the gauze and roll down his face. On more than one occasion, we had to stop our conversation and help him stuff a painkiller down his throat.

For the next hour or so, it was an excruciating experience for me to sit there and watch this guy. Every time he moved around in his chair, I could see the pain shoot through his body like a jolt of electricity. But none of this seemed to have bothered him in the least. In fact, he was having a ball. Finally, one of the studs at our table asked him why was he so damn happy, since he was obviously in such great pain and discomfort. In between several gulps of beer, the guy told us that he had just arrived in Vietnam about three weeks earlier. During that short time, he had been wounded on three different occasions while serving with the 5th Marines. So by an act of Congress, he was going home before he had even gotten his first gook sore.

Completely stunned, we just sat there for a second and looked at him in total disbelief. The silence was deafening, especially from the L.A. studs. We kept glancing back and forth at each other, as if we couldn't believe our ears. At that point, this guy suddenly looked up at the ceiling and started yelling, "Look out, Mom, the kid is coming home." With the help of a lot of alcohol, it didn't take long before his enthusiasm had spread throughout the entire club. We began singing and laughing together as if we were going home, too.

Later, I had an opportunity to talk to the guy who had returned to Nam. He didn't make any bones about it. Going back to the States had been a real disappointment for him. He said there wasn't anyone back home he could really relate to any longer or share his feelings with. His former school chums hadn't changed very much. They still acted as if they were in high school, obsessed with their cars and their acne. His parents had treated him as if he had never left and that nothing had really changed between them. In their eyes, he was still a punk-ass kid who didn't have the needed skills to even make a decent living. Then his old girlfriend had gotten pregnant and had to marry some guy who had punctured one of his eardrums in order to avoid the draft. He said that the whole atmosphere was so completely alien to him that he felt lost and alone in a world he didn't understand any longer. Then he muttered something that really got my attention. Looking straight into my eyes, he said in a wistful manner, "You know man, the world changed for me while I was in Nam. But it didn't seem to have affected anyone back home."

While in Hawaii, Mom and I had a wonderful time trying to cram seven days and nights into a lifetime. We must have hit every bar and restaurant in Honolulu. When we weren't drinking our way into oblivion, we were either seeing the sights or stuffing our faces with the local cuisine. The place was absolutely beautiful. Filled with pearly white beaches, green mountains, and crystal clear waters, it resembled a geological wonderland. It seemed that the women were all running around half-naked and tanned, which made the scenery even more pleasurable.

During our stay together, I really didn't have an opportunity to talk to her. In our Old Irish tradition, we lived it up nonstop for seven straight days and nights until the opportunities were far and few in between. But I guess it was all for the best. She knew me better than I knew myself. Things might have looked bleak from where I was standing, but she possessed an indomitable faith that somehow I would come out of it. In her own way, she let me know that whatever I had to do to survive, no matter how dreadful, it was okay with her and that she would always be there for me, come hell or high water.

Boot Camp picture.

Author home for Christmas, 1968.

Author sighting in a 81mm mortar at Khe Sanh, 1968.

Author in his bunker at Khe Sanh, 1968.

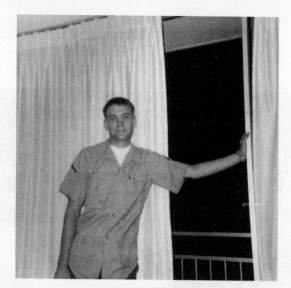

Author in Hawaii on R&R, 1968.

Author on R&R in Hawaii, 1968.

Author with lady friend in Hong Kong, 1968.

Author on R&R in Hong Kong, 1968.

Author and brother while on leave in 1968.

Author outside his barracks in Da Nang, 1969.

Author on guard duty in Da Nang, 1969.

Author and mother after he came home from Vietnam, 1969.

Author in 2005.

Chapter Eight

Gypsy

**"Truth might be the first casualty of war,
but sweet reason comes in a close second."**

By the time I had returned from my R&R in Hawaii, the American people were still reeling from the shock over the assassinations of Martin Luther King Jr. (April 4) and Robert F. Kennedy (June 5). Within two short months, our nation's leading advocates for getting out of Vietnam had been suddenly cut down in the prime of their lives. To millions of Americans, they represented the hopes and dreams of a whole generation, a bridge between the wrongs of the past and the promises of a bright new future.

During this turbulent period, I had no idea as to the impact of their tragic deaths. As grunts, we lived with death and suffering all around us. So when we heard the news about their assassinations, our attitude was one of almost callous indifference. While I was in the field, I had overheard more than one person remark, "Well, better them than me." It's not that we didn't admire and respect these men for their accomplishments; it's just that for many of us, we had run out of tears.

Sometime in the middle of June, Westy was rewarded for his efforts by being kicked upstairs to the Pentagon. His replacement was Gen. Creighton Abrams of World War II fame. Revered throughout the U.S. Army as a tough-minded, no-nonsense type of commander, he had earned his spurs while commanding Patton's 3rd Army spearhead during the relief of Bastogne. Although he was a tank expert by training, Abrams had an astute knowledge of the particular problems facing our infantry in Vietnam. In an effort to get a clearer picture, he would interview many of the Army's top soldiers. Without question, his presence was a stabilizing force around a mountain of growing doubts. Of course, like every other commander in Vietnam, he had a tiger by the tail that was prepared to go the distance.

With the help of the People's Republic of China and the former Soviet Union, the North Vietnamese were prepared to drag the war into the next millennium. Time and space were on their side and they knew it. Thus Abrams found himself in an impossible situation. After overseeing the Vietnamization Program, the American troop withdrawals, and the invasion of two neutral countries (Cambodia and Laos), he left Vietnam knowing full well that it was not our kind of war. Insurgencies, counter-insurgencies, black ops, helicopter extractions, free-fire zones, and bombing limitations were concepts completely alien to the World War II generation.

Ever since the U.S. Army moved up to I Corps, the air bases at Da Nang and Phu Bai had gone through several changes. The dirt roads were widened and paved, new facilities and camps were built, perimeters were expanded, and the entire area was brimming with Army personnel. Much like my experience with the 1st Air Cav in *Operation Pegasus*, I was in complete awe of their organizational wealth. These guys knew how to fight a war. Besides bringing an impressive array of weaponry, tanks, and fighting vehicles to the battle, they also brought with them pizzerias, beer gardens, pool halls, air-conditioned movie theaters, PXs, and bath houses. In no time at all, they had the place looking like a part of home.

Guerrilla, or rather counter-insurgency, wars are very difficult to wage, because they tend to become self-perpetuating affairs. An army just can't expect to grab the enemy by the testicles and hope that their hearts and minds will follow. The nature of the game in Vietnam was unlike a conventional conflict like World War II, where an army's success is based upon its ability to gain ground and to induce massive casualties. From the very start, we had to win over and possess the center of gravity, which happened to be the South Vietnamese peasant. Whoever won the majority of their support would eventually come out on top. In essence, the NVA couldn't have initially succeeded without the support of the Viet Cong and the Viet Cong couldn't have operated without the support the South Vietnamese peasants. In fact, we were so busy trying to undermine the enemy's will to fight that we missed the whole point of the conflict.

As history has shown in this type of struggle, the winning of the hearts and minds of the populace can only be achieved through political stability and the economic improvement of their everyday lives. In actuality, the widespread use of military forces in any civil or counter-insurgency conflict will only interfere with those objectives and perpetuate the conflict.

In general, people don't like foreigners moving them out of their villages, ransacking their homes, arresting their relatives, killing and maiming their children, or putting large craters in their front yards. These tactics will only produce a constant source of new enemies. For every innocent civilian that we happened to kill in Vietnam, we created ten new enemies among his or her outraged relatives. In point of fact, any military tactics we employed would have eventually failed. Because no matter what new grandiose schemes we had devised, the enemy would have eventually drawn us into their sleepy villages and watched us blow the hell out of our friends and foes alike. With our ever growing body counts, the situation in Vietnam was such that our military forces were actually generating newer enemies faster than we were killing off the old ones.[1]

To everyone's dissatisfaction, our military commanders were placed at a decisive disadvantage by the rules of engagement. Similar to our Korean War experience, they became frustrated over the restrictions placed upon them. Not wanting to escalate the conflict into a world war over a piece of dirt in Southeast Asia, our politicians back in Washington had expected them to adapt to the situation and fight within those restrictions. Of course, this was an impossible expectation on the part of the politicians, because an army can't just change its spots any more than a leopard can.

As in the case of Vietnam, our government was asking the Pentagon to put down their expensive weaponry and fight the enemy on their own terms. During the prior three decades, our Army had been trained to fight a wide-open, fast-paced mechanized war with the Soviet Union. To have expected them to ignore their previous training and wage a slow-paced guerrilla war may have looked good on paper, but the actuality was quite unrealistic.

In effect, industrial armies can't fight counter-insurgency type wars very effectively. They have been trained to fight highly mechanized conventional ones, based upon pure and simple attrition. The idea of not being able to engage the enemy in a conventional battle was completely alien to us. We like to fight our wars quickly and decisively, using our tanks, airplanes, helicopters, aircraft carriers, and heavy artillery. Around the sleepy villages and rice paddies of South Vietnam, we found ourselves pitted against an ill-equipped agrarian army quite prepared to avoid the big battle and bide their time in the jungles. Armed with assortment of outdated weapons, punji stakes, and homemade mines, their intention was to slowly spread out our forces much like a huge hand and then use their infantry units to hack off our fingers. Thus it was a totally unrealistic expectation for us to have fought the NVA/VC on their own terms, because their terms were actually from another century.

Besides our military problems, our armed forces could have never succeeded in that kind of politically charged environment. Being a civil conflict between two religious and sectional factions, we unknowingly also made it a racial conflict as well by our mere presence. Within every village and district lurked a dedicated enemy, determined to undermine our efforts to control their country. Contrary to many media commentators' interpretations, the North Vietnamese could not have cared less about exporting communism to Chicago or Atlanta. Nor were they prepared to let Moscow or Beijing tell them how to run their own country. Hiding within the jungles and among the general population, they fought the war on their own turf, striking us whenever and wherever they could. In this manner, they were able to keep the initiative, and thus dictate the pace of the war.

Militarily, our only hope was to keep the enemy off of the South Vietnamese's back long enough for them to learn how to defend themselves. But because the enemy was able to work both sides of our perimeter, it made even this task impossible. In the long run, the majority of the population in the south was never going to support a corrupt minority (Catholic) government, funded by white foreigners. The nationalistic fervor that had spread throughout the world after World War II was such that they were prepared to fight for a couple of generations in order to reestablish an independent Vietnam, under one flag, and controlled by the Vietnamese. In the final analysis, there wasn't any way we could have won the war without the South Vietnamese stepping forward and taking control of the situation. It was their war and we made the mistake of making it ours.

When General Abrams took command in mid-1968, his first order of business was to abandon Khe Sanh. It was his intention to pull the Marines back towards the populated areas, while he unleashed his mobilized Army units into the A Shau Valley. Knowing full well that he wasn't going to get permission to invade Laos with American troops and cut the Ho Chi Minh Trail, Abrams had decided to block the NVA's invasion routes leading into South Vietnam.

In theory, it was good idea. Under his command, we built a string of firebases on or near every major supply route that the NVA had been using. From one end of the country to the other, American foot soldiers humped the bush trying to create a shield around the South Vietnamese people. The only problem with this strategy was that the NVA knew it was just a matter of time before we would be forced to return home. So from 1969 to 1973, they continued to nit-pick us to death with their small engagements, while preparing their conventional forces for the final showdown with the South Vietnamese Army.

After my unit had successfully destroyed and evacuated the historic combat base at Khe Sanh, I eventually caught up with them stationed along the coast at a place called Cua Viet. Situated near the beach just south of the DMZ, it was a beautiful area, if a person didn't take into account the numerous craters, empty ammo casings, and burnt-out villages. Apparently, the higher-ups had decided we needed a break. So while I was there, they issued us a supply of warm beer and let us go swimming in the Cua Viet River. The guys were having a ball splashing around the water as the war continued around them.

It was about this time that I became determined to part ways with the 2nd Battalion, 1st Marines. Being back with a gun crew, I was still being treated as the guy who couldn't hack it in the bush. Even through there was nothing personal in my decision, I felt it was time for me to move on to another unit. In the previous months, I had grown considerably in my outlook. I knew that I wasn't afraid of the bush or the enemy that lurked there. I just wanted a chance to prove myself again without having to get myself killed in the process.

On about my second day back, I finally summoned up the nerve to approach my platoon lieutenant about transferring to another unit.

He had been swimming in the river with the rest of the officers, so I thought I might catch him with his pants down in a manner of speaking. Somewhat taken aback by my request, he stood there for a minute and listened to my reasons for wanting to leave the unit. Up to this point, the Marine Corps had never really given me anything except a hard time, and I didn't figure this guy was going to be any different. But then, he did something extraordinary for a Marine Corps officer. He began to talk to me as though I was a real human being.

"Short, I thought you got a raw deal when you were with Hotel Company. But there was nothing I could do about it at the time. I have been aware of your problems with the other guys in the unit, and quite frankly, I understand your discontent. Ever since you've been in this unit, you have always done a good job for me. Personally, I would like to see you stick around. But if you really want to leave, let me do you a big favor."

I hesitated for a second and then I said, "What's that, sir?"

"Instead of going to another 1st Marine battalion, let me transfer you to the 27th Marines near Da Nang, which protects the surrounding rear areas there," he said. "I have always liked your style and I would like to see you eventually survive this war."

Well, after he had uttered those magical words of *Da Nang, rear area,* and *survival,* I was ready to go. As far as I was concerned, Da Nang was the Mecca of Vietnam. Thanks to the Army, it had everything a person needed: ice-cold beer, female companionship, and hot chow. After thinking about it for a second or two, I proudly snapped myself to attention and said, "Lieutenant, I would be honored to step forward and volunteer to serve my country with the 27th Marines."

With a nod of his head, I knew that I was going south, but before he walked away, he turned around and said, "Oh, by the way, you've just been promoted to lance corporal."

The Marine Corps was always unpredictable like that. They would screw with your mind until it felt as if it was about to explode. Then out of left field, they would do something extremely humane or rational. On more than one occasion, I would find myself in a tight spot and they would come to my rescue as if I was a part of a big family. Then if I screwed up on something as insignificant as a dirty belt buckle, they would have me digging ditches well into the night. Most of the time, I never thought that they even knew my name, much less cared about me. The senior NCOs and the officers lived in a different world than the enlisted men, so I never really got a chance to know any of them well. They operated as if over-familiarity was a sin written in stone and being inherently uptight was a way of life. Yet underneath their dress blues and shiny swords, they knew my name and they actually did care about my growth as a young man.

Before I took off for Da Nang, I went to say goodbye to everybody. Davis and Georgie were still treating me as if I was a leper, so they didn't have much to say. In their minds, I guess they thought that I was a non-hacker. But it didn't bother me anymore. The way I figured it, the line between being a non-hacker and a survivor was getting foggier by the day.

As for Perez, Wallace, and Dee, they were sorry to see me go. That night, we talked and laughed about all the crazy things we had experienced together. Sitting there watching those guys cut up together in the moonlight gave me the strangest feeling. I knew in my heart that I would never see them again. Life was going to take us different directions and there was nothing we could do about it. Back in those days, it was considered very unmanly for two males to hug each other, because nobody wanted to be labeled a pansy. So we just stoically shook hands and said our goodbyes. Up to this day, those three fellows have always remained a very precious part of my memory. I still get a chuckle out of remembering the expression on their faces back in Con Thien, when they saw my claymore mine pointed at their heads.

After hitching a ride to Dong Ha, I walked over to the air base's terminal to see about catching a plane to Da Nang. As luck would have it, I was told there would be a C-130 cargo plane landing within the hour. So with a broad smile on my face, I picked up my boarding pass and went outside to wait for my ride.

Knowing that Dong Ha was within range of the NVA's artillery, I wanted to be as near to a bunker as possible, in case the enemy decided to hit the airstrip again. Early in the war, one of our divisions had made the mistake of moving their headquarters to Dong Ha. Within a matter of a few months, the brass got so sick and tired of running to the bunkers and dodging the shells that they eventually packed up their gear and moved everything down to Quang Tri.

As I walked around the area, looking for the safest place to hang out, I suddenly saw the oddest sight. Standing all by herself next to the terminal building, I came upon a Caucasian woman. Wearing dark sunglasses, a brown overcoat, and a red scarf around her head, she was somewhat tall, medium built, and probably in her mid-60s. I got the impression that she didn't want to be recognized. So out of curiosity, I walked over and asked her if she had a light for my cigarette.

As she reached into her pocket, I looked at her with my baby-blue eyes and asked, "What's a nice girl like you, doing in a place like this?"

Displaying a slight grin across her face, she replied, "Honey, you wouldn't believe half the crap I've gone through just to end up here."

After sharing a good laugh together, we talked for a little while, until our plane finally arrived. I didn't ask her name, because she wasn't offering it. But I knew who she was from watching the old movies on television as a kid. She had a wonderful way about her and a tremendous sense of humor. I bet in her younger days, she had the guys draped all over her. However, she did mention to me that she was working with the USO show in I Corps and that she was in Dong Ha visiting friends. The fact that I didn't believe her story didn't make any difference. As I stood there and looked into the tired eyes of Gypsy Rose Lee, I kept thinking about how tough the entertainment business must be on a soul. One day you're a star, and then after a few bumps and bruises, you could find yourself in the USO next to the DMZ of all places.

Following a few days at Phu Bai, I was finally able to get a flight to Da Nang. Knowing I had a few days to kill before I was expected to report to my new unit, I walked out of Marine transit and hitched a ride to Freedom Hill. Heading in a westerly direction, we drove through a small residential area called Dog Patch. Lined up on either side of the road were all kinds of Vietnamese shops, cafes, and cat-houses. With the help of the black market, a guy could buy almost anything there including marijuana, Coca-Colas, watches, radios, and a good case of gonorrhea. For over a half-mile or so, the Vietnamese kids would stand next to the road and yell out at the bypassing vehicles. To this day, I can still remember hearing their cheerful little voices echoing through the sounds of the traffic. "You want my sister for five dolla," "Number one boom-boom right over here, mister," or "Hey GI, give me a dolla for my sick mama-san."

After travelling farther down the road, we drove by the same building that I had stayed in before I went to Hawaii. Called the Serviceman's Hotel, it was used to billet the servicemen coming and going on their R&Rs. Constructed with dark red wood and located near a huge rice paddy, it was actually a fairly large two-story barracks with real bunk beds and showers. Since the hotel was always full of American personnel, I discovered that it was a good place to find a bunk and enjoy the fruits of the rear area.

Situated on the southern slope of Hill 327 and not far from the 1st Marine Division's Headquarters, Freedom Hill was probably one of the most secure compounds in I Corps. A guy could actually walk around the place without having to worry about getting killed by the local VC. Just inside the gate was a USO building where American girls (Donut Dollies) served coffee and donuts to the servicemen. Dressed in their bright blue outfits, they did their best to cheer up the troops with their beautiful smiles and pleasant conversations.

The rumor was that many of them would share their pleasures for a person's combat pay ($65), but I didn't believe it. They didn't walk, talk, or act like any hookers I had ever run across.

Then inside the compound was a huge building complex, which housed a PX, cafeteria, barbershop, and a post office. Besides sending letters home and getting our ears lowered (haircut), it was fairly common for everyone to hang around the cafeteria's juke box and listen to the music of the Beach Boys, the Rolling Stones, Johnny Cash, Merle Haggard, or Smokey Robinson and the Miracles. On occasion, the jukebox could create a few racial problems. The Black troops loved to hit the reset button every time the white guys had played one of their country songs and vice versa. In terms of modern conveniences, the compound wasn't all that great, but it did have a wonderful feel about it. After eating a hot meal, browsing the PX, and talking to the USO gals for awhile, it made a lonely boy feel like a civilian again.

However, the best part about Freedom Hill was located behind the PX. After the Tet Offensive, someone had erected an air-conditioned movie theater and an honest-to-goodness beer garden. The movies they showed us were usually old westerns or Beach Party nonsense, but the air-conditioning was terrific. I used to spend hours on end in the theater, sleeping or chatting with other guys while enjoying the cool, crisp air. One afternoon, someone actually got the bright idea to bring in an USO polka band of all things. After hearing their first song, the audience was unceremoniously driven back out into searing heat.

Overall, I would have to say that the beer garden was my favorite place in the whole wide world. For the average grunt in Vietnam, ice was a luxury almost impossible to come by. The officers and the staff-NCOs were snatching up the ice machines as fast as they were being unloaded from the docks. So the only way an enlisted man could quench his never-ending thirst in the plus-hundred-degree heat was by drinking warm water. Some of the fellows mixed the water with Kool-Aid in order to improve the favor, but it still tasted terrible. But when the higher-ups constructed a real beer garden, which actually served ice-cold beer and sodas to everyone, it was like finding the fountain of youth.

The very next morning, I went to the Marine transit building and caught a ride to the 27th Marine Regimental Headquarters. Driving in a westerly direction, we passed nothing but smelly rice paddies, water buffaloes, and small villages. The experience was completely different from traveling around the DMZ, where it was a free-fire zone. And quite frankly, I had never seen so many Vietnamese in all of my life. They seemed to be everywhere, in the fields, outside their huts, and along the dirt roads.

After journeying about five or six miles, we finally stopped at the Regimental Compound, which also happened to be 1/27's Battalion Headquarters. Surrounded by huge rice paddies, the first thing that caught my attention was the lack of security. I didn't see any deep trench lines, huge bunkers, or tanks in the area. In fact, it was as quiet as a graveyard. Everybody was walking around without their helmets and flak jackets, as if they were back in the States. The whole scene didn't make any sense to me. It was as though I wasn't even in a war zone.

As part of the 5th Marine Division, the 27th Marines had been stationed in Hawaii. Sometime during the Tet Offensive, someone in Washington had gotten the bright idea to activate the unit and send them directly to Vietnam as part of the 1st Marine Division. These men were solid, dedicated Marines, but they were not at all prepared for what they eventually encountered. From what they told me, one day when they were all sitting around on their sofas watching football, drinking a few beers, and arguing with their wives and kids, they unexpectedly received a telephone call to report for combat duty. Then within a matter of a few days, they found themselves in Hue City, neck-deep in the biggest offensive of the war. In all honesty, they had been thrown to the wolves. Ordinarily, it takes several months of combat duty before a unit finally learns how to function as a well-organized team.

Once I had gotten my gear squared away, I was told to assemble the new guys for an introduction class. Being a freshly minted lance corporal, I rounded them up and marched them over to a small outside theater near the mess hall. Upon arriving, a big, burly captain gave us a wonderful speech about how we lived in the greatest country in the world and that we were going to win this conflict and go home. I kept looking at the other guys sitting around me and rolling my eyes up in the air as if to say, "What distant planet is this guy from?"

Of course, these new guys had just gotten into country, so they didn't know what to think. Then an old crusty first sergeant by the name of Burtsell stepped onto the stage and began rambling about his days in the Korean War. He spoke of the value of teamwork and discipline as a means to survive in the harshest combat situations, and that as Marines, we could only depend upon each other. Then he began to reminisce about the good old days, his deep love of country, and his horses that he left back home. While listening to him, I immediately liked the old fart, because he had a way about him. He was obviously way too crazy to be a civilian. But I'll never forget the last thing he told us. After stammering around for a minute or two trying to find the right words, he suddenly blurted out in frustration, "Now goddamn it, we're going to go out there and hunt down these little yellow bastards and you're just going to thoroughly enjoy yourselves."

To my surprise, I had been assigned to Alpha Company's 60mm mortar section as part of the 1st Battalion. It had never dawned on me that I might be placed in another unit besides the 81st. As I was standing there in the headquarters shed, the clerk tried to ease my disappointment by saying, "You're very lucky to be in the sixties, because every company in the battalion is in need of ground-pounders." So I wasn't that disappointed in the change. Compared to the other weapons, the 60mm mortar didn't strike fear into anyone's heart, like the NVA's fifty-one-caliber machine guns or our own quad-fifties. But it was a very effective weapon, if one happened to catch the enemy out in the open. Then after receiving my new assignment, I began walking around the area collecting all the extra canteens, M-16 magazines, and field bandages I could get my hands on. Knowing that I was going back out into the bush again, I wanted to be ready.

I don't really remember where the truck driver actually took us, but we must have driven for at least another five miles out into the boonies before we finally reached another compound. Unlike the regimental/battalion area, this place was bad news. Bulldozed all around the perimeter was an eight-foot-high wall of dirt, which everyone called a berm. Separating us from the surrounding villages, its sole purpose was to protect us from the snipers.

Then positioned about every twenty feet along the berm was a bunker manned with an M-60 machine gun and a starlight scope (night vision device). Outside the rolls of concertina wire stretched a thick minefield laced with claymores and anti-personnel mines. There was also a tall metal tower constructed near the helicopter pad for observation. Although everyone slept in a nice, dry tent surrounded by a wall of sandbags, there were shallow bunkers everywhere in case of mortar attacks. After I had an opportunity to talk to several different Marines, I was informed that the only time to sweat an enemy attack was during the nighttime. It seems that during the day there was a vested interest by everyone involved not to interfere with the farmers' work on their all-important crops.

Before I finally caught up with Alpha Company, I ran across a Vietnamese fellow named Rice Paddy Bob. In almost every outpost and installation in Vietnam, there were guys like Bob everywhere. With a huge smile and a sparkling gleam in their eyes, they would bend over backward trying to please the American servicemen. If there was anything you needed or wanted, these guys could deliver it for a price. Ranging from the ages of thirteen to seventy, every one of them, it seemed, had an inordinate burning desire to learn about our culture and about America in general. Their questions were endless and they made no qualms about wanting to go back home with us. Normally, they hung around our bases in the hopes of making a buck, but when they weren't stealing everything that wasn't nailed down, they were usually hustling some poor sap out of something.

Old Rice Paddy Bob lived in a small, dirty hut about a quarter of a mile from the compound. Almost every day, he would get on his overloaded bicycle full of junk and ride up to our gate looking for work. Sometimes our commanding officer had a job for him, so the sentries would let him enter and give him the run of the compound. Being so friendly and helpful, one couldn't help liking him. If there was a messy job to do, he was always ready and willing to do it.

On the day that I met him, he was wearing a pair of black pajamas, Ho Chi Minh scandals, and a red baseball cap, which read, "Come to Disney Land." As he stood there sizing me up, he had a sneaky way about him, which reminded me of a double-talking politician. He kept trying to hold my hand, a sign of Vietnamese friendship, and convince me of his undying hatred for the VC. But when I asked him if he could point out the local VC commander for me because I intensely wanted to show the guy my new rifle, his eyes suddenly widened into a distinct harshness.

"No, VC here, Americans number one," he said, after pausing for an uncomfortable minute.

Similar to the rest of the farmers in Vietnam, he possessed a set of wiry bow legs, crooked teeth, and a breath, thanks to a rotten fish sauce called Nuoc Mam, that would have knocked over an intoxicated vagrant. Back in the States, he would have made a great salesman. He could spot a sucker from a mile away and sell him everything from a broken watch to a bottle of gin filled with water. Of course, the majority of these guys were actually Viet Cong agents. They would collect mountains of information about the compounds and our routines and then pass it on to their operators. Nevertheless, they certainly played their roles well. And just like in the old World War II Hollywood movies, they all acted as though they wanted to be little GIs.

To the average American, getting used to the Vietnamese people and their way of life was a very difficult matter. They didn't walk, talk, or even act like anyone we had ever known back in the States. Their clothes looked funny, their language sounded like it came from the North Pole, and I doubt very seriously if I could have lived on their meager diets. Despite the fact that their history and traditions went back a couple of thousand years and were rich in literature, drama, and the arts, the people still looked poor, underfed, and primitive. It appeared to us as if they were not only stuck in a different century, but also on another planet as well. Since Vietnam was one of the poorest countries in the world, we took it for granted that they were also destitute in every other aspect of their society. Thus we totally ignored the beauty, the power, and the logic behind their way of life.

In terms of understanding the Vietnamese people, our government failed to realize that we weren't dealing with the average Westerner. Shrouded in ritual and ancient traditions, completely assimilated within a particular group, and culturally homogeneous, their lives were centered upon the upholding and the honoring of their unique relationships between each other in reverence to their community's harmony. Instead of economically competing against each other or struggling to keep up with the Joneses, their culture strived for collective cooperation, defined social roles, and personal self-control. While worshiping their ancestors and struggling in the rice fields, they couldn't have cared less about our astronauts reaching the moon. In their minds, why would someone want to go to the moon, when heaven is here on earth?

In 1963, hundreds of angry college students and discontented Buddhist monks began to hit the streets in Saigon and Hue City to protest President Diem's American-supported regime. The world was shocked at the scenes that were to follow. To the absolute horror of the television watchers around the world, several of the monks were doused in gasoline and then ignited with a match in a whirlwind of flames and smoke. Without even cringing from the pain or blinking an eye, these poor fellows disintegrated into a heap of smoldering ashes right before our very eyes. What our reporters and commentators had failed to realize was that their sacrifices were more than just a protest. At the time, the Buddhists were trying to convey a message, or rather a warning to the American public about their culture and their willpower.

Tragically, it was a message our media whitewashed away by proclaiming the monks were on drugs. In actuality, the monks were exhibiting to us the power and the discipline of their two-thousand-year-old culture. Within a torrent of searing flames and burning flesh, it was their intention to demonstrate their cultural and individual willingness to sacrifice themselves for their national harmony. By alerting the international media beforehand and dying in front of the cameras in such a grotesque manner, they were actually revealing the strength of their determination.

As a highly industrialized nation, we mistakenly assumed that their goals were as immediate and self-serving as were ours. Within the smugness of our supposed superiority, we couldn't understand why they didn't think as we did or even value the same things. Amazingly, we fought the entire war believing the Vietnamese would be willing to throw away their ancient beliefs and traditions for a motorcycle and a few tractors, and that they actually harbored dreams of living in Oklahoma next to some drive-in movie theater.

But in actuality, they weren't very impressed with our technological culture. In fact, many of their scholars would view us as only a collection of uncivilized marauders, temporarily interfering with their ongoing history. One might have thought that after fighting three different wars in Asia within a thirty-five-year period, we would have understood the Vietnamese mind better. Sadly as long as we continue to measure the value and the accomplishments of a society by its wealth and productivity, then we're never going to understand anyone beyond our borders.

Chapter Nine

The Wild Bunch

"If citizens really wanted to eliminate war, they could enact a law that would require their political, religious, and financial leaders to personally lead them into battle."

For the next couple of months, I found myself sloshing through the rice paddies, searching villages, and patrolling the surrounding darkness. Being the middle of summer, the work was hot and rugged. Since I was used to climbing up and down the mountains, I was a little surprised to discover how tough it was to wade through a rice paddy with fifty pounds on my back. The mud was so thick and gooey that it would literally ooze up my legs and into my crotch area. On more than one patrol, I would have to stop, strip off my gear, and walk back out into the paddy in order to get my damn boots. Between the incessant heat, humidity, and the insects, I began to appreciate what our other units had been facing in the lowlands and especially what the U.S. Army units had to endure in the Mekong Delta. There may not have been any heavy artillery or rocket barrages to dodge, but the living conditions were far worse than what I had faced up north. And yet in many other ways, it could be just as deadly.

During this time, I don't think that I spent a day without being completely soaked and covered with mud. But what really fried my buns was the unorthodox way in which the enemy fought us. Instead of confronting us like the NVA were accustomed to doing, the Viet Cong would sit back in their huts and let their booby traps do most of the work. Looking back, it was one of the most frustrating experiences of my entire life. While on patrol, it was quite common for us to lose half a squad without making any contact with the enemy. The surrounding trails were literally covered with booby traps and punji stakes to the point where it would take us several hours just to move a couple of hundred yards.

That was one of the strangest aspects about the Vietnam War. Unlike our previous wars, there was never any continuity on the battlefield. The enemy's tactics and the nature of the combat itself would change from district to district. It seemed that every geographical location in the country featured a unique way of fighting us.

After I had transferred to the 27th Marines and moved south, I discovered that everything was different. The rules of engagement were stricter, the enemy's weapons were cruder, and the combat was less intense. Around the populated areas, we had to deal with what was left of the local Viet Cong. They would usually come out at night to set up their ambushes or bury their booby traps. But during the days, they would rarely confront us in force. Most of the time, they were either in their fields working away as honest citizens or they were in their tunnels making weapons. Unlike the fighting in the DMZ, the nature of the combat could suddenly change from area to area, depending upon the Viet Congs' resources and their leadership. Some areas were full of snipers and booby traps, while just across a river or around the next set of villages, we had to sweat their ambushes and occasional mortar attack. Hell, we weren't fighting the Vietnam War; we were fighting the Vietnam Wars.

However, the enemy did employ one particular tactic throughout the country to great effect. For months on end, they would lull our troops to sleep in our base camps with long periods of inactivity. As far as our daily patrols could ascertain, there hadn't been an enemy soldier in the area for years. The days and then the weeks would pass without so much as a hint of their presence. Due to the boredom, everyone in the camp would become somewhat lax and careless. Thus it became quite common for us to settle into a predictable routine, believing the war had passed us by.

Then suddenly one night, when we least expected it, the enemy would show up around our perimeter with a battalion of troops and overrun the place as easily as falling off a log. In response, our reinforcements would be rushed to the scene only to find the enemy had disappeared into the surrounding terrain. As a battlefield tactic, there is nothing more effective than convincing a unit that they aren't in harm's way and then unexpectedly hitting them while they are in their ponchos dreaming of home.

While I was in Alpha Company, I had been attached to a rifle platoon as a mortar section leader. For my first command, I was put in charge of two 60mm mortars and a crew of three new guys (cherries). When I first met them, they looked at me as if I had been heaven sent. Not surprisingly, they were scared to death and constantly wondering what to do next. I quickly discovered that no one had bothered to tell them what to do or even whom to ask. So the first thing I did was to sit them down and explain how I wanted things done. Unlike my first section leader, I knew that I wasn't going to be able to gain their respect unless I got down in the dirt with them. In my mind, this entailed standing watches with them and helping out with the everyday chores or work details. Besides conducting daily drills on the guns, I also tried to share with them the knowledge that I had picked up in the DMZ. They were eager to learn and happy to discover that there were certain things one could do to survive and still get the job done. Like everybody else during their first few months in Vietnam, all they needed was someone to show them the ropes.

The fact that I had been at Con Thien and Khe Sanh had made me somewhat of a celebrity. Ever since the Tet Offensive, Alpha Company along with the rest of the battalion was in dire need of experienced people. Most of the original staff-NCOs and officers had been blown away or shipped home for whatever the reasons. As far as I could tell, the company was operating at half strength with corporals acting as sergeants and sergeants acting as platoon leaders.

Somewhere or somehow, I had come to accept my death or dismemberment as a possibility that I had very little control over. The fear that had been gnawing at my insides was suddenly gone. I didn't know if it was my faith in God or the eventual acceptance of my doom that led to this transformation. All I knew was that by the time I joined the 27th Marines, something inside of me had changed. If I was going to have to die in this god-forsaken place, I had decided to go down fightin'.

In essence, I had become the hunter, instead of the hunted. The days of sitting around and dreaming about home were gone. When I wasn't asleep or on a work detail, all I could think about was the different ways to improve my skills and knowledge as a grunt. The idea of beating them at their own game had become a challenge and nothing gave me more pleasure than to implement a plan and watch it successfully unfold. Besides studying the local terrain, I also began observing everything around me. Whether I was out on patrol or visiting a nearby village, I was beginning to study the enemy and learn his weaknesses. In short, I was finally becoming an infantryman.

Due to the company's depleted state, sometimes we were ordered to go out on patrol with the grunts or to help them stand watch on the perimeter. Earlier, I had made a deal with the acting gunnery sergeant, who was actually a staff sergeant, that my 60-mortar crew wouldn't be sent out on patrol without me. At the time, I didn't feel that my three cherries could survive a tough firefight. Thus I was able to convince him of my need to keep an eye on them. This wasn't showboating on my part by any means. If I had learned anything from watching the NCOs and officers in 2/1, it was that leadership is all about attitude and audacity. In the long run, it doesn't matter what the size of the unit a person is commanding or even his rank; he has to have a certain demeanor to be successful or his men won't fight for him.

From what I observed, if a combat leader didn't walk around with an air of fearlessness and supreme confidence about him, his unit was eventually going to become timid and ineffectual. Unlike managing a corporation, a factory, or a government bureaucracy, a person can't operate a combat unit by hiding out in his office. A combat leader must personally lead by setting an example to his troops. He must share their pain and hardships before they will blindly follow him.

Ultimately, the success of any combat unit is based upon the dedication and motivation of its leaders. Their enthusiasm and determination will spread throughout a unit like wildfire. Unfortunately in Vietnam, the basic motivation for fighting the war was lacking at almost every level but the air-conditioned top. Try as they might, the Pentagon and our political leaders were never able to convince the average grunt and the NCOs of the gravity of the conflict. Although we weren't the smartest guys in the world, it didn't a take a genius to realize that the war we were waging against these peasants had nothing to do with our national security or preserving our way of life.

Since the fighting in our area wasn't as intense as I had experienced up north, I began to walk around with a renewed strut and determination. In the past six months, I had gained enough combat experience to know how to do my job and how to do it well. I could also tell the difference between a good plan and a bad plan or recognize a fool from someone who knew what they were doing. With my growing confidence and the general lack of experienced personnel within the company, I began to exercise my authority with even more self-assurance.

If a sergeant or a lieutenant was about to do something really stupid, I would stand up and let him know about it. It didn't sit well with many of them, but at least they started listening. But what really impressed the new and old guys alike was when I would stand out in the open and adjust our mortar rounds onto the target. After being trained as an FO, I had learned to accept the danger as part of the job. Still, it really freaked them out when I would ignore the occasional sniper's pot shot and continue to go about my business. Everybody would get all excited and start yelling at me to get down. But I would just smile back at them and say, "Nah, this ain't nothing, wait till the big shit comes in."

In order to cover a much wider area, each platoon was assigned a particular sector for patrolling. From what I could figure out, because we were never told anything by anyone, it was our responsibility to keep the enemy from shelling the airstrip at Da Nang. As night approached, we would break up into squads and either set up an ambush or roam around the countryside looking for trouble. Normally, if an enemy unit did happen to walk into our ambush, the procedure was to wait until their point man was about to pass the end of our line and then let them have it. Once the firing stopped, the idea was to stay in our position until first light. Then as the sun began to rise, we would search the area for casualties, blood trails, and equipment. Under the best of conditions, a well-placed ambush could be quite deadly. Unfortunately though, it didn't always work out that way.

One particular night, we set up an ambush along a well-traveled trail. The underbrush was thick and wet, but it was suitable for our purposes. Because there were nine of us, we stretched out along the bushes and began taking turns staying awake. After I had stood my watch, I closed my eyes and tried to get some sleep. The insects weren't that bad, so I was able to doze off within a few minutes.

Then sometime around two o'clock in the morning, I felt a hand touch my arm. Slowly rolling over onto my belly, I raised my rifle into position and began to look around. Among the deep shadows, I could see about four or five guys walking down the pathway towards us. They were carrying their weapons over their shoulders as if they were strolling in the park. Suddenly, just as I was about to ease the safety off of my rifle, all hell broke loose. Up and down our line, everyone in our patrol began unleashing a barrage of deadly rifle fire as our lone machine gunner traversed his tracers all along the trail. Within a matter of seconds, those poor bastards were blown into the next county.

Almost immediately after the order had been given to cease fire, we started receiving rifle fire from farther down the trail. Recovering from the momentary shock, I looked through the moonlight and observed about thirty enemy soldiers coming towards us. Several of them were shooting at us, while the rest of them were trying to maneuver around our flanks. Then, I heard our squad leader yell out, "I'll see you boys back at the hooch," as he jumped up and took off through the bushes like a bat out of hell.

Before I could say anything, three figures ran out of the bushes and jumped into my small foxhole with me. As I was turning my rifle in their direction, they yelled, "Hey damn it, it's us." By the sound of their voices, I instantly realized it was the cherries. Amid all the confusion and mayhem, we just sat there for a minute and watched the rest of the guys bugging out in every different direction. They were moving so fast that all we could see were these vague images disappearing into the darkness. Then as one of the cherries yelled out, "Oh shit, here they come," several enemy soldiers were moving closer to us. Reaching down into my pants pocket, I pulled out a smoke grenade and threw it down the trail. Then I jumped up through a mass of tangled arms and legs and yelled out, "Let's get the hell out of here."

In one small wave of flying feet and abandoned equipment, they followed me through the bushes and onto a nearby road. Not to be too cautious, we kept on running until it was almost daylight.

To this day, I have no idea how far we actually ran that night, but the scenery definitely changed. It must have been around noon the next day, before we finally found ourselves standing on a major road. While hitchhiking back to the camp, the cherries were all excited about having survived their first close encounter with the enemy. However, when we finally did make it back, the lieutenant was pissed off at everyone involved. He must have chewed on our asses for a solid hour. But personally, I felt that we had done the right thing. Much like a bad marriage, sometimes things don't happen as one would expect, so the best thing a guy can do is cut his losses and run like hell.

During the middle part of July, our platoon had established a base camp in an area along the beach, just south of Marble Mountain. The place was covered with thick shrubs, windswept gullies, and mounds of sand. As we patrolled the area, we didn't find anything except a few booby traps and lots of insects. Occasionally, we would lie in our ponchos at night and listen to the enemy firing their mortars or rockets into the Da Nang airstrip. The experience always gave us the jitters, because we never knew if the outgoing rounds were being aimed at us.

In Vietnam and especially along the coast, the countryside was full of rice paddies, which were surrounded by thick hedgerows. Much like what our troops had experienced in World War II during the Battle of Saint Lo (1944), the fighting centered in and around those damn bushy obstacles. Early in the war, it was quite common for our troops to wade across these mud-filled paddies in order to reach the next hedgerow. Not ones to miss an easy target, the enemy made it a habit of ambushing us right in the middle of those death traps. Stuck in the mud and surrounded by walls of vegetation, a unit didn't stand a chance in that kind of situation.

Then after awhile, it began to dawn on our commanders to keep our troops out of the rice paddies and have them walk along the hedgerows. Invariably though, the enemy would respond to this change in tactics by constantly booby trapping them. Within a maze of waist-deep mud, slippery dikes, and interlocking thickets, I doubt if anyone could have created a more deadly environment. To this day I'm not sure what was worse, getting ambushed in a rice paddy or walking through one of their booby-trapped trails. In either scenario, we paid a very high price.

It was at this point of my short military career that I began to exhibit some very peculiar behavior. It seems that somewhere within the inner workings of my mind I had decided to become a British commando. Since the Marine Corps had prohibited any form of individual expression such as wearing beads, patches, or peace symbols, I began to express myself in a totally different fashion. Instead of showing any kind of resentment towards the war by wearing anti-war paraphernalia, I began to express my individuality in the other extreme. By dressing up like a British commando, I sought to put a little dash in my appearance and thus in my demeanor. To my surprise, it didn't seem to bother anybody that I was turning into Errol Flynn.

In preparation for each patrol, I found myself going through the same ritual. After tying a thin strip of leather around my wrists and above my elbows and knees, so as to inhibit the bleeding in case I got wounded, I hung a grenade or two from my flak jacket. Then I would strap a K-bar knife onto one of my legs, toss a bandoleer of ammunition across my chest, and fasten my cartridge belt around my waist.

Then once we moved out on a patrol, I would walk around with a long stick (cane) in one hand and a Dr. Grabow's unlit pipe hanging from my mouth. Shaped like one of Sherlock Holmes' pipes, it hung down below my chin and curled upward towards my half-grown handlebar mustache. Along with wearing a pair of dark sunglasses and my old salty boots and pants, I would go into the bush thinking that I was invincible.

However, almost everyone in my platoon agreed that the best part of it all was my helmet. Unlike the German-style helmet (Kevlar) our soldiers are forced to wear today, we wore the all-American World War II-type of helmet. When I was stationed at Khe Sanh, I had cut out a strip of material from a green and yellow parachute, which had been dropped during the siege, and wrapped it around my helmet as a decoration. Hanging off to one side was a little knot or bulb from the parachute that looked like a camouflaged braid. It was all so very commando like. While walking around in the bush, I not only looked like one of Britain's Gen. Orde Wingate Chindits of World War II fame, but I also began to act like them.

But I guess the most amusing part about the whole charade was that I had even begun to talk like a British commando. I started saying things like, "Cheerio, bloody savages, and well done, chaps."

At one of our temporary base camps, near the Cam Le Bridge, we were situated next to a group of huts overlooking a huge rice paddy. The heat was relentless and unforgiving. During the days, we would sit under our ponchos and intentionally try not to breathe through our noses, so that we wouldn't have to smell the unforgettable aroma of human feces emanating from the rice paddies. One day after we had finished policing the area, I looked over at the front gate and observed a young woman and a kid setting up a small vendor's stand next to a couple of ice chests. It didn't take long before we meandered over to see what they were selling. The young female was in the middle of starting a small fire for cooking, as the kid was busy building a small table. Curious, we pitched in and began helping him nail the pieces together. Naturally, we were more interested in what was in the ice chests than her Vietnamese cuisine.

Suddenly, she looked up from under her *non la* (cone-shaped hat) and said, "You wantie chop chop [food] and koo-beer?"

In almost perfect unison, we replied, "Yessssss, ma'am."

At thirty-five cents a can, the beer was rather expensive by Vietnam standards, but we didn't complain. It was cold and refreshing.

After a few minutes of conversation, we discovered that they were brother and sister. She was short and slender, possessing long black hair, olive skin, and piercing brown eyes. A genuine warmth radiated from her smile that made one feel immediately at ease. Being the oldest offspring in her family, she said, her name was Lan and she was in charge of their little business enterprise. She and her brother Danh were trying to help their parents support a family of ten. Then after we had introduced ourselves, Danh stepped forward to shake my hand. I figured that he was about fifteen years old, due to his overall shyness. Wearing a pair of yellow tennis shoes, thick nerd-looking glasses, and a dark-blue baseball cap, he could have been mistaken for any American high school student. In spite of the fact that he was awkward and unsure of his appearance, there was a certain maturity about him.

Since we had trouble pronouncing Danh's name, we started calling him Danny. Displaying a bright smile, deep brown eyes, and an infectious laugh, he was constantly joking around with us about the war and the craziness of it all. As a person, I grew to like him a lot. He had an easy manner about him that I found very reassuring. But I guess what really caught my attention was his obvious intelligence. He could not only speak very good English, but he also liked to recite Vietnamese poetry as well. From what he told us, it was his intention to become something other than a lousy dirt farmer. Apparently, the idea of spending the rest of his life working in the rice paddies wasn't on his agenda. His dream was to eventually save enough money so that he could bribe his way into college. During our time together, all he could talk about was his burning desire to teach literature and history, so that someday he could help his mother and father move into the city. In many ways, he reminded me of the average American servicemen. Young, naive, and possessing an uncertain future, he ferociously clung to his dreams.

Over the next couple of weeks, we made it a habit of going to their stand almost every day around noon. Even though we couldn't afford to buy but one or two beers a day, it really helped our morale. Besides enjoying the cold beer, Danny would teach me some basic Vietnamese words and their customs, while Lan sat around and cooked up her dishes. Surprisingly, I found her food had a strange odor about it. Full of noodles, chunks of water buffalo meat, and lots of peppers, the only way I could actually eat the stuff without gagging was to blow the foul-smelling fumes away from the bowl before I stuck it into my mouth. Yet it was a pleasant time for all of us. We talked and laughed our way through the humid afternoons while sitting under a huge shade tree.

On more than one occasion, I would watch in amusement as my three cherries tried to woo Lan. Of course, they didn't get very far in gaining her affection. She was much too intelligent for that. As for myself, I didn't even bother. The Vietnamese women had a way about them that I found generally unattractive. Even if they were young or wealthy enough to have avoided the hard life of working in the rice fields, there was still something about them that failed to inspire the lover in me. Overall, they were just too scrawny, hard looking, and flat-chested for my taste. Yet I must admit that after the war, when the South Vietnamese finally came to America and began to fatten themselves up on carbohydrates, I began to appreciate their beauty.

One muggy morning, while we were in the middle of a work detail, a huge explosion unexpectedly mushroomed through the palm trees about a half-mile away from our perimeter. Jumping into a jeep, several of us rushed to the scene in order to get a situation report (sitrep) for our lieutenant. As we drove up to a cluster of huts, we observed a large smoking crater where Rice Paddy Bob's hut used to be located. It took some time, but with the help of some engineers, we were finally able to determine what had happened.

Evidently, Rice Paddy Bob had dug up and then dragged a 250-pound bomb dud into his underground bunker, which he had dug underneath his hut. Obviously working for the local Viet Cong, he was right in the middle of trying to extract the explosives from the bomb, when all of a sudden, he was blown into little bitty pieces of hair and bone. Considering that everybody liked the fellow and mourned his loss, it was decided to say a short prayer over the smoldering crater. Amidst the surrounding smoke and burning trees, we solemnly stood there with our caps off and our heads bent low, wishing old Rice Paddy Bob a quick and painless journey to wherever the hell he ended up.

Due to Rice Paddy's demise, we should have known something big was about to happen. Under normal circumstances, I doubt if he would have been so careless. But at the time, none of us made the connection. We just went about our business, completely unaware that the enemy was about to launch the third phase of their 1968 Summer Offensive.

On August 22, I had been sent back to the Regimental/Battalion Compound to clear up some administrative matters. It seems the battalion clerk wanted to make sure everything in my records was up to date. That evening, after I had made my way to the Enlisted Men's Club, I unexpectedly walked into a huge celebration. Everyone was excited and talking up a storm, because the word had been circulating that the 27th Marines were finally going home. Of course, we didn't know if that applied to everybody. For those of us with several months left to serve in country, the prospects of returning home looked bleak. At the time, I just couldn't believe that the Marines were going to let anyone go home early. But it didn't matter to me. Somebody yelled, "Let's party," and I jumped in with both feet.

Later that night around midnight, everyone in our tent was sound asleep, when all of a sudden we were awakened by a chorus of screams to get out of our cots and man the perimeter. By the urgency of their voices, one would have thought we were being overrun. Half-drunk and still drowsy from the party, I quickly put on my gear and rushed out to the nearest post.

Once my head had cleared a little bit, it didn't take long before I realized our perimeter wasn't in any immediate danger. However as far as the eye could see, it looked as if everybody else around Da Nang was getting the hell knocked out of them. Inasmuch as our compound was situated on a main road that ran generally east to west, I could turn my head in either direction and hear a firefight raging just a short distance down the road. Then peering off to the south and then to the north, I noticed there must have been a half dozen or so Puff the Magic Dragons (C-47s) in the air, dropping their flares and spewing their deadly fire. They literally lit up the sky like a New Year's Eve party. From where I was standing, it appeared as if every compound around us was under heavy attack. Unquestionably, it was an eerie feeling having to listen to everyone around us fighting for his life. Yet I instinctively knew that our compound was safe from an enemy attack. Whoever had selected this particular position knew exactly what he was doing. There wasn't a tree line or a village within a half-mile of the place.

After about an hour of watching the light show and listening to the surrounding gunfire, I decided to get some shuteye. From my experience, I knew that if the enemy were going to hit our compound, they would have already done it. Moreover, I knew that once the sun reappeared, we would be in for a long violent day. So I rolled myself up into a little ball at the bottom of the open bunker and told everyone to wake me up if some fellows in black pajamas happened to show up.

As the sunlight began to shine through the entranceway, I suddenly awoke from a deep sleep. The distant firing wasn't quite as intense as earlier that night, but I could still hear the occasional crack of an AK-47 from off in the distance. Opening a can of beans and weenies, I eagerly wolfed down the food, knowing full well that we would be moving out shortly.

Then just as I was about to finish up a cup of warm coffee, a fat sergeant came around and ordered us to muster on the main road. Within a matter of a few minutes, about thirty of us were assembled in front of the motor pool. Most of the guys were upset, because they thought everybody was going home. However, I knew better than that. Standing off to one side, First Sergeant Burtsell stepped forward and introduced a captain by the name of Moore to us. I knew and liked Burtsell, but I didn't know Moore from Adam. As crazy as it may seem, I found out later that the guy was actually my company commander.

Although everyone on the road was hung-over and half-asleep, we still tried to look as military as possible. Yet I had never seen such a collection of misfits, scoundrels, and oddballs in all my life. We looked like an outfit from *F Troop*, which was a popular television series about a bunch of misfits. The rear-area NCOs had been forced to gather up every warm body in the perimeter, including clerks, cooks, truck drivers, and sick bay hounds. They had even grabbed a couple of guys who had been under house arrest and were awaiting their trials. Under military law, they didn't have to participate in any form of duty. But in the finest tradition of the Corps, it didn't matter to them. If there was a Marine in trouble, they wanted to pick up a rifle and help. To my discomfort, only a few of us were actually grunts. As far as I could tell, most of guys didn't even have a proper weapon, much less a helmet or a flak jacket. I remember one poor fellow, who hadn't been issued his rifle yet, was carrying an old Korean War 3.5 bazooka.

None of this seemed to bother anybody as the captain began telling us what was expected of us. From what he had been informed by headquarters, an enemy force of unknown size had captured Cam Le Bridge, just south of the Da Nang airstrip. Since most of our units in the area had been hit that night and had their hands full, our ad hoc group was being ordered to help retake the bridge. The plan was for us to attack the bridge from the south, while Delta Company attacked it from the west. Not knowing the full extent of the enemy's intentions, I knew something wasn't right. Why would the enemy capture and then hold onto a bridge right next to one of our largest military installations? Normally, they would have shot up the place and then melted away into the background. However this time around, they were actually holding their objective and waiting for the fury that was sure to come.[1]

It was at this point that Burtsell walked over to me, and said, "Well, what do think, Short?"

After looking around at the other fellows for a second, I replied, "Top, I don't think these blokes could fight their way out of a ruddy whorehouse."

Nodding his head in agreement, he sarcastically replied, "That's why I want you to take up the rear and keep an eye on this wild bunch. I don't want any of them skedaddling back to the compound."

"Roger that," I said with a smile.

As we made our way out of the gate and across the rice paddies, it occurred to me that my platoon was positioned not very far from the southern end of the bridge. I kept wondering if they were going to be all right. At the time, I didn't realize that they had also been ordered to attack the bridge at about the same time that we had left the compound. Even under the best of circumstances, it was going to be a tough nut for them to crack. Besides being surrounded by deep foxholes, rolls of concertina wire, and an open field of fire, the southern part of the bridge was protected by a thick cement bunker that had been built by the French. Unbeknown to everyone, a detachment of Marine MPs had already recaptured the northern end of the bridge earlier that morning. Thus with the enemy still controlling the southern end and having nowhere to retreat, my platoon was going to run into a very desperate and entrenched foe.

It must have been about eight o'clock in the morning, when our ragtag outfit reached an intersection in the road, just south of a small village called Cam Nam. Standing in the crossroads, I could see several U.S. Army personnel pointing down the road at the village to the north. After bringing up the rear, I approached Moore and Burtsell to report that everybody was present. Then the three of us walked over to where the Army guys were standing.

To this day, I don't know if what we did that day ever became a part of Marine Corps lore, but it probably should have. Exhibiting once again the United States Marine Corps' indomitable fighting spirit, it would become one of the proudest moments of my life.

When we walked up to their group, we encountered an Army major, his master sergeant, and their radioman. Looking down a nearby pathway, I spotted what I thought was a platoon of their soldiers. Throwing a hand out, Captain Moore introduced myself to the major and then asked him the direction to Cam Le Bridge.

Motioning in the direction of Cam Nam, the major replied, "It's about a half a mile on the other side of that village, Captain. But believe me, you don't want to go there. It's full of NVA."

But in actuality, we were about to confront the 402nd VC Sapper Battalion.

"Well, major," Captain Moore replied, "I don't give a damn how many NVA are in that village. My orders are to retake the bridge and that's what we are going to do."

While they began arguing with each other, I noticed the Army's master sergeant and his radioman glancing over at our ragtag group with the strangest expression on their faces. In their amusement, they kept rolling their eyes up in the air and nudging each other with their elbows. Obviously, they weren't catching us at our best. In fact, two of our people had just gotten off R&R and were still half-dressed in their civilian clothes. I'll never forget one of them would spend the whole day running around in his dress shoes.

Finally, right in the middle of their heated discussion Moore blurted out, "Major, my orders are to retake the bridge. Now, if you want to join us that's fine and dandy. But if not, move your people out of the way and let us do our jobs."

In a moment of frustration, the Army master sergeant stepped forward and said, "Captain, we've been told that there are over four hundred NVA in that village. You can't expect to go through the village and then reach the bridge with the number of people you've got here."

Suddenly, Burtsell leaned over and spit on the ground in front of the master sergeant, and then said, "Shit man, that's good odds." Then Moore abruptly turned to Burtsell and bellowed, "Move them out, Top."

As our undermanned, ill-equipped outfit paraded by the Army major and his master sergeant, they looked as if they were in a state of shock. Shaking their heads in disbelief, I could tell that there was no way they were going to follow us down that road. It was just too crazy. Being the last guy to walk past their group, I waited until I was several yards down the road before I turned around and yelled, "Tallyho, mates."

After making our way to within four hundred meters of the village, Captain Moore received a radio message to stay in position, until our Battalion Commander could call in some support for us. Then he was ordered to divert one of our squads to a nearby CAP unit, thus reducing our numbers to about twenty Marines.

For the next hour or so, we sat around and chewed the fat. As days go, the weather was beautiful. The sky was clear and bluish, the wind was calm, and the enemy was not running away. I remember talking to one black fellow, who kept shaking his head in disbelief.

"Why in the world would they want to make a stand here of all places?" he said in exasperation. "They're all just going to die for no reason."

"That's bloody well true, mate," I replied, "None of this tommy-rot makes any sense to me."

Then while I was checking my rifle, a most beautiful sight came rumbling down the road towards us. Our Battalion Commander had called in five tanks from Bravo Company of the 5th Tank Battalion. Besides showing up to the party with four M-48 tanks and their 90mm cannons, they also brought along a flame-thrower tank, which everyone referred to as a "Zippo." Viewed from the side of the road, they were simply unbelievable machines to behold. Mounted with a high velocity gun and two machine guns, I don't see how anyone could have stood up to them. Within a matter of seconds, they could pump out a helluva lot of firepower. Glancing over to my right, I noticed Burtsell had a big smile etched across his face. Puzzled, I couldn't understand why he was smiling. Then I remembered he once told me that there was nothing more exciting than going into combat with tanks. While describing them to me, he persistently used the words, "extremely deadly."

Following several minutes of consultation between Captain Moore and the tankers, it was decided that the tanks would remain on the road, while we positioned ourselves on their flanks for protection. Then as one coordinated group, we would attack northward through the village and eventually reach the bridge.

As I positioned myself on the east side of the road with my rifle at the ready, Captain Moore waved his arm in the air and gave us the order to attack. Without a doubt, it was the most breathtaking spectacle that I had ever witnessed. As the huge tanks lurched forward towards the village, we advanced through the surrounding rice paddies. The roar of the tank engines was almost deafening as we determinedly marched forward.

Then without warning, an intense array of firepower began to erupt across the front of our formation in one panoramic outburst of violent eruptions. Our artillery and mortar rounds had been so perfectly placed that they literally created a protective wall of fire and steel between the village and us. As we slowly moved behind the deadly barrages in one synchronized mass of men and machines, I doubt if an attack could have been managed any better. Combined with the openness of the ground and the fury of the explosions, the scene was right out of the Halls of Montezuma.

By and large, I was overwhelmed with exhilaration. Instead of being ambushed along a jungle path or having to walk through the enemy's booby traps, we were actually going to fight these bastards on our own terms. It was all so incredible and invigorating that I could almost hear the Marine Corps hymn being played in the background.

Then as we got within ten meters of the first hut, the enemy suddenly opened fire upon us with everything they had and the music abruptly stopped.

To this day, I have no idea what had inspired me to walk next to the lead tank. I can only guess that I thought a person would be safe there, next to one of those green, forty-nine-ton monsters. I would never make that mistake again.

For when the enemy had finally decided to open fire, they had intentionally concentrated their weapons at the lead tank and thus at me. Just as I was about to unclick the safety on my rifle, a huge wave of B-40 rockets, machine gun tracers, and AK-47 fire smashed into the lead tank and flew past my head. I instantly hit the dirt and began rolling away from the road. While I was twirling myself across the ground, I could hear the rounds hitting all around me. Their impact was so loud that I kept rolling until I had almost rolled into the next rice paddy.

Stopping to catch my breath, I suddenly looked up and realized a B-40 rocket was coming right at me. Mesmerized by the sight, I watched it sail directly over my head like a football and land in front of a lieutenant who was lying several yards behind me. And where he and his unit had come from, I had no idea. They had just appeared behind us out of nowhere. Luckily though, the shrapnel didn't hit either one of us. I was stunned by the dreadful roar of the cannons and the rattling of the machine guns, so I just lay there for a minute with my face pressed against the warm earth.

Our tanks began unleashing a torrent of cannon and machine-gun fire into the nearby structures in response to the enemy's burst of fire. At point-blank range, it was impossible for them to have missed their targets. As I watched their rounds slam into the sides of the huts, the concussions from the 90mm shells were so powerful that they were blowing huge chunks of debris back towards me. Since most of the huts were made of cement and brick, the tank gunners had to fire more than one round into them in order to penetrate the walls. After being blasted by a couple of salvos, a section of wall would collapse and expose a group of terrified occupants scrambling for their lives.

On more than one occasion, I happened to witness two tanks firing simultaneously into the same hut. The result was absolutely devastating. Once the rounds ripped through the thick walls and exploded within the rooms, a deluge of dense smoke, bright flashes, and ungodly screams bellowed out from the windows and through the open doorways. Looking up, I could see the roofs of the structures flying up into the air with an assortment of Vietnamese furniture trailing behind them. In a blink of an eye, the huts were being reduced to a mass of smoldering rubble.

However, none of this seemed to have deterred the enemy's counter-fire. Between the blasts from our cannons, we could still hear their bullets and see their B-40 rockets ricocheting off the tanks. Then just as I thought that I had seen the height of destruction and mayhem, our Zippo tank went into action.

Spitting out a long line of burning hot napalm, the tank's flames literally splattered against the walls of the huts, creating a whirlwind of fire and blistering heat. As the crew traversed their deadly barrel across the neighborhood, the tank's machine gunners were firing their guns at anything that moved. Struggling to save themselves from the holocaust, several people were heaving pails of water onto the burning window ledges and then jumping through the openings. I remember one elderly lady was defiantly standing in her front yard, waving a blanket around trying to put out the fires. But it was all for naught. Within a matter of minutes, the outskirts of the village were ablaze in an inferno of cinders and burning huts. At times, the heat from the napalm was so intense that I had to shield my face.

During the initial attack, I didn't realize that Echo Company from the 2nd Battalion (2/27) had come up from our rear and was supporting the attack. Earlier, I had observed several groups of Marines were pinned down along my side of the road and in the rice paddy. But I figured they were just part of our unit. Then as I lay there wondering what I was going to do next, I heard someone whistling in my direction. Looking back over my shoulder, there was a lieutenant from Echo Company waving at me to come towards him. He was the same fellow who had dodged the B-40 rocket just a few minutes before. Somewhat irritated, I turned around and crawled about fifteen feet in his direction to see what he wanted. The enemy's rounds were zinging all around us when he asked me the whereabouts of Captain Moore.

Pointing at the lead tank, I yelled, "You'll probably find him over there, sir."

Then he put his hand upon my shoulder and yelled back at me, "I want you to go find him for me and ask him where he wants my unit positioned?"

After pausing for a second, I replied, "Then I suppose you want me to come back and report to you?"

"Yep, that's it exactly," he said with a small grin.

"Now, let me get this straight," I shouted, "You want me to run all the way over there and back?"

At the time, we could both see the area was being swept by enemy fire.

"That's right, damn it," he answered, "We'll cover you."

There was something about this conversation that just didn't sound right to me. He must have had over thirty other Marines in his unit lying around him, and yet he wanted me to carry his lousy messages for him.

"Now, let me get this straight," I shouted again, "You want me to run all the way over there and back, while you're covering who?"

At this point, the lieutenant was getting pissed off. So he leaned over into my face and yelled, "I gave you an order, Marine, and you had better carry it out."

Instantly leaping to my feet as a good Marine would, I took a couple of steps towards Captain Moore's position before a burst from an AK-47 whizzed past my head. Realizing that I was on a fool's errand, I quickly turned away from the road and ran to the nearest tree line, located about twenty meters farther to the east. While I was running for my life, I wondered for a second if the lieutenant was going to have me arrested for disobeying a direct order. But at that point, I couldn't have cared less. I figured if the message was all that damn important, he should have taken it himself. He didn't look all that frickin' busy to me.

Crashing through a maze of tangled vines and shrubs, I discovered a deep ditch inside the tree line, which ran parallel to the road. Sitting next to the dirt walls were about six or seven other Marines taking a breather. To my surprise, one of them was the kid with the bazooka. He had become so frustrated because his weapon wouldn't fire that he was almost in tears. All I could do was chuckle to myself as I began to make my way down the ditch. Trying not to step on anybody, I could hear the enemy's rounds clipping the tree limbs above us. Then suddenly, an F-4 Phantom came roaring out of the sky and began strafing the village.

This gave me an opportunity to stick my head up and get a better view of the situation. From what I could tell, the majority of the houses in the village were on the other (western) side of the road. Thus there were only a handful of structures to our immediate front. In particular, I could see a large, blue house looming in the distance. Unknown to us at the time, Delta Company of 1/27 was also attacking the village from the west. Under heavy fire and pinned down, it would take them several hours just to reach the outskirts of the village. However, once they were able to reach the huts, they would join us and turn their attack in a northerly direction towards the bridge.

As our tanks inched their way down the road, Captain Moore and First Sergeant Burtsell assisted them in finding their targets. Every time an enemy's position was located, they radioed the tanks to blow it into a pile of rubble. Unfortunately though, every time one of their positions was destroyed, another enemy gunner popped up from another location and continued to pin us down. The only problem we were facing on the eastern side of the road was the blue house. From the edge of the ditch, we must have spent at least a couple of hours pouring rifle fire into the windows and walls. Almost like a cheap western movie, we would pop up and shoot at them for awhile and then they would pop up and shoot at us for awhile. During all this time, the smoke from the burning huts was becoming so thick that it was difficult for us to see, much less to breathe. Lacking water and running low on ammo, three of us decided to run back down the ditch and circle around to see if we could approach the blue house from another direction.

After holding our breath and retracing our steps, we jumped through some bushes and ran across an adjacent rice paddy into another tree line on the extreme eastern end of the village. While keeping as low to the ground as possible, we then maneuvered our way to the side of the blue house.

At this point, it took us several minutes to figure out what to do next. In the background, we could hear our tanks' fifty-caliber machine guns firing into the nearby huts, so we decided to get off our asses and surround the place. Pulling out our grenades, the other two fellows crept around to the front of the house, while I crept around to the back. In almost perfect unison, we tossed our grenades into the windows and ran back around to the side of the house. With a loud boom, the explosions rocked the house, sending shrapnel everywhere.

As I peeked around the corner, I noticed several of our guys from the ditch began running up to the house and shooting into the front door and windows. Surrounded by smoke and rifle fire, the three of us joined the rest of the guys and prepared to throw some more grenades. But before we could pull the pins, the strangest thing occurred among all the confusion. Approximately thirty to forty wide-eyed civilians suddenly ran from across the road in our direction. With their children in their arms and a few valuables strapped to their backs, their only desire was to get the hell out of Dodge City. Temporarily stunned by their unexpected presence, we didn't know what to do. None of us wanted to turn our backs on them while in the middle of a firefight.

Suddenly, I spotted Burtsell lying by the side of the road, so I yelled at him, "Hey Top, what do you want us to do with these people?"

Then in one of the typical ironies of the Vietnam War, he yelled back, "Check their IDs."

As comical as it may seem, we actually were able to stop several of them and check their identification cards. However, this madness quickly came to an abrupt halt when one of the VC from a nearby hut ripped a line of rounds right through the middle of our group. Scattering like a covey of quail, the Vietnamese ran one way as we ran the other.

Upon entering the blue house, we saw blood strains, empty rifle casings, and soiled bandages strewn all over the floor. Yet there weren't any bodies. The rooms had been stripped of all personal belongings and several holes had been cut into the walls as passageways. The absence of their belongings indicated to me that this fight had been carefully planned. Every hut in the village that was strong enough to withstand an attack had been manned and prepared with great care. Yet I still didn't understand the purpose for what would eventually end up being a week's worth of heavy fighting around the Da Nang area. Tactically, the enemy wasn't achieving anything, except maybe freaking out the local peasants and our folks back home. At the time, we didn't realize that as part of the strategy behind Tet Offensive, the NVA intended to continue their attacks along the populated coastline throughout most of 1968, so as to keep our attention away from the Ho Chi Minh Trail.

Once our attack had reached the middle of the village, the VC became extremely desperate. Several of them started driving their vehicles onto the road in order to create an obstacle for the tanks. In a flurry of surrounding rifle fire, we rushed out of the blue house and tried to shoot them down before they could get out of their vehicles. Between the tank's machine guns and our M-16s, the noise was almost unbearable.

Then I heard someone yell, "Here comes another one." As I looked up, I saw this white vehicle speeding towards the road. Then all of a sudden, the driver tried to leap out of the cab. However, he must have failed to put the gear into neutral, because when he jumped, the vehicle suddenly stopped dead in its tracks, thus slamming him into the doorframe and knocking him out cold in the middle of road. Amid the whirling smoke and the sporadic rifle fire, we must have laid there laughing and arguing with each other for several minutes as to whether or not we should shoot the poor dumb bastard.

Then emerging from the other side of the road, a jeep filled with about three or four VC came barreling onto the road and headed in the direction of the bridge. For a split second, it looked as if they might make it, until one of our tanks turned its deadly turret in their direction and unloaded a 90mm shell right into their back seat. The ensuing explosion ripped through the steel chassis with tremendous force and blew the doors and the roof high into the air. Incredibly, what was left of the burning vehicle and the VC inside of it began to sizzle and crackle, much like the sound of popcorn.

Soon afterward, one of our tanks turned its cannon at the other vehicles parked on the road and blew them out of the way. After realizing that the fellow who had been knocked unconscious in the middle of the road had vanished, we moved closer to the last hut and began lobbing our remaining grenades into the windows. After a succession of explosions, a couple of our guys ran into the hut only to find a couple of VC bodies.

With the village destroyed and the enemy retreating in the direction of the bridge, we walked up to the tanks and asked their crews for some water. After about nine hours of fighting, our thirst was so intense that we would have drunk anything wet. To our delight, one of the tank members handed us down a jerry can full of water. While we were satisfying our thirst, Burtsell came over and ordered us to help evacuate the dead and wounded. Gesturing towards a rice paddy next to the blue house, he said a helicopter would be landing there shortly and that he wanted us to make sure all of our casualties were on it. During the fight, we had suffered several wounded and two KIAs (killed in action). In the larger scheme of things, I didn't have any idea of how many people our other units had lost.

Once we set up a small perimeter, somebody pulled the pin of a green smoke grenade and threw it into the nearby rice paddy. Suddenly out of the sky, a UH-34 helicopter came soaring over a tree line and into the LZ. Within seconds, the ship's crew began to frantically unload boxes of ammo out onto the ground, while a detail of stretcher-bearers moved our dead and wounded to the doorway. As I stood there at my post and watched our kids being loaded into the belly of the chopper, I felt a sense of deep loss and remorse. The tears streamed down my cheeks and onto my flak jacket as I tried to retain my composure. In spite of the fact that I had carried the dead on many different occasions, it was something that always made my insides ache. In my mind, they had given their blood and their lives for something much more important than the mere politics of the Cold War. They had sacrificed themselves for their leaders, for their loved ones, and for the other kids around them. Ironically, they would represent the best that our country had to offer, even though the overwhelming majority of them had come from our poorest neighborhoods. And tragically for the ones who had survived, they were the least appreciated and understood veterans that had ever returned from an American war.

It seemed that only a few minutes had passed before we made our way back to the road and renewed the attack towards the bridge. From this point, we could actually see the bridge and the French bunker off in the distance. Instead of walking beside the road next to the tanks, I instinctively moved farther out into the rice paddies. At the time, I did not intend to get killed by another ricochet. However, it didn't take long before the enemy's machine gun and rocket fire began to land all around us. Luckily, the air was so full of smoke from the burning village that their rounds were off the mark. As we moved closer though the haze, we could actually hear the VC screaming at each other. Though I had no idea as to what they were saying, their voices sounded urgent and strained. Strangely, they sounded like a bunch of kids.

For the next hour or so, our tanks pumped round after round into the French bunker. It seemed that every time we silenced one of their machine gunners, someone else would pop up and take his place. Between the tanks' salvos, we had an opportunity to maneuver closer to the enemy's position. At one point, as I was lying behind a dike, these two fellows came running out of nowhere and slid down right next to me. As they were trying to catch their breath, I noticed one of them was wearing a pair of dress shoes. Then the other guy muttered, "Man, this is bad shit. I haven't seen this much crap since I've been here."

Glancing at the bunker for a second, I turned my head towards him and replied, "Well, it could be worse. The tanks could be firing at us."

Meanwhile, the guy wearing the dress shoes rolled over on his back and responded in his best southern drawl, "Damn fellers, in three more weeks I'm gettin' out of this green machine (USMC) and you can kiss my young ass goodbye."

After struggling over the dikes and through the stalks of rice, it took us a while before we finally made contact with one of the squads from my platoon. They were scattered all over the place. I had to individually call out their names so that we wouldn't shoot each other. Then after a quick exchange of hellos, the order was given to prepare ourselves to rush the French bunker. Even though I could barely walk from the fatigue, I approached several people and asked them the whereabouts of my cherries. None of them could help me, so just as I was about to ask another fellow, everyone around me suddenly jumped up and began running and firing at the enemy's last position. Not to be left behind, I took off with them.

As I was making my way up an incline, I came upon a small ditch, so I stopped to see if there was any VC in it. As I pointed my rifle down into the hole, my three cherries suddenly poked their heads up with a big grin plastered across their dirty faces and yelled out, "Where in the hell have you been?"

In response to their exuberance and the craziness of it all, I stood there for a second with a reassuring smile and then bellowed out, "Exciting, ain't it?" Then I quickly turned away and ran up towards the bunker. Within minutes, we were able to flush out the surviving VC and end their military careers.

As the tanks began to turn around and leave the area, there was a sense of satisfaction that prevailed among us. I could see it in every-one's faces and in the way they looked at each other. After what seemed like an eternity, we had finally secured the bridge.

Out of our small unit, there were only thirteen of us left stand-ing. As for the other guys in my original platoon, they had spent the entire day pinned down in front of the French bunker. Without any fire support, they had walked right into the enemy's line of fire that morning. Later, I was informed by one of the cherries that the enemy's machine-gun fire had been so intense that they had ended up digging into the ground with their fingers in order to hide. If I remember cor-rectly, they had lost about four or five guys that day, trying to capture the enemy's position.

As I wearily sat down between Captain Moore and Burtsell, I pulled out a cigarette and tried to enjoy our victory. Flies began gathering around the VC bodies lying all over the place, while the parts of others were hanging off the bridge. Looking around for a moment, I noticed one of the VC bodies in a nearby ditch was consumed in flames. Then as I was about to make a wisecrack about it to Burtsell, the chicoms that were strapped to his back began to explode what was left of him into the air, thus turning him into a fine red mist. It was all so very gruesome, but exhilarating at the same time. We had fought the enemy on our own terms for once and they had paid a very high price for their tomfoolery.

In the meantime as Captain Moore was radioing headquarters for a re-supply helicopter, a truck filled with ARVNs drove up. We weren't very happy to see them, because as far as we could tell, they hadn't fired a shot all day. But instead of greeting us as allies or just going about their business, these assholes decided to show us how tough they were. One by one, they walked over to the VC bodies and began shooting them in the heads at close range. The idea of these creeps' mutilating the enemies' bodies was just too much. We may have blown them to bits, but their remains still deserved our respect. They had fought like men and they had died as men.

As Burtsell and I began to stand up to kick some asses, several other Marines locked and loaded their rifles and aimed them at the South Vietnamese commander. For a slight moment, it appeared as if this idiot was going to challenge us. He stood there with his hand tightly gripped around his pistol with a smirk on his face. Then Moore finally stood up and yelled at him to get his lousy men out of the area. Reluctantly, the ARVN commander ordered his troops to move away from the bridge, until we had left.

Exhausted, hungry, and in a daze, our ragtag group had been ordered to follow my platoon back to our original camp, located just down the river. Meanwhile, I had been walking around the nearby bushes looking for a few souvenirs. Finding an NVA flag, a Russian Makarov pistol, or a Simonov SKS rifle was considered a real prize in any man's army. Of course, I had heard stories about how some of our guys would hack off pieces of the enemy's bodies as mementos. Personally, I found the idea repulsive. Who in the world would want to walk around with an ear in his pocket?

Nevertheless as I was stumbling around, I happened to come across another VC body. Half hidden in the bushes, he had a B-40 rocket launcher clutched in one hand and a hole in the back of his head about the size of a baseball. Then after looking at him a little more carefully, I suddenly noticed that he was wearing a pair of yellow tennis shoes. As I edged closer towards him, I felt my life's blood drain from my body. Overwhelmed with a sense of utter futility, my breathing became deep and uncertain. No one back in Camp Pendleton had told me that we would be killing human beings. They were all supposed to be just a bunch of nameless, unfeeling gooks.

Kneeling down and placing my hand upon his shoulder, I remember whispering, "Oh Danny, what in the hell did you think you were doing?" After several minutes, I returned to the bridge and found a poncho with which to cover his body. Then I mumbled a brief prayer and walked away. It was the second time that terrible day that I had found myself wiping the tears off of my hardened face and feeling as if I had been kicked in the guts.

Needless to say that ended my days as a would-be British commando.

Later that evening, after we had staggered into camp, the mood was grim and hushed. There wasn't any joking or kidding around. Everyone just wanted to eat a little something and find a place to sleep. As for myself, I was dreading the coming of the next day. I kept wondering to myself, what in the world could I possibly say to Lan. Would she understand or would she begin looking at us with absolute contempt and loathing in her eyes, like so many other Vietnamese people did. Fortunately, it was something that I wouldn't have to deal with, because she never returned to her little stand.

On September 12, 1968, the 27th Marines left the shores of Vietnam for good to be replaced by none other than my old unit, the 2nd Battalion, 1st Marines. To this day, I have no idea of how many people actually went home, because everybody in my unit was transferred to another outfit. But I guess it made for a lot of good publicity for the folks back home to believe that we were making a substantial troop withdrawal. Nevertheless, after standing in front of the headquarters shed for several hours, I was finally given my walking orders. To my absolute dismay, I had been transferred to the 3rd Marine Division.

The fact that they were operating in the DMZ didn't bother me that much. I knew the terrain and I understood the hardships. And quite frankly, I was getting sick and tired of dealing with the VC and their lousy booby traps. However, I was disappointed and rather confused about being assigned to another division. Considering myself a 1st Division man, I found the decision illogical. Why go through the trouble of moving a guy to another division, when the other units in his division were also in need of replacements? Disappointed, I took my orders like any good Marine and carried on the best that I could. Yet I must admit that to this day, whenever I hear the 1st Marine Division's theme song, "Waltzing Matilda," I still get teary eyed.

Later that afternoon, a short, stocky corporal suddenly approached me and asked, "Where in the world did they stick your ass?"

When I told him the 3rd Marine Division, he responded by saying, "So long as they don't put you in the 1st Battalion, 9th Marines, you'll be all right. Those poor bastards are always walking into the shit."

Chapter Ten

Walking with the Dead

*During a conventional war, seeking out the enemy
is normally a sound strategy, but in Vietnam, it only
created a lot of unnecessary casualties.*

Once the truck had come to a screeching halt, I reluctantly jumped down onto the hot pavement and ventured into the Marine transit building to get my orders processed. The weather had finally cleared up from the typhoon to where I could catch a flight to the 3rd Marine Division Headquarters in Quang Tri. Seated at the division's counter was probably one of the most disinterested human beings I had ever seen. He kept yawning and stretching his backside as if he didn't have a care in the world. However since he was in the position to send me to any regiment within the division, I tried my best to be as friendly as possible.

Somewhat nervously, I kept asking him about his lovely family and the beautiful girlfriend he had left behind in the hopes that he might give me a break and assign me to some out-of-the-way outfit. Of course, it was all wishful thinking on my part. All I knew at the time was that I didn't want to be a member of the 9th Marines, especially their 1st Battalion. As a hard-luck unit, they had become infamous for always being at the wrong place at the wrong time. It seemed like every other week or so, there was a story on the front page of the *Stars & Stripes* about one of their companies stumbling into an ambush. It was even rumored that they had lost more people than any other battalion in Vietnam, including those in the U.S. Army. Still as I stood there in eerie anticipation, I figured the odds were in my favor. With the addition of the 26th Marines in 1966, the 3rd Marine Division had been operating with four different regiments (3rd, 4th, 9th, and 26th), instead of the usual three.

Then after the clerk had conferred with his lieutenant for a little while, he nonchalantly walked back over to the counter and said, "Sorry pal," as he stamped my orders for the 9th Marines. Glaring back at him as if he had just sold me down the river for a handful of trinkets, he meekly responded, "Look buddy, the 2nd and 3rd Battalions are excellent outfits, but it's the 1st Battalion that you want to avoid. They ain't called the 'Walking Dead' for nothing."

Besides the fact that he had significantly lowered the odds for my survival, I still felt good about my chances. With my mortar specialty, I figured that I would probably be assigned to some 81mm mortar section, which in my mind wouldn't have been all that bad of a proposition, considering my experience with the weapon.

Later that afternoon, I was able to catch a C-130 transport to Quang Tri with a group of Army personnel. Located about twenty miles north of Hue City on Route 1, Quang Tri was one of the biggest Marine combat bases in I Corps. Much like the base at Phu Bai, it was a mixture of old run-down tents, starched uniforms, snappy salutes, and uptight NCOs. Upon entering the 9th Regimental Headquarters, I immediately approached another counter with another disinterested clerk sitting behind it. But before I could even shake his hand and offer to buy him a few beers afterward, he grabbed my orders and stamped them for the 1st Battalion. I just stood there for a minute flabbergasted. At that instant, I remember wondering to myself, why me? I've always tried to live a decent and somewhat righteous life. Then after he realized that I wasn't going to happily go away as if I was some ignorant cherry, he finally looked up and in a gesture of relieving his own guilt, he said, "Look here, the 1st Battalion is a good outfit. They have excellent officers and NCOs. It's Bravo Company that you want to avoid. They tend to walk into the shit wherever they go. So cheer up and look at the bright side. The other companies in the battalion need men, too."

Of course, I knew he was full of it. Bravo Company may have been infamous for getting the hell knocked out of them, but in my mind, the other companies weren't any better. During the fighting around Khe Sanh earlier that year, the battalion had suffered almost six hundred casualties out of approximately eight hundred kids. Though my math wasn't that great, I knew that anyway you looked at it, the whole outfit was bad news.

By the time I walked into the 1st Battalion Headquarters, I was clutching a Bible in one hand and a string of juju beads in the other. I honestly couldn't believe that my luck had run out to the point where I would even be standing there in the first place. After I handed my orders to another disinterested clerk, I just kept looking up at the ceiling in frustration, with my hands on my hips and shaking my head in disbelief.

Then I heard him mutter, "Well, I see you're coming from the 27th Marines. We sure can use all the replacements we can get." In one vivid flash, I suddenly realized what was coming next. It was as if the clouds had finally cleared and I could see for miles. So instead of trying to fight what was obviously my fate, I decided to get to the point.

"That doesn't surprise me in the least," I replied in a sarcastic manner. Then as I continued to look up at the ceiling, I said, "Now let me guess, you don't need any eighty-one mortarmen."

"That's right," the smiling clerk responded, "How did you know?"

"And you don't need any sixty-millimeter mortarmen either," as I continued to prophesize.

"Hey, that's right again," he replied, "You're really a sharp fellow."

"But let me guess, Bravo Company is in need of ground-pounders," I said, as I looked down at him in absolute contempt.

With a devious grin smeared across his face, he replied, "Boy Howdy, nothing gets past you, does it?" as he gleefully stamped my orders for Bravo Company.

To this day, I really don't remember what platoon, squad, or even what fire team I was actually assigned to in Bravo Company. It had gotten to the point where all that had become rather meaningless to me. For the next several months, I just humped the bush and tried to bring my professionalism to bear. Once a unit had gotten the mark of Cain placed upon it, it wasn't an easy matter to remove it. As I had observed in 2/1, some companies could hump around in the most distant enemy infested areas for weeks on end without losing a man. Yet a hard-luck unit could trigger an ambush just outside their perimeter in what was supposed to be a secure area.

The rumor circulating around the Enlisted Men's Clubs was that when the 1st Battalion, 9th Marines had first entered the country back in the mid-sixties, they had a bad habit of mutilating the bodies of the enemy dead and not taking any prisoners. It was also rumored that in retaliation, the NVA would regularly assign one of their regiments in their area to make life as miserable as possible for them. Of course, I didn't know if any of that stuff was true, but it wouldn't have surprised me in the least. The NVA and VC had a way of keeping score with our units' atrocities. Almost immediately upon entering any particular area, they knew exactly what unit they were up against and that unit's history.

It didn't take long before I was finally able to catch a helicopter ride to our forward base camp at LZ Stud. Staring out through the window and into the hazy clouds, I was completely frustrated and bewildered about the war. It just didn't appear as if we were making any progress. Out in the field, we continued to conduct our operations and build our firebases, without accepting the fact that our strategy wasn't working. This situation had nothing to do with the meddling politicians back in Washington. This had to do with our commanders' inability to tactically adjust to the situation. Almost to a man, they continued to conduct the war as if they thought we were winning. With the exception of a few maverick officers and civilian bureaucrats, there was never any doubt in their minds about the effectiveness of our methods.

As the chopper gently touched the ground and I walked down the ramp, it was like a homecoming of sorts. In spite of the fact that I hadn't been there in five months, everything looked about the same. The airstrip, the tents, and the outlying bunkers were all where I had remembered them. I had always enjoyed myself at LZ Stud. As a combat base, it couldn't have been built in a more perfect location. Not only was it out of range from the enemy's artillery located in Laos and the DMZ, but it was also inaccessible to their forward observers as well. Located deep within an emerald valley and surrounded by outposts along the nearby mountaintops, it was part of a string of firebases guarding Route 9. Unlike the combat bases at Khe Sanh and Con Thien, LZ Stud wasn't exposed and isolated. The terrain was such that it would have been very difficult for the enemy to move their troops into the valley without being trapped. We had firebases to the north, south, and to the east of us, ready to chew up any force attempting to overrun the place.

With the rain beginning to fall, I entered the headquarters tent and reported for duty. A burly sergeant assigned me a place to sleep and said that I would probably be choppered out to Bravo Company within a day or so. He also mentioned that they had been operating from a hill west of the Rockpile and that I needed to be prepared to leave at a moment's notice. Thus I picked up my gear and made my way through the downpour to the enlisted men's area. After entering a tent, it took a few minutes for my eyes to adjust to the darkness. Hearing the sounds of laughter, I noticed six or seven black guys were sitting in one corner playing cards around a small table. Then I noticed a small group of whites were sitting by themselves in another corner, while a group of Mexican-Americans were sitting by the rear entranceway. This type of voluntary segregation wasn't unusual in Vietnam, but it always gave me the creeps.

As we played cards late into the night, one of the black guys kept everyone in stitches with his antics. He was the type of fellow a person would come across in almost every outfit. Big, fat, and jovial, this guy loved being the center of attention. If he wasn't ranting and raving about one thing or another, he was constantly cracking jokes or trying to mooch candy bars off of everybody. Sporting a huge innocent grin and a stomach the size of a bowling ball, he came over to where I was sitting and introduced himself to me as Fuzzy. It was obvious to me by his indifferent demeanor that he had no intention of leaving this earth on a serious note.

In fact, he had no intention of doing anything at all. When he wasn't hiding from the NCOs or trying to cut in front of the chow line, he was always kidding around and displaying a total disdain for any kind of responsibility. Even before I had joined Bravo Company, it had become common knowledge around the outfit that if there were an important job to be done or a dangerous mission to be performed, one could always count on Fuzzy not being there. On a personal level, I learned to like these guys, because they tended to keep everyone loose and at ease with their constant bantering. Yet surprisingly enough, when things got hot, many of them would stand up and be counted.

After forcing down a hearty breakfast of powdered eggs and chunks of half-cooked Spam, we were ordered to get our gear together and report to the headquarters tent. It took a little while for us to get our stuff together, but once we got there, we were informed that a helicopter was on its way to take us to our company. Since there was only one jeep and the twelve of us, the driver began shuttling us to the LZ in groups of four. Fuzzy and I happened to be standing in the last group when the jeep suddenly pulled up and the driver yelled for us to hurry up. He said the helicopter was waiting on the pad and that we didn't have any time to waste. As the four of us piled into the jeep, Fuzzy ended up sitting in the back seat on top of our equipment. He looked kind of silly, perched up in the air like a big old teddy bear and wearing a helmet that was way too small for his head.

In our haste, I had just sat down next to the driver when, all of a sudden, he gunned the engine and we began to race down the road like a bat out of hell. In Vietnam, everyone drove like a maniac, so it didn't surprise me that this guy wasn't any different. As he was fanatically changing gears and stomping on the clutch, we zoomed around the corners and bypassed the other vehicles as if we were in the Indy 500. With every tight turn and near miss of an approaching vehicle, I kept holding my breath. I just knew he was going to lose control of the vehicle and get us all killed.

At one point, we could hear Fuzzy in the back seat screaming to the high heavens. "Stop this goddamn vehicle. Hell, I'll get out and run to the LZ, if it's all that important."

Then suddenly as we went into the last turn, it became painfully obvious to me that we weren't going to make it and I grabbed hold of the dashboard with both hands. The jeep went sailing off of the road like a missile and plowed into a huge mound of dirt. The impact was so abrupt that it propelled the vehicle's rear end high up into the air and catapulted Fuzzy right over the mound. Evidently, he was right in the middle of tearing open another candy bar when, without warning, he found himself flying through the atmosphere as if he had been shot from a circus cannon. To our amazement, he must have somersaulted about twenty feet before he finally hit the ground with a loud thud, producing an upheaval of powdered dust and scattered leaves.

In fact, the impact was so great that it had knocked everyone out of the jeep and onto the ground.

Shaking my head in disbelief, I realized that I had injured my knee. It felt as if something had snapped inside the joint after I had hit the ground. In a near panic, the driver restarted the vehicle and yelled for everyone to get back into the jeep. While the other guys were collecting their gear, I informed the driver that I had hurt my leg and that I couldn't walk. In exasperation, he yelled for me not to move, so that he could come back and take me to the aid station, once he had taken the rest of the guys to the LZ.

At that instant, Fuzzy stumbled out from behind the mound and gingerly got back into the jeep. He was covered in dust and cussing up a storm, when he suddenly looked over at me sitting on the ground and asked the driver, "What's up with that dude?" As the driver was trying to put the gearshift knob into reverse, he told him that I was hurt and I wouldn't be going with them.

Pausing for a second, everyone stopped what they were doing and slowly turned around towards Fuzzy. Even though he wasn't the sharpest guy in the world, we knew he wasn't going to miss this golden opportunity. Finally, after taking a few seconds to collect his thoughts, Fuzzy's eyes suddenly lit up and he began to yell, "Now, wait a damn minute, I think I hurt my back." We all started giggling and chuckling to ourselves as the driver shook his head in disbelief. Meanwhile, the more Fuzzy complained about his newfound injury, the more ridiculous it looked. Every time he turned around and showed the driver where it hurt, we couldn't help but burst out laughing.

Since the other two guys in the jeep weren't all that dumb either, one of them suddenly realized that he had hurt his arm. Then almost as a signal, the other fellow began moaning about his neck. Witnessing this outbreak of injuries, I couldn't keep from laughing till there were tears in my eyes. As the other two guys were moaning in pain and accusing the driver of almost getting everybody killed, Fuzzy began yelling into the sky for an ambulance. I'll never forget the look of disgust on the driver's face when he finally realized that he wasn't going to get any of us to the LZ that day.

I don't think it surprised anyone when the doctors discovered that we weren't hurt that badly. But after Fuzzy had raised so much hell about being hurled over a portion of Quang Tri Province, I don't think they had the nerve to proclaim us fit for duty.

For the next couple of days or so, we lay around in our cots and played cards, until two of the platoons from Bravo Company came walking into the perimeter. They had been out in the bush for several weeks and they looked beat to hell. Since our platoon had been flown to one of the nearby mountaintops, Fuzzy and I had been informed that we would be joining them the very next morning. I didn't realize it, but the outpost had been receiving incoming on a regular basis. From down below in the valley, I didn't even know there was a war going on. I had spent our time hanging around with Fuzzy, dodging NCOs, and complaining about the war.

When Fuzzy and I jumped out of the helicopter the next morning, we were hurriedly directed to a set of bunkers on the perimeter. As far as we could tell, the place was in total chaos with several people running around in a near panic. The sergeants were screaming and yelling at the top of their lungs. At the time, we couldn't understand the urgency of the situation. There wasn't any incoming hitting the outpost, nor were we under attack. Being somewhat confused, Fuzzy and I just kept looking at each other with the dumbest expression on our faces.

Then out of nowhere, a skinny corporal stuck his head into our bunker and ordered us outside for a work detail. Without any hint of emotion or strain in his voice, he told us to look around the area for anything that might resemble what was once a Marine. It took a few seconds for us to recover from the shock of his words. Then Fuzzy finally broke the silence and asked him in a quivering voice, "What the hell is going on here, man?" The corporal just shook his head and told us to look around to see if we could find a missing man.

Apparently, right before Fuzzy and I had landed, a group of Marines had been waiting to board a helicopter when, out of nowhere, an enemy shell from a 85mm artillery piece screamed into the small LZ and hit one of the guys directly in the chest. The ensuing explosion had not only wounded several nearby Marines, but it had also vaporized the unlucky fellow who had gotten hit. The survivors of his platoon had been frantically looking around the area for any part of him, when Fuzzy and I had arrived. Everyone was not only freaked out about the way the guy had died, but also by the way he had just disappeared into nothingness. From what I understood, his teary-eyed platoon sergeant was refusing to leave the outpost, until he had found out which one of his boys had been killed.

Finally, we heard someone yell from across the hill that he had discovered fragments of a boot and something that resembled an arm or a leg. It was during the middle of this morbid commotion that I was initially introduced to my new squad. Of course, I wouldn't learn more about them until later.

Ever since I was a little kid, I've always been attracted to eccentric people. I don't know if it is because I like their unpredictability or if it is because I'm a nonconformist at heart. But for whatever the reasons, I always enjoyed watching them with great anticipation and amusement. At this point of the war, I had already given up trying to get to know the officers or the staff NCOs on a personal basis. They all seemed about the same to me. It was as if the government had a machine somewhere and was stamping them out in duplicates. However, my new platoon sergeant was one of those unforgettable characters. Covered in tattoos, bald-headed, and possessing a huge handlebar mustache, he was arrogant, unscrupulous, and completely self-possessed.

While sticking out his rugged hand and introducing himself as Staff Sergeant Redburn, he made the off-hand comment to me about being the best damn sergeant in the entire U.S. Marine Corps. As I was peering into his clear blue, steely eyes, I could tell something wasn't right. They had that weird glare about them, as if he looked through people instead of at them. Calling himself Red, he actually loved being in the bush and running around the countryside. As far as I could tell, he didn't view the Vietnam War as being a political struggle between two different ideologies, but rather, as a place where he could express his inner need to blow things up without being labeled a menace to society.

My new squad leader was a twenty-one-year old stocky fellow named Boyd. He had been assigned to 1/9 in January, when they were undergoing the siege of Khe Sanh. He had a crop of brown wavy hair that dangled in his eyes and a ruddy complexion. He had come from the hills of Kentucky, dirt poor and politically incorrect. With the help of the legal system, he had joined the Marines under the government's new "36 Plan." A district judge had given him the choice of either serving three years in the Corps or six years in prison. At least he hadn't been a part of McNamara's "Project 100,000," implemented in 1966. [1]

Robert Strange McNamara, the Secretary of Defense, had intentionally lowered the IQ and health standards for 100,000 prospective military recruits, so that the local draft boards wouldn't have to draft the more privileged teenagers. Referred to by the military brass as "McNamara's Moron Corps," over 354,000 of them would eventually be accepted into the military by 1971. Needless to say, the majority of them were actually mentally handicapped or possessed numerous physical problems. While 40 percent of them were African-Americans, their average reading level was that of a sixth grader. Inexplicably, the national media continued to ignore this shameful issue throughout the entire war.

Privately, I had to take my hat off to Boyd, because he had seen a lot of action without suffering a scratch. Yet I could tell that his good fortune had its negative repercussions. If there was ever a classic case of "Survivor's Guilt," Boyd had it. On occasion, he would wake up in the middle of the night in a cold sweat, screaming out the names of his dead buddies. But if that weren't bad enough, sometimes he would even sleepwalk out towards the perimeter as if he subconsciously wanted someone to put him out of his misery. To say the least, it had a chilling effect on everybody, especially the new guys. As a squad leader, he knew his job and he did it well. As long as someone watched over him while he slept, he seemed to be able to function without any problems.

Then there was this one particular fellow everyone mockingly referred to as M&M (Mean Mother). He was tall and lanky with short sandy hair and thin shoulders. Unlike the majority of us, he was in his mid-twenties, very well educated, and somewhat feminine in his gestures. He was the type of guy that had no business being in the bush.

Reared in a high-strung, upper-middle-class environment, he just never got used to living in the filth or being surrounded by the constant danger. He was always jumping at shadows and pissing in his pants whenever things got exciting. Presumably on the day he was about to become a full-fledged Catholic priest back in New York City, he flipped out and joined the Corps as an infantryman. From what I had heard, his parents were so pious and influential that they had even met the Pope once. When I first met M&M, he didn't smoke, drink, or even cuss. In fact, he was extremely proud of the fact that he was still a virgin.

However after a few months in the bush, he was smoking two packs a day, drinking like a fish, cussing like a sailor, and obsessing about the prospects of meeting a very cooperative lady. To this day, I have always wondered how his saintly parents reacted to him after he finally made it back home.

One of the most interesting fellows that I have ever had the pleasure of meeting was a guy named Huff. Similar to M&M, he had come from a very affluent background when, all of sudden, he just flipped out and joined the Corps. Standing about six-foot-two and weighing over two hundred pounds, he was a big, clumsy fellow with broad shoulders, short black hair, and green eyes.

Reared in New Jersey, right across the street from his state senator, he seemed to have a bad habit of getting wounded whenever the shit hit the fan. By the time I met him, he already had two Purple Hearts with another one shortly to follow. It's not that he didn't try to be a good infantryman. It was just that he was way too educated to be in the bush. Soldiering is all about instinct and teamwork, attributes that a higher education tends to expunge from an individual.

At the tender age of nineteen, Huff had already obtained his master's degree in literature from Yale University, when his parents decided to ship him off to England to further his education. I don't know exactly what happened, but something inside of him had snapped. After flying home for Christmas break, he suddenly walked into a Marine recruiter's office and signed his life away. There to greet him at the door was an immaculately dressed staff sergeant who offered him the world in terms of going to Officer Candidate School and eventually working at the Pentagon. But Huff would have none of it. He told the bewildered staff sergeant, "Either you sign me up in the infantry as an enlisted man or I'll go talk to the Army."

Over time, I learned to admire and respect Huff as a person. He had a wonderful sense of humor and a laid-back disposition. Although he didn't have any street sense, he seemed to be much more intelligent and informed then many of our officers.

Then there was this guy named Roger, who had been voted by his boot camp platoon to be the person most likely to get himself killed. Small in stature, awkward, and skinny as a rail, he had an odd-shaped head and a pair of bulging eyes that stuck out almost to the end of his nose. If one didn't know any better, a person would have sworn that he had a nervous disorder. Born and raised in Philadelphia, he used to drive everyone crazy with his constant fidgeting and whining. It's not that Roger lacked intelligence or the desire to be a good Marine; it's just that he was a walking disaster waiting to happen. He was extremely absent-minded and accident prone while possessing the unique ability of turning the simplest task into a full-blown calamity. It was as though the guy had been cursed. Once when the platoon lieutenant had ordered him to go burn the company shitters, the poor kid ended up burning down the shitters, the headquarters shed, several nearby tents, and half of the base camp.

As for the rest of my squad, they were a collection of underprivileged kids from all over America. Inspired by their patriotism and the need to get out from underneath their parents' thumb, they found themselves right in the middle of a war. Calling themselves Zit, Morgan, Rodriquez, Wills, and Jacobs, they were just a group of fellows trying to survive the surrounding chaos. But I guess the most outstanding thing about them was that they were just regular guys. The Marine Corps might have made them arrogant and cocky, but underneath their macho images was a group of young men who just wanted to get the job done and go back home to their loved ones. They didn't harbor any dreams of becoming a general, a politician, or even a national hero. All they wanted was to serve their country with pride and hopefully live long enough to tell their grandchildren about it.

Sometime in late September 1968, our platoon was ordered to move down from the mud-filled bunkers above LZ Stud to link up with the rest of the company. Of course, we didn't stay there for any length of time, just long enough for everyone to get one hot meal and a full night's sleep. By early the next morning, in the midst of all the grumbling and bitching, the whole company was suddenly choppered to a semi-barren mountaintop. From the direction of our flight, I figured we had been dropped somewhere south of LZ Stud. Within no time at all, we had set up our perimeter and began placing flares in front of our foxholes. Everyone seemed to be on edge, including Red. The surrounding jungle was so thick and foreboding that he kept going from position to position to make sure the perimeter was airtight. Looking out over the landscape, it didn't look to me as if anyone had patrolled this area in years. The deep valley below us was rich in vegetation without a bomb crater in sight.

As soon as the base camp was set up, the Skipper began to schedule our twenty-four-hour routine. On a nightly basis, a fire team from each platoon was expected to go out a short distance from the perimeter in order to establish a listening post (LP). Taking along a radio, it was their job to give an early warning to the rest of the company in case the enemy was preparing to attack our position. Sometimes the kids in an LP could save everyone's life, and then sometimes, they could keep everybody up all night by shooting at shadows. One never knew how a person was going to react to the creepy sounds coming out of the jungle.

However, the biggest problem we faced was trying to stay awake during our watches. The nights were long and it was very difficult for us to keep our eyes open. Having to sit up every night for three or four hours at a time for weeks on end was extremely hard on everybody. After awhile, it became so exhausting that a person learned how to catch a few winks, here and there. During my year in the bush, I had looked into the night sky and counted the stars so often, that I probably should have become a frickin' astronomer.

On a routine basis, we were expected to earn our pay by searching out the enemy. Before the sun had risen each morning, a squad from each platoon would saddle up to patrol the surrounding valleys and mountainsides. Sometimes these excursions were easy to hump. But most of the time, they were a real test of wills. While climbing up and down the hidden ravines and the steep slopes, we had to continuously slash our way through the dense barriers of plant life. Because of the intense heat and the thick vegetation, I found myself completely covered in sweat and blood before we had moved even a couple of hundred yards. The terrain was so rugged and impenetrable that the jungle would literally grab a person and tear him to bits in its web of sharp thorns, barbed underbrush, and prickly vines. Looking back, I realize that our daily patrols were more involved with fighting the elements, than they were with actually reconnoitering the area.

Of course that was when the going was good. If it happened to be raining that day, a patrol didn't stand a chance of moving anywhere very fast or even moving very far. The mud was so thick and slippery that it was almost impossible for us to keep our feet. One of the things that I had learned during my months of patrolling was that the jungle has its own ways. A person just can't push his way through it like a bulldozer and ignore its awesome presence. It was always better to go with the flow.

During these daily patrols, one of our responsibilities was to look for any indication of NVA activity in the form of beaten trails, discarded equipment, or freshly broken tree limbs. The idea behind this tactic was to follow their different signs in the hopes of locating their base camps. On most occasions, their trails didn't lead anywhere except to another trail. This didn't really disappoint anybody, because the last thing we wanted to do was to attack a unit of well dug-in NVA. Since this part of I Corps was so inaccessible and everyone involved was forced to use the same trails, booby traps were not a concern. The majority of our casualties occurred from either trying to dodge the enemy's incoming barrages or making contact with one of their entrenched base camps. Yet the few times that I had an opportunity to exchange fire with the enemy in the jungle, I found it a very frustrating experience. Due to the thick vegetation, uneven terrain, and poor visibility, it was almost impossible for anyone to locate a good target, much less for someone to call in accurate fire support.

While we were positioned on this particular mountaintop, two events took place that have stuck in my mind over the years. The first one occurred as we were patrolling an area east of our base camp. As usual, the going was tough and everyone was complaining. The heat was so unrelenting that we had to stop every half an hour or so, just to take a water break. At the time, the enemy didn't seem to be anywhere in the vicinity. Then suddenly, as we made our way down to the bottom of a small gorge, we came upon something that made my blood run cold.

Running along the ravine and up to an adjacent mountaintop was a freshly used NVA trail. However, it wasn't the usual trail. It looked more like a service road than a pathway. Besides being several meters wide and well kept, there must have been at least a couple of hundred freshly imprinted footsteps in the moist ground. Upon closer examination, Boyd thought at least a battalion of NVA had used the trail just the night before. Looking up at a nearby mountaintop, I felt a cold chill shoot up my spine. I just knew there was an enemy bunker complex up there waiting for us. Then Fuzzy finally spoke up and said, "Hey man that sure is a big ass trail. Maybe we ought to get the hell out of here and report this to the Skipper."

Being the new guy in the outfit, I just stood there for a minute and watched the other guys' reactions. Morgan, Roger, and Huff were all gung-ho to follow the trail and kick some ass. Roger kept saying, "Screw these gooks, we can handle them." But I could tell Boyd was uneasy. He kept clearing his throat and fidgeting his shoulders. Then he looked up at me and asked, "What do you think?"

After taking a deep breath, I replied, "I think you would be a damn fool to lead these guys up that trail." Then without any emotion in my voice, I made it quite clear to anyone else as to what I thought about their fighting prowess or the obvious lack thereof.

Turning towards the other guys in the squad, I said in my finest Texas drawl, "If you dumb asses want to follow that there trail, y'all go right ahead. I'll be glad to take up the rear and send your remains back to the world [stateside]. But personally, I don't think any of you guys know what in the hell is going on here."

M&M started scratching the back of his head in a nervous manner, when he suddenly found his voice, "Well, if you feel that strongly about it, maybe we ought to go back."

Getting to his feet, Boyd gazed up the trail for a second and said, "To hell with this nonsense, I'm way too short [near the end of his tour] for this shit. Let's head on back."

It was at that instant that I realized Boyd knew his way around the bush. Survivor's guilt or not, he still understood the difference between taking a reasonable chance and committing outright suicide. But as far the other fellows were concerned, they confirmed my suspicions that they didn't have a clue as to how to operate in the bush.

After hearing about the trail, the Skipper ordered one of the other platoons to check it out. Amusingly when the lieutenant returned from his patrol, I overheard him tell the Skipper that he wouldn't dare go up that trail, unless he could take along the whole regiment and part of the 101st Airborne as well. In exasperation, he finally said, "Skipper, I haven't seen so many gook signs, since I went on R&R to Tokyo."

The second memorable incident occurred a few nights later. Just as the sun went down, three of the guys in my squad had been ordered to go a hundred meters down the slope and set up an LP. Zit was carrying the radio, while M&M and Fuzzy took along their ponchos and rifles. As they moved through the perimeter, I could tell everyone was on edge because of the discovery of the trail. Even the Company Gunny had come down to our area to make sure everybody was alert. If I remember correctly, the night was moonless and a person couldn't see ten feet in front of his face. However, it was during the nights like these that I had learned to use my ears instead of my vision. Setting my helmet to one side and closing my eyes, I was always amazed how much I could hear at night. The surrounding sounds would echo through my brain like a freight train, and if the wind wasn't blowing, it seemed that I could even hear the sweat roll off of my face.

That next morning, as I was lying in my poncho and dreaming about eating a big turkey dinner with all of the trimmings, I was unexpectedly awakened by an anxious Red and Boyd. In an urgent voice, Red informed me that our LP hadn't been heard from since midnight. Fearing the worst, they figured the NVA had crept up on them and cut their throats. It took me a few minutes to clear my head but, when I finally did, I realized that they wanted me to go out there with Roger and find out what had happened to them. I just looked at them as if they were both nuts and thought to myself, Jesus Christ. new guys never get a break.

After I had collected my gear and smoked a quick cigarette, I told Roger to walk directly behind me and under no circumstances was he to accidentally shoot me in the back. Pale and obviously scared shitless, he didn't seem like the same guy who had several days before wanted to go running up the mountain after the NVA. But that's the way it was in Vietnam. Some days, it felt like you could go out and kill a tiger with your bare hands. Then on other days, it felt like you were going to end up being tiger shit before morning.

Once everyone along the perimeter had been informed of our movement, I led Roger down the slope as quietly as possible. I didn't know what to expect, but I did know that if an enemy soldier happened to show his miserable head, I was going to blow his brains all over the countryside and haul ass back up to the perimeter.

Using all of my senses to detect the enemy, I slowly crept down the slope to their position. Nothing seemed out of the ordinary but, just to make sure, I went from bush to bush in order to hide my approach. With my rifle at the ready, the only thing I could hear was Roger's heavy breathing. It sounded as if he was about to have a heart attack, when I suddenly stopped and signaled him to kneel down onto the ground. Then it dawned on me that he was going to be more of a hindrance than a help. So I inched my way back to where he was kneeling and whispered in his ear to stay put until I returned. Then as I quietly moved forward into a row of bushes, I suddenly heard the strangest wheezing sound. It sounded like someone was gasping for air, as if he could hardly breathe. Pausing to catch my own breath and to swallow what spit I had left in my dry mouth, I slipped through a mass of dangling leaves and came upon a most chilling sight.

Lying next to each other with their arms and legs entangled, it didn't look like Zit, Fuzzy or M&M had put up very much of a fight. Their bodies were serenely cradled in a small hole with their chins resting upon their chests. Instinctively, I looked around for a second to see if there was anyone else in the area. Oddly enough, there wasn't anyone in sight nor did I see any signs of a struggle. Whoever had sneaked up on them was very professional. They had been able to approach their position without disturbing the surrounding vegetation.

Glancing back down, my eyes began to fill with tears as the futility of the moment grabbed my insides and turned them inside out. Engulfed by a wave of sadness and grief, it appeared as though they had all died in their sleep without knowing what had hit them. Almost in a state of shock, I couldn't believe that they could have been so stupid. In my mind, only a complete idiot would have gotten himself caught in that situation.

Then suddenly, Fuzzy effortlessly reached up and swatted a fly off of his nose. To this day, I don't know which emotion overcame me the most, the relief that they were all still alive or the anger that they had been cutting Zs (sleeping) on my time.

So instead of waking them up, which would have been the decent thing to do, I sat there for a minute trying to think of a really neat way to teach them a lesson. Then like a thunderbolt, it hit me. Positioning myself in between Zit and M&M, I quietly moved their rifles out of their reach and started jabbering out Vietnamese phrases as if I was talking to someone else. I said things like, "Dong moo-ah fat wah, sin do-ba toy, nook loc su-way dung, cow'tew noy dow." Naturally, I didn't have any idea as to the meaning of these words. I had heard them spoken on the streets of Da Nang. But I must say in all truthfulness, it did have its desired effect.

In one quick motion, Zit and M&M suddenly jumped up all groggy-eyed and began searching for their rifles in a near panic. For a few enjoyable seconds, I sat there and watched them running around their little hole like a couple of chickens with their heads cut off. They just kept looking at each other in bewilderment, and then they would pause for a second, rub their eyes, and then look back at me.

"Holy Saint Christopher, where in the hell did you come from?" M&M finally shrieked in desperation.

With a big grin spread across my face, I handed them their rifles and replied, "You boys had better come up with a good story for Red or he is going to kick your butts into the next hemisphere." Incredibly, Fuzzy just lay there out like a light, during all of the commotion. He seemed to be totally impervious to the fact that he was right in the middle of a war.

After rousing Fuzzy to his feet and sabotaging the radio, we made our way past Roger and up the slope. Confronting an angry Red and Boyd with their hands upon their hips, Zit told them that their radio had quit working, so they had decided to remain at their post. Knowing full well that he was probably lying, Red informed them that if he ever caught them sleeping while on duty, he was going to put his foot so far up their butts that it was going to take a naval surgeon to remove it.

Sometime in the middle of October, the helicopters unexpectedly arrived to take us to another mountaintop. Everyone was apprehensive, because we didn't have any idea as to where we were going. In what was to be called *Operation Dawson River*, our companies would be individually sent out into the bush to fend for ourselves. Unlike the major operations in the spring, when we were employed in battalion-sized units, this was a totally different experience. For the next couple of months, we would stay about two weeks on a mountaintop, before we were ordered to move out again. What made it so frustrating was that as soon as we had made the camp livable and learned the surrounding terrain, the choppers would suddenly appear and take us to another mountaintop.

To many of us, it appeared as if we were being intentionally used as bait. Isolated and exposed with very little ground support, we were being dangled in front of the NVA in the hopes they might come out and show themselves. Fortunately though, the enemy's main battle units had already left the area. Since Khe Sanh had been abandoned in June, we didn't realize that the NVA had moved their major units south into the A Shau Valley. As far as Hanoi was concerned, the biggest threat to the Ho Chi Minh Trail was coming from the U.S. Army's efforts to control the valley. Consequently, the major engagements would slowly shift from the DMZ to the Laotian and Cambodian borders. However, this didn't mean that the NVA had completely disappeared from our AO (Area of Operation). There were still enough of them hanging around to keep us occupied.

"Holy crap, here they come again," Huff yelled, as he buried his head into the dirt.

Amid the roar of the diving jets, I looked up just in time to see one of our F-4 Phantoms release two canisters of napalm. Constructed of bright metallic casings, they tumbled through the sky and crashed into an adjacent hilltop, thus leaving a path of fiery destruction in their wake. Just minutes before, we had been safely inserted into the LZ when, all of a sudden, a line of green tracers swept over our area. Jumping into a nearby crater, we sat there for awhile and watched our planes unload their deadly canisters. The heat from the nearby napalm explosions was so intense, I could feel the skin on my face begin to redden.

Napalm was probably the most feared weapon in our arsenal. It was a gasoline-infused jelly (*Na*phthene-*Palm*itate) that would spatter all over the target, igniting it into an inferno of blistering flames and screaming victims. Much like an onrushing tidal wave, the exploding flames would engulf an area before anyone could escape its wrath. If a poor fellow wasn't immediately burnt to a crisp by the firestorm, he usually choked to death from the absorption of the surrounding toxic air.

For an eighteen- or nineteen-year-old boy, I cannot think of a more shocking experience than having to walk through a position after it had just been hit with napalm. The scene was right out of Dante's *Inferno*. The once beautiful trees, bushes, and flowering plants were all reduced to cinders within a matter of seconds. Among the glowing ashes and smoldering debris, everything seemed to be crackling and sizzling from the intense heat. The ground itself was black and sticky with tiny pieces of fused glass lying all over the place.

After being forced to step over the grisly remains of the incinerated bodies, I couldn't imagine anyone surviving this man-made holocaust. Everywhere I stepped, my boots made a weird crunching sound as the sickening smell of gasoline lingered in my nostrils. On more than one occasion, we were ordered to rip open the top of a bunker, only to find the terrified expressions of the dead staring back at us. Between the stench of the burnt flesh and the devastated landscape, it was a struggle just to keep one's lunch down.

After looking out from our crater, it didn't appear to me as if the NVA soldiers were seriously attempting to threaten our landing. Usually when they did fire a few rounds into our LZs, they were trying to divert our attention from something else in the area. They usually employed just one machine gun and a few sharpshooters to distract us long enough for their main body of troops to get away. Of course, it would take a couple of painful years before our commanders began to understand the enemy's tactics. Unlike a conventional war setting, where utilizing brute force has been the basis for our success, we had to learn a whole new set of rules.

Then a few days later another incident indicated how the enemy was able to use our tactics against us. While we were eating our C-rations, a company from the 4th Marines had made a landing several hills over from us. Our radioman instantly switched his radio to their frequency, so that we could listen to their chatter. As we gathered around his handset, we could hear one of their lieutenants screaming into his radio set that they had spotted a small group of NVA soldiers near a clearing. For the next few minutes or so, Boyd and I just looked at each other in anticipation. The two of us had been in the bush long enough to know that something didn't sound right.

Then the lieutenant came back on the air to report that they had blown away two of the NVA and that they were chasing the others down a bloodstained trail. To this day, I'll never forget the lieutenant's last words echoing over the radio, "We finally got some gooks and we ain't leavin' till we get some more." In one loud chorus, the other guys in our group around the radio started whooping and hollering, "Get some, motherfuckers." However as I was shaking my head in disbelief, Boyd abruptly stood up and just walked away. Tragically, we both knew what was coming next and there wasn't a damn thing we could do about it.

It didn't take more than about twenty minutes before the NVA were able to lure that aggressive lieutenant and his fine platoon into an ambush. The enemy had placed a row of command-detonated claymore mines all along the trail and then waited for their decoys to bring the onrushing Marines into their killing zone. Hidden within their camouflaged bunkers, the NVA troops detonated their mines and unleashed a torrent of firepower before the platoon even knew what had hit them. Thus the Marines suddenly found themselves caught in a death trap. Later, we were informed that the brave lieutenant and four other Marines had died trying to rush the enemy's bunkers.

While we sat there in silence and listened to the surviving platoon sergeant call for help over his radio, the other guys around me became very demoralized. They couldn't understand how something like this could have happened to the finest military organization in the world. One minute, the guys of the 4th Marines were in the middle of a victorious charge, when all of a sudden, they found themselves trapped by their own aggressiveness.

Without question, our overly aggressive World War II training didn't help matters. Because our troops had been trained to quickly overcome an objective and overwhelm an opponent with an aggressive gung-ho spirit, it actually played right into the enemy's hands. All they had to do was lure us into their area and then ambush our onrushing forces. Moreover, the rotation system we employed in Vietnam was one of the major factors behind our inability to adapt to the circumstances. For some reason, our officers were rotated out of the bush every six months. In fact when they were just beginning to get their feet on the ground, headquarters would yank them out of the bush and then put them behind a desk, thus leaving his platoon in the uncertain hands of an amateur.

Actually, there are two seasons in Vietnam. There is the hot, dry season during the summer months and then there is the winter monsoon. It was during the monsoon season that the fighting would usually ease up, so that each side could rebuild their units. Of course, this didn't stop us from patrolling the surrounding areas. But it did make the patrols shorter and the contact with the enemy less likely.

Between September and February, the warm winds would come off of the South China Sea and collide with the higher cooler air, thus creating rainstorm after rainstorm. Like in the Mekong Delta and the Central Highlands, it could constantly rain for months on end. But unlike the other regions, it did get somewhat cold up in the mountains near Laos. The elevation was so high that sometimes it was difficult for us to breathe the thin air. Also, there were times when it seemed as if we were never going to see the blue sky again.

During the monsoon season, it was almost impossible to move through the terrain, because it was so wet and slippery. We found ourselves slipping and sliding along the steep inclines until we became so frustrated that we would just sit down in our tracks. And even if we had run into an enemy patrol, I doubt very seriously that we could have seen anything to shoot at. The visibility was so poor that on more than one occasion, we got lost and wandered around the countryside until we finally made in back.

Of course, none of us was overly concerned about an enemy attack. If they had been able to climb those slippery slopes, we would have given them a medal. The mud had become so mushy from the constant rain that we couldn't even keep the walls of our foxholes from collapsing. During the nightly watches, a person had to lie on top of the ground without any protection from the incoming rounds. But I think the most difficult part about the whole affair was being constantly soaked to the bone. For some reason, I could handle the hunger and the backbreaking work, but dealing with the unceasing wetness was an ordeal in itself. Besides being unable to sleep, write letters home, or heat one's C-rations, my skin had begun to puff up and peel off in layers, much like snake would shed its skin. Then making matters worse, my toenails had become so soft from the moisture that they would swell up and become infected.

It was at this point of the war that I began to take stock of my situation. I realized that I was still somewhat healthy, mature for my age, and extremely lucky. Yet the gut-numbing loneliness that I was constantly feeling just wouldn't go away. No matter how hard I tried to ignore it, a terrible emptiness filled my heart. I longed to see my brother, my parents, and all of my friends again. Walking underneath the pecan trees and smelling the scent of freshly cut grass, I so wanted to hear their voices and to rejoice in their smiles. In spite of the fact that I still believed in the importance of our mission in Vietnam, I had the nagging feeling that I was missing out on a lot of important things, things that I had taken for granted when I was a civilian. The warmth of a girlfriend's embrace, the joy of playing football with my friends, the love of my dog, and Mom's Sunday dinners were all experiences that I held dear.

I knew that by joining the United States Marine Corps, I was expected to sacrifice my youth and my innocence. I didn't mind giving up those things. In my mind that was the price one paid for defending his country. Yet I was beginning to realize that I was sacrificing much more than my mere naiveté and adolescence. At the time, I couldn't describe it in words. But in essence, I sensed that the people back home were actually involved with living their lives. They had futures, foreseeable dreams, and real aspirations. Their reality was one of building a better future for themselves and for their loved ones. While I was sitting around waiting for the next round to take my head off, I realized that I was just existing. My life had become a bottomless, unfulfilled moment where there wasn't any room for dreaming or any aspirations of the future. It was a place of very little mercy, where might made right, and where the shroud of death hung over everyone's shoulder.

During the first part of November, my unit was given several days' rest. Instead of being sent to a real rest area, we were choppered to an Army artillery base in order to guard their perimeter. In all truthfulness, it wasn't all that bad of an installation. Our commander had flown in some beer and we were permitted to use the Army's chow hall at least once a day. To my surprise, the base was located in the strangest place I had ever seen in Vietnam. I didn't even know a place like this even existed. Extending for miles, it was located on a beautiful grassy plain, much like one would see in Kansas. The tall grass was everywhere with not a rice paddy or a village in sight. Staff Sergeant Redburn figured we must have been flown to a stretch of land several miles west of the coastal plains, southwest of Phu Bai.

As we were being assigned to our positions around the perimeter, everyone was astonished at the wide-open spaces and the quality of the Army's bunkers. Constructed with huge wooden beams, thick walls, and watertight ceilings, these bunkers were built solid, just like the command bunker at Khe Sanh. These Army guys sure knew how to spend their money. Unlike the cramped Marine artillery bases, they had the resources and the manpower to spread out their bases so the enemy couldn't hit anything with ease. But what really blew our minds was when they told us that we didn't have to patrol the surrounding area or conduct any listening posts. With a big grin smeared across his face, an Army lieutenant told us that their helicopters provided most of the security around the perimeter. And sure enough, the few nights that we were there, the helicopters zoomed around the perimeter, pointing a huge spotlight at the ground. Of course, we didn't have the heart to tell them that if the NVA really wanted the place, they could have easily shot down the brightly lit helicopters and gone through their perimeter like shit through a goose.

I'll never forget the first time that they let us eat at their mess hall. We had been told by several of their personnel that the food was inedible and that most of them were refusing to eat there. However when we went through their chow line, they filled our trays with fried chicken, mashed potatoes and gravy, green beans, and a slice of real apple pie. It was great. We had grease and chicken crumbs all over our faces in no time at all. As the Army guys sat around and picked at their food in disgust, we eagerly gobbled down ours and then asked if we could have theirs, too. In all fairness, I'm sure that if I had to eat their recently thawed out or canned food every day of the week, I would have probably gotten pretty sick of it myself.

On our second day there, several Army personnel approached us about buying some marijuana. Knowing the terrain was non-threatening and we didn't have to patrol the area, we went ahead and bought a packet-full of joints. In between the one hot meal a day, the somewhat cold beer, and the marijuana, we thought that we had died and gone to heaven. We would pass the days getting stoned, cleaning our weapons, and talking about the upcoming presidential election. Most of the guys, like myself, didn't know the difference between a Republican and a Democrat, but that didn't stop us. We would argue with each other for hours over issues that we personally didn't understand and probably never would.

One night while we were all sitting around getting stoned and drinking some beer, Staff Sergeant Redburn and an Army first sergeant came staggering down the perimeter checking the lines. Frantically scrambling to our feet, we started stashing the empty beer cans and dousing the joints. Everyone was holding his breath as they approached us. We didn't know how bad they were going to freak out over our obviously impaired condition. While dealing with NCOs, one just never knew what they were thinking. Standing almost at attention, Red started sniffing our clothes as the Army sergeant began looking around the area. The muscles in the back of my neck and shoulders began to tighten up, because they seemed to be acting very strangely. I just knew they were going to have us all arrested and thrown into the brig.

Then suddenly, the Army sergeant wobbled over to us, swirled around in a circle and muttered, "Honey, I'm home." Then he fell flat on his butt, passed out dead drunk. We were giggling till our sides began to hurt, then Red staggered over to where he was lying and hollered, "Get up, you non-hacker. This ain't any way to show my boys how tough you are."

It wasn't very long after we had left the Army base, when Red approached our squad and asked us if anyone wanted to go to Hong Kong on R&R. There was an opening on the next flight and it needed to be filled. Considering that I had already taken my R&R in Hawaii back in June, I didn't say anything. We were only supposed to have one R&R per tour. Then to my astonishment, none of the guys spoke up. They all just stood there and mumbled that they had made other plans. I couldn't believe it. I had always heard that Hong Kong was a great place to party with beautiful women everywhere.

Then Red suddenly looked over at me and said, "Short, have you taken your R&R, yet?"

I don't know what I was thinking, but the words just rolled right out of my mouth. "No Sergeant, I haven't, but going to Hong Kong sounds okay by me."

Chapter Eleven

America's Finest

"Fundamentally, wars are an economic struggle between
the ruling classes of nations. But it's the common people
that have to pay the terrible price for their avarice."

One of the truisms that I learned in Vietnam was that a grunt shouldn't
hang around his company's rear area while he is awaiting orders. The
spit-and-polish NCOs would seek him out and put him to work at
the first opportunity whether he is in dire need of rest or not. To my
absolute disgust, it took about ten minutes after I had landed in Quang
Tri before some sergeant stuck his head into the tent and ordered me
to collect my gear in order to stand watch on the perimeter. But instead
of blindly following his orders, I began to argue with the guy. I had lost
all patience with the REMFs (Rear Echelon Mother Fuckers). As far as
I was concerned, they didn't give a damn about our welfare and they
sure as hell couldn't have cared less about what we had been through.
It was obvious that many of them enjoyed screwing with the grunts.
Whether it was from some deep-seated resentment on their part or
from some inbred anger they had acquired as a kid, I had no idea. But

at this point of the war, I was getting extremely tired of being harassed by every lame NCO who had spent his entire tour surrounded by rows of barbed-wire fences while living in air-conditioned hooches.

Of course, I'm not implying that all of the guys stationed in the rear were complete jerks. Most of them were good Marines who just wanted to serve their country without any hassles. However, since it had been customary for our commanders to treat the grunts as cannon fodder, a lot of guys unknowingly jumped on the bandwagon. Consequently, the conflict between the rear-area personnel and the front line troops was much more intense than anyone cares to admit. In fact, whenever there was a major disturbance among the troops in Vietnam, it generally occurred in the rear areas.

After losing my argument with the sergeant, I found myself sharing a bunker with two cherries fresh from the States, who had been trained as helicopter mechanics. I don't really remember their names, but they acted as if they had never seen a rifle before. The myth that every Marine was a rifleman may have sounded good back at Camp Pendleton, but the reality was quite different. These two guys had been way too pampered in their training to be grunts. They kept whining about the dirt, the bugs, and the lack of toilet paper.

Nevertheless after getting my gear situated, I walked up and down the perimeter in order to get a feel for the position. Our bunker was located about three hundred yards from a small village, which overlooked a huge rice paddy. Off in the distance, I could see several Vietnamese farmers working the fields with their children at their side. Then as I walked back to our bunker, one of the cherries handed me a box of C-rations for dinner. Snatching the box out of his hand, I couldn't help but shake my head in disgust. Here I was in the rear area surrounded by several mess halls and I was stuck having to eat frickin' C-rations again.

Similar to the perimeters around Da Nang and Phu Bai, the bunkers were well constructed, but the positions had been poorly manned and neglected. The Marines' policy of rotating whatever personnel were available that day wasn't any way to secure a perimeter. Nobody seemed to understand his responsibilities or even who was in command for that matter. Instead of rotating our infantry units in and out of the perimeter on a regular basis, we rotated individuals. On any given night, the perimeter could be manned by just about anyone, including the rear-area types who didn't know what they were doing. As I continued to look around, I also noticed the detonators to the claymore mines were old and rusty, the concertina wire was in need of repair, and the sandbags needed replacing. At the time, I didn't let any of this stuff bother me. I was going to Hong Kong in a few days, so my mind was on wolfing down a thick steak and possibly meeting an attractive woman. Thus as I lay down that night, I wasn't at all concerned about having to defend the perimeter. Life was good and I would shortly be sleeping between two clean white sheets.

It must have been around three o'clock in the morning when I was suddenly awakened by the sounds of 122mm rockets whistling through the air. From the impact of the distant explosions, I figured the NVA gunners were trying to hit the airstrip, which was located on the other side of the base. Confused and terrified, the other two guys in the bunker with me kept diving to the ground every time a rocket sailed over our heads. I tried to tell them that we weren't in any danger, but they refused to listen.

Then as I gazed through the rows of concertina wire, I noticed in the dim moonlight something real peculiar. The rice paddy out in front of us had miraculously grown several new bushes since I had last looked out there. As I slowly lifted my rifle onto my shoulder, the hairs on the back of my head began to stand up and bristle. I quietly leaned down and whispered to one of the guys that we had movement to our front and that I wanted him to man the claymore detonators. But instead of following my instructions, he refused to do anything but hide at the bottom of the bunker. So with my rifle in one hand, I reached over, grabbed a detonator, and then waited to see if the bushes started moving again. And sure enough, it took about five minutes before I spotted two more bushes slowly creeping out of the dry creek bed and into the open field.

As the sweat began to roll down my forehead and into my eyes, a cold chill suddenly ran through my entire body. At that instant, my heart was pounding so hard that it felt like it was going to jump out of my chest. Then just as I was about to kick the ever-lovin' shit out of the guy sitting at my feet, I heard a blast and then the swooshing sound of an RPG rocket. Instinctively falling to my knees, I heard the rocket make a loud thud as it glanced off of our bunker and exploded several yards behind us. While I was attempting to stand up and return fire, a surge of rifle fire suddenly erupted across our position, driving me back down to my knees again. Unaware of what the other two guys were doing, I began to frantically pump the detonators to the claymore mines. Within a matter of seconds, I was able to discharge a couple of them in quick succession. Even though one of them was a dud, I could feel the back-blast from their concussions slam into our bunker.

Pausing for a few seconds to catch my breath, I poked my head back up and peered out into the field. I had never seen anything like it. There were these little bushes running all over the place, as if it was a Chinese circus. Just to give them a little encouragement, I began firing at them with short bursts from my rifle. Amid the dark shadows, I could see pieces of leaves and twigs flying in every direction as I continued to spray the field. It was at that instance I distinctly remember yelling out into the night, "Gotcha, you gook bastards." Then as I bent down to pick up a hand grenade, I felt the strangest sensation. All at once, a feeling of complete abandonment swept over me. Quickly glancing around the bunker, I realized that the two mechanics had bugged out immediately after the RPG had exploded and left me to my fate.

Trembling from the rush of adrenaline, I picked up a phone connected to a landline and tried make contact with headquarters. Either they were asleep or the phone was dead, because I couldn't get anyone on the line. Frustrated, I moved out of the bunker and jumped into a small nearby trench. I figured since the enemy knew my position, I had better find another location. In the bush, the NVA had become infamous for probing a position just to find out where our weapons were located. Then once they had us pinpointed, they would readjust their RPG and machine-gun fire toward our positions.

As I stood in the trench, I kept wondering where everyone had gone. Normally when there was firing on the perimeter, all kinds of people would be hauling ass down to the bunkers to find out what was happening. But on this occasion, I found myself having to sit there all alone until morning. I couldn't get anyone to answer the phone and I didn't see anybody checking the perimeter. After awhile, I was beginning to think that everybody back in headquarters was either dead or really intoxicated.

Luckily though, whoever was out there that night prowling around in the darkness had decided to withdraw. I figured that it was probably a squad of VC probing our position in order to collect some intelligence data or possibly a few POWs. Whatever they had in mind though, it didn't work. But that was the way it was in combat. Without exception, a combat operation is probably the most difficult human endeavor an organization can undertake. People get confused, orders become unclear, and the opposition rarely behaves as predicted. In fact, a battle could be defined as two terrified masses of confused soldiers, trying to obey their commanders' orders without having to sacrifice their lives in the process. It is this paradox that creates many of the difficulties for the commanding generals. Men want to be good soldiers, but they don't want to be good dead soldiers. With very few exceptions, something always goes wrong in an engagement and everybody usually ends up having to wing it.

Shortly after the sun had risen, a first lieutenant and his driver drove up to my position in a cloud of dust. In all truthfulness, I expected a well done or at least a pat on the back. As far as I knew, I could have single-handedly repelled another Tet Offensive. But what happened next took me completely by surprise.

Leaping from his jeep, a second lieutenant began screaming at me as if I were a child, "Who in the hell gave you authorization to fire your weapon?"

Somewhat stunned, I replied, "Sir, I wasn't aware that I needed authorization. I'm just here to clear up some paperwork for going on R&R and no one told me about needin' any authorization to defend my position."

Then as I tried to explain to him what had happened, he suddenly interrupted me and said, "That sounds like nonsense to me mister. I've got two Marines back in headquarters who claim that you flipped out and began shooting up the place."

It was at this point that I felt completely drained. I was tired, hungry, and all I wanted to do was go to Hong Kong. As I looked at the lieutenant, dressed in his shiny new boots and his starched uniform, he represented everything I hated about the war. He didn't give a damn about the people under him or getting the job done. All he was concerned about was looking good to the higher-ups, so that he could get another undeserved promotion.

Stepping up into his face while tightly gripping my rifle, I replied to him in a tense sarcastic voice, "Lieutenant, I don't give a damn what America's finest told you back at headquarters. And I don't really give a damn about your rules of engagement. We were probed here last night and those two chicken-shits couldn't get out of here quick enough. Now if you want to arrest me on some kind of charge, you go right ahead. I'll be glad to explain everything to the Battalion Commander."

To my surprise, he mumbled a few words, jumped back into his jeep, and then told his driver to drive on.

That day, I learned two very important lessons about dealing with irate higher-ups, especially the ones who have their priorities all screwed up. First and foremost, if you stand up to your supervisors and boldly voice your opinion, both clearly and honestly, they will usually respect your sincerity and take into account what you have to say. They may not agree with you, but their tone will change to one of civility and concern. Hence I discovered that it is only through meaningful dialogue that they will begin to acknowledge your rights as a professional member of the team. Given the chance, they will be more than happy to take your expert opinion into account.

Secondly, it also helps to be gripping a fully loaded M-16 when you decide to make your feelings known to these assholes.

After standing muster that morning in November of 1968, I began preparing for my R&R by getting my shots updated, finding a pair of khakis to wear, and stashing my combat gear at the supply tent. Then before anyone could blink an eye, I did my disappearing act. From sunup to sundown until I left for Hong Kong, the only time that I could be seen in the company area was during morning and evening chow. In this manner, I could avoid being unduly harassed by the NCOs. Usually, I would find a deserted out-of-way bunker and sleep through the day. Or I would hitch a ride to the other side of the base and visit the Army's area as if I was just one of the boys. Then sometimes, I would venture outside the gate and visit the nearby village of Quang Tri. The Vietnamese had set up a variety of shops and cat-houses all along the road for our entertainment. However, I always kept my nose clean whenever I wasn't in Da Nang. There was something about the people in these villages just south of the DMZ that gave me the creeps. I had the feeling that they would cut your throat for a mere dollar and then throw your remains into the nearest river.

Similar to the overwhelming majority of Americans in Vietnam, I had a hard time relating to the Vietnamese people. Although they were our allies and we were supposed to be in Vietnam trying to help them create a democratic society, I discovered that we had very little in common with the average citizen. Keeping in mind that they lived in a completely different world from what I had known, it was still very difficult for me just to be around them. On a personal level, they were unwashed, unmotivated, and appeared to be quite devious. As far as I could tell, they hadn't attempted to improve their way of life for over a thousand years. Unlike the industrialized and modern Japanese, the Vietnamese culture seemed to revolve around eating fish heads, working in the smelly fields, and chewing betel nut. Without any form of sanitation or water purification system, they lived and worked amid the unhealthiest conditions. As Americans, we had been thrown into a completely different culture, where any form of meaningful communication or mutual respect was almost impossible to achieve. Our value systems, personal habits, and political beliefs were just too different and worlds apart. All the good intentions in the world weren't going to change that fact.

Contrary to what our leaders chose to believe, there was a huge gap between what the average Vietnamese wanted to get out of the war and what we wanted. While trying to keep the landlords from repossessing their small plots of land, most of them tilled their fields and raised their children without any concern for the struggle raging around them. They couldn't have cared less about stopping the spread of communism or creating a democratic government. Their world was one of fighting the elements, revering their ancestors, and praying for a good harvest. The idea of establishing political parties, forming constituencies, and voting on a regular basis was never on their agenda. Their political tradition had always been to put their trust in the individual and not in the institution.

In their minds, the mandate to heaven or rather, the right to rule their society, could only be bestowed upon a person or a family who was prepared to act and then rule in the Confucian tradition—a tradition based upon one's virtuous thinking and proper behavior. Only in this manner could the wheels of government be controlled by their culture and not by some separate entity unto itself, such as foreign investors. Of course, none of this made any sense to our political leaders. They had arrogantly assumed that everybody in the world wanted to be like us.

After spending a few wonderful days in Da Nang, a large group of us were finally loaded into a cattle car and taken to the airstrip. As we stood there on the tarmac awaiting our plane, I noticed one of the guys on my flight looked very familiar. So I walked up to him and said, "Hey is that you, Bobby?" With a big smile stretched across his face, he immediately recognized me. As fellow Texans, we had not only come from the same part of the state, but we had also gone through boot camp together back in San Diego. It was good to see someone from home again. Even though he looked a lot older and leaner, he still had a boyish way about him.

Standing about five-feet, eight-inches tall and weighing close to one hundred forty pounds, he had straw-colored hair, drooping shoulders, and deep brown eyes. Like me, he had quit school at the age of seventeen and joined the Corps. While serving with an artillery unit near Hue, his war had been one of pumping rounds into a 105mm howitzer, filling sandbags, and burning shitters. The thing I remembered the most about Bobby was that while he was speaking to someone, he had a peculiar habit of constantly clearing throat and tugging on his crotch.

One of the most beautiful sights that I have ever witnessed was when our plane began its approach to Kai Tak International Airport in Hong Kong. The sun was just beginning to set as its rays skipped across the ocean waves. Moored in the harbor below us, I could see the ships and junks lined all along the docks as their crews unloaded their precious cargoes. The city itself was a hive of activity among the twinkling lights and towering skyscrapers. Off in the distance, the mountains loomed high in the air, covered in mist and mystery. Knowing full well that beyond those ridgelines was Red China, I couldn't help but wonder what evil lurked behind those bluish peaks.

As I continued to look out the window, Bobby was more concerned with planning our R&R together than with the scenery. Much like my first R&R, he wanted to fit a lifetime into five short days and nights. I tried to explain to him before we had landed that I intended to take things easy and enjoy myself. I had learned in Hawaii that when I stayed up every night and partied until dawn, and then tried to see all of the sights the next day, I ended up being too exhausted to really enjoy myself. Thus I came to realize that it actually took a couple of R&Rs before a person could learn how to relax and enjoy his unique surroundings. But it was all a waste of time on my part. I could tell that Bobby was determined to suck out every bit of marrow that Hong Kong had to offer.

Since Bobby and I had decided to share the cost of a room together, we registered in one of the finest hotels in Asia. Decorated in a Victorian-style arrangement, the accommodations didn't have any trouble living up to their famous name, the Grand Hotel. Beneath a string of crystal chandeliers was a massive staircase made of pink marble and brass railings. The floors leading up to the spacious rooms were covered with a thick, reddish carpet. Overlooking a street corner was a pair of huge bay windows, decorated with a set of dark-blue curtains. The walls were trimmed with strips of hardwood and covered in wallpaper made of velvet. In the hallways, I could see vases of exotic flowers and green foliage all along the corridors, thus creating an aura of gentility. Then, positioned in almost every corner of the hotel, there was a sculpture of a Greek or Roman statesman. I must say that for two young Texas boys from Hicksville, the experience was overwhelming. The bellboys and attendants were literally fighting each other for the sole privilege of attending to our primitive and inexpensive needs.

As far as I was concerned, the first order of business was to wire my parents and ask them for some more money. After making only a hundred and fifty bucks a month in the bush, I didn't have enough money to stay in Hong Kong for two days, much less for five. So the first thing we did was to make a beeline to the nearest telegraph office. It took a couple of days, but God bless her, my mother was finally able to come up with the dough. For whatever the reasons, she didn't have the heart to ask my stepfather for it, so she ended up asking my brother, David. He had spent the previous summer working in a grain elevator, instead of running around raising hell with his friends. To this day, David and I still get a big laugh about him sending me the money. In spite of the fact that he had been vehemently against the war in Vietnam, he graciously supported one of its most destitute fighting men.

One of the things I had learned while living in Asia was that Westerners just don't have any idea as to how to properly serve a customer. For instance, when Bobby and I entered a clothing shop the very next day to buy some civilian clothes, two grinning Chinese tailors met us at the door. Their enthusiasm was something to behold behind their gold-plated teeth and dark-rimmed glasses. Instead of idly standing there and waiting for us to pick out our clothes, the first words that came out of their mouths were, "Do you GIs want a cold beer?"

Taken aback by their offer, we replied, "hell yes." Then one of them quickly scurried over to a small icebox in the corner of the shop and pulled out a couple of cold ones.

As we drank our beer and looked at the clothing, these two guys went out of their way to make us feel as comfortable as possible. They kept patting us on the back and telling us how handsome and virile we looked. Then every time we picked out something to buy, they would congratulate us on making the wisest and most stylish choice anyone had ever made. At the time, I was utterly amazed at how they were able to turn a simple business venture into a pleasurable experience. They went out of their way to personally get to know us and make us feel good about ourselves, something I had never experienced back in the States. In fact, they were so slick that I ended up buying a maroon sports jacket, which I didn't really need or want.

Later that afternoon, Bobby took off to visit the sights, so I went down to one of the hotel's cocktail lounges. The Viking Club was located in the basement, right next to the hotel's restaurant. Designed as a traditional British pub, the atmosphere was quite different from what one would find in an American bar. Everybody just sat around and conversed with each other in a civilized manner without having to endure the sounds of loud music or the rattling of video games. To my enjoyment, the people who congregated there were some of the most interesting folks that I would ever have the pleasure of meeting. Besides running into an assortment of jet-fighter pilots, ship captains, ambassador's aides, and movie screenwriters, I also met and befriended the manager of the Viking Club. He was a middle-aged, distinguished-looking gentleman from Perth, Australia. Highly respected by all of his patrons, he introduced himself to me as Stanley Beasley.

Almost every afternoon for the next five days, Stanley and I would meet in the bar and have a few drinks. While reminiscing about World War II, he told me that he had been a sailor in the Merchant Marines. During the long voyages, it was their responsibility to transport supplies to our troops in the Pacific Theater. Within a three-year period, Stanley had two ships shot out from underneath him by the Japanese Navy. In a matter-of-fact tone, he jokingly mentioned that was where he had first learned how to swim. To this day, I have no idea as to why he enjoyed my company. Knowing that I was in the Marine Corps and a grunt in Vietnam, I guess that he felt a special kinship towards me, since the Marines had helped repel the Japanese from Australia during World War II. Nevertheless, I really enjoyed listening to his stories about living in Asia and sailing the seven seas.

It was during one of my afternoons with Stanley that I had an opportunity to meet a group of Israeli paratroopers. I don't remember any of their names, except that one of them was a major, another one was a captain, and two of them were sergeants. While on special assignment, they said that they had been touring South Vietnam by invitation of the U.S. Army. Up to that point, all I had ever heard from my father and many other American officers were how much they greatly respected and admired the Israeli Army. In their minds, there was no finer army in the world. Outnumbered and surrounded by several hostile nations, the Israelis had already defeated several Arab nations on three different occasions (1948, 1956, and 1967).

Over several beers, we must have spent the next four or five hours discussing our combat experiences, the enemies we had faced, and the weapons we had used. Overall, I found them to be highly professional and competent in their military knowledge. And no doubt about it, they were well trained, organized, and motivated. Yet there was something about these four Israeli paratroopers that was missing from their demeanor. As infantrymen, they just didn't have the look of murder and mayhem about them that I had seen in our own grunts.

It must have been on our third day in Hong Kong, when Bobby came storming into our room with a French girl named Elaine. She was a twenty-six-year-old schoolteacher of all things with a plump body and long dark hair. I learned later that she spoke six languages, loathed French men, and regarded the war in Vietnam as a big waste. Though she wasn't a raging beauty, there was still something about her that I found very appealing and classy. At this point, I couldn't figure out why she was with Bobby. She obviously wasn't a hooker or a party animal, but more like a woman on a mission. Whatever it was about her, I knew that I wanted her in the worst way. So after our brief introduction, I began to turn on the old Short charm by telling her how young and beautiful she looked and how attracted I was to women who were intelligent enough to form their own opinions. I figured that would turn her head. Yet before I could even offer her a cocktail, Bobby began ripping off his clothes and telling me to get out of the room, so that they could have some quality time together.

Feeling forsaken, I went down to the Viking Club for a while to talk to Stanley. As I sat there on a stool nursing a beer, I began to fiendishly plot and connive about how I was going to get Elaine away from Bobby and then possibly take her out for a few drinks. Not being a Casanova type fellow, I had discovered that my chances for romance were greatly enhanced whenever I could get the lady somewhat intoxicated and distracted.

As fortune would have it, it didn't take long before I was able to be with the enchanting Elaine. After about thirty minutes or so, she and Bobby came down to the bar with their hair all messed up and their clothes out of line. To my surprise, neither one of them had much to say, as they sipped on their drinks and glared at each other in pure disgust. Then suddenly, Bobby abruptly excused himself from the table and said, "She's all yours, buddy. I'm going to go find me a party." As he stomped out the door, I was both confused and elated. Turning towards Elaine, I asked her, "What in the hell is wrong with him?"

Somewhat reluctantly, she told me that they had been in the middle of a lovers' embrace when things unexpectedly turned sour. Evidently, she had made the mistake of crying out for more, when she suddenly realized that Bobby had already given his all. Due to the fact that they had just been together, I didn't figure it would be a good idea to invite her back up to the room for another go at it right away. So instead, I asked her if she wanted to go to a flick (movie) or a museum. Shaking her head in disagreement, she said, "No, let's go sightseeing."

Hong Kong was the first British colony that I had ever visited and I was truly impressed. The streets were clean, the buildings were modern, and the people were very hard working. Obviously, a person could make a lot of money operating there. Everywhere I looked, there were rich European and Japanese bankers running around in their expensive business suits and carrying black umbrellas. In spite of the fact that the place was extremely crowded, I was amazed at how considerate everyone was to each other. Courteous and always smiling, the people seemed to be in harmony with the hustle and bustle of city life. They just went about their business as if they didn't have a care in the world. Apparently, life was good and there was plenty of money to be made with the constant arrival of hundreds of U.S. servicemen every five days.

As we were walking down a narrow street and I was admiring the beauty of her eyes, a young French fellow came up to Elaine and grabbed her by the arm. As I stepped towards him, they started arguing with each other in their native tongue. Sensing that I had been caught in the middle of a lovers' quarrel by the urgency of their tone, I held back and let the guy speak his piece. Of course, I had no idea as to what they were actually saying to each other. But it seemed obvious to me that he was asking her forgiveness for some transgression he had committed.

By the character of their argument and by the way she had unhesitatingly bedded down with Bobby, I put two and two together and figured she had recently caught him with another woman. Since I wasn't overly anxious for them to kiss and make up at that particular moment, I started thinking of a way to get rid of him. Then as their conversation was becoming alarmingly more congenial, it hit me like a bolt of lightning.

Stepping next to her, I leaned down and whispered in Elaine's ear, "I wouldn't believe this guy. He looks like the type that has a string of chicks all over this town."

At that instant, her face turned red from recalling his wrongdoing and she grabbed my arm and said, "Screw this gigolo, let's go back to your hotel room."

I'll never forget the despondent look on that poor guy's face as we sashayed down the street. But the way I figured it, catching women is like catching a fish. Once a fellow feels a nibble, he had better snatch her up or she'll be gone.

Before I jumped into the sack with Elaine, I jokingly promised her the most exciting three minutes of her life.

Realizing I was being just plain silly, she replied, "Well, don't shoot till you see the whites of my eyes."

Then we embraced each other and fell into bed, laughing and giggling like a couple of kids. In all honesty, I gave her one of my best performances. If someone had been giving out Oscars that night, I would have gotten one. Suave and caring in my caresses, I tried to be as sensitive and as loving as possible. The unbridled passion I had unleashed that evening were something that had been building up in me for a very long time. The very texture of her creamy skin and her distinctive fragrance made my blood boil. Responding to her every touch, we created our own idyllic rhythm, submerged in an alliance of sweat, moans, and pounding hearts. For a second, it felt as if we had exchanged our souls. The sensation was one of complete harmony and contentment. Afterward, I even held her in my arms for several minutes, before I finally jumped up and said, "Let's go get some chow."

After enjoying several drinks in the Viking Club, we decided to check out the hotel's restaurant. Without question, we must have been a sight to behold, while we strolled past a long line of people waiting to enter the restaurant. I was wearing a pair of dark sunglasses, a flowery shirt, wrinkled slacks, and an old baseball cap. My hair was sticking up in the air and I had gook sores all over my arms and neck. As for Elaine, she was decked out in a pair of old blue jeans, dirty sneakers, and a bright yellow jacket that read on the back, "Hong Kong is for Lovers." A long line of high-ranking diplomats, military officers, movie producers, and corporate executives were awaiting their turn, until Stanley could find them a table. At the time, I hadn't seen so many big shots in all of my life. Several of the guys were even wearing black tuxedoes, as their dates were showing off their long, glittery evening gowns. I remember one particular lady was wearing a set of diamonds around her neck that looked like the crown jewels of England.

I don't think we stood in line for more than ten minutes, before something truly wonderful happened. Unknowingly, it would become the beginning of an extraordinary evening that will always remain in my memories. As I was standing there talking to Elaine, I looked up and saw Stanley at the doorway of the club waving at us to come towards him. Not suspecting what he wanted, I grabbed Elaine by the arm and we made our way to the front of the line. To say the least, I didn't feel very comfortable about having to walk past all those big shots.

Nevertheless, once we reached the entranceway, Stanley gently put his hand on my shoulder and said, "Mr. Short, I've reserved the best table in the house for you and your lady friend. So order whatever you desire, because it's all on me."

Completely shocked by his generosity, a group of eager Chinese waiters suddenly appeared and led us to a small cozy table next to a guy playing the piano. Without question, Elaine was thoroughly flabbergasted by my newfound clout. She kept looking up at me as if I was a movie star or something. Then unexpectedly, Stanley walked up to our table with a bottle of their finest champagne and suggested that we order the Hong Kong lobster, which was smothered in a buttery Cantonese sauce and mushrooms. With a huge smile plastered across my face, I replied, "That sounds wonderful, Mr. Beasley, but can I also get a steak on the side?"

He just grinned at me and said, "Anything for America's finest."

Being from the lower side of Fort Worth, I never had the opportunity to attend any classy social events while I was growing up. My family's social schedule had evolved around going to barbecues, bowling alleys, or drive-in movies. As a child, I had been instructed in the mysteries of using a knife and a fork. Moreover, I was even encouraged to use a napkin when the occasion arose. However, I was completely

in the dark when it came to exhibiting any other form of social ameni-
ties. Luckily though, Elaine was there to guide me through my more
awkward moments. And I must admit that I rather enjoyed being
pampered. Of course, it did freak her out a bit when I began tossing
olives up into the air and catching them with my mouth. But she was
a good sport about it.

While we began to eat our shrimp cocktails, Elaine started play-
fully kissing me in between the bites of shrimp. At first, I didn't
think anything about it, because I figured it was just a French thing.
Then with a piece of shrimp in her mouth, she unexpectedly leaned
over and kissed me again. Only this time, she gently pushed her
shrimp deep into my mouth. Never experiencing anything like
it back home, I found it extremely arousing. Before the waiters
had even gotten around to serving us the second course, we were
kissing and exchanging the food in our mouths as if we had been
lovers for years.

In between the gulps of champagne and the erotic kisses, I began
to get with the program. With each new kiss, my hands would roam
all over her delicious young body and end up on her firm breasts. At
any moment, I expected to get slapped across the face. But instead, she
would just giggle and smile at me in a way I had never been smiled at
before. Then later, as we were in the middle of exchanging pieces of
lobster with one of our kisses, she reached down under the table and
began stroking my manhood. Oddly enough, the movement of her
hand was so exhilarating that I found myself trying to speak French.
Burdened by my southwestern drawl, I kept saying things like "viva
le Francie" and "parle vouie francè."

As she continued to slowly stroke me, I became even more aroused.
In a flood of sexual excitement, I could feel the blood in my veins
rush down into my feet and back up to the top of my head. Overcome by a surge of pure ecstasy, the expression on my face must have
resembled something out of a goofy Jim Carrey movie. The harder

she stroked, the more difficult it was for me to breathe, much less to keep a straight face.

Undoubtedly, Elaine was an extraordinary woman. She had a way about her that made every minute special. Throughout the rest of the evening, she laughed and talked with great charm and gaiety. Most of the time, I didn't understand a word she was saying because of her superior education. But I didn't let it bother me. Like so many other women in Texas, she exhibited a hardness about her that would occasionally reveal itself at the oddest moments. Lurking underneath a polite veneer of Victorian decorum was a woman who knew what she wanted and wasn't afraid to get it. One minute, she could be extremely feminine and gracious in her demeanor, and then the next, she would burst out laughing in a hearty masculine voice and slap everybody on the back as if she was just one of the boys. As I gazed into her hazel-tinted eyes, I found her even more alluring because of this contradiction. There was something about her that made me feel whole and appreciated.

For the last two days of my R&R, I had a wonderful time with Elaine. We went everywhere together as she showed me the sights. It was during our most intimate moments that I made an effort to get closer to her. Dazzled by her sophisticated European ways, I definitely wanted to deepen our relationship. Unfortunately, she was old enough to realize that my future was uncertain and not at all promising. Thus whenever I referred to us as a couple, she would quickly respond by changing the subject or by ignoring me altogether. Yet being so young, I was rather hurt that Elaine wouldn't even give me her address so that we could at least exchange letters. I guess she figured that in the long run, it would be better for the both of us.

On the day Bobby and I were scheduled to fly back to Nam, the atmosphere was filled with one of regret and sadness. I knew that I wouldn't be seeing Elaine again, and quite honestly, I was rather upset about it. While she was sitting on the bed watching us pack our clothes, two Navy guys suddenly knocked on the door and introduced themselves. They had just arrived in Hong Kong for their R&Rs, so they were ready to party. I remember one of them was a tall, black fellow and the other one was a skinny Caucasian.

Excusing myself, I stepped out into the hallway and explained to them that we had to catch a flight back to Nam. Then the black fellow stepped forward and offered to buy everyone a drink before we left. Not being in the mood to be sociable, I declined his offer and then unexpectedly asked them if they wanted to meet a French lady. While they were mumbling something unintelligible, I went back into our room and returned with Elaine. Literally handing her over to them, I briskly turned around and walked back into the room without saying a word. Then as I was about to shut the door behind me, I heard her say in a regretful voice, "Take care, cowboy, it's been fun."

Sensing that something was wrong, Bobby asked me if I was going to be all right. In an off-hand manner, I replied, "I'll be okay, as soon as I get to shoot somebody." For some reason, Del Shannon's hit song, "Runaway," kept running through my brain like a freight train.

It must have been about five or six days after I had last seen Elaine, when a row of 82mm mortar rounds came slamming along our perimeter. As I dove into a nearby foxhole, one of the rounds landed in the hole next to mine. Luckily for Roger, if he hadn't been on a work detail, he would have been blown to bits. Amid the swirling smoke and the smell of burning cordite, I could hear the screams of the wounded and the desperate yells of the survivors. Red was running around trying to find the corpsmen, while everyone else hid in their holes.

During my absence, Bravo Company had been positioned on top of a mountain near Hill 881 South. Inasmuch as the area had been routinely fought over for the last couple of years, the NVA had every inch of our outpost zeroed in with their guns. They could have easily hit any foxhole they wanted, so we spent the rest of the day medevac-ing the wounded and digging deeper into the ground.

For the next several days, we patrolled the surrounding valleys and muddy slopes, knowing full well that the enemy was watching our every movement. Although they had stopped dropping their mortar rounds into our position and there wasn't any sign of activity, we still didn't feel very good about the situation. The Ho Chi Minh Trail was just several ridgelines away from us and we knew that the NVA had several major units operating in the area. I do remember that we weren't at all happy about our unit being used as bait. Positioned in the enemy's front yard like that, they could have overrun our perimeter anytime they so desired.

Predictably, we kept asking each other the same question, "Why in the hell were we even in this part of Vietnam, if we weren't going to commit enough troops to do the job?"

Then someone in a very distant headquarters decided that our company should move down from our mountaintop, cross the bar-ren valley floor down below, and occupy the adjacent mountaintop. Gazing across the valley, our objective looked like any other mountain near Laos. Sections of it were scarred with bomb and artillery craters, yet there was still enough vegetation left on it to conceal a fairly large enemy unit. So early the next morning, we packed our gear and began moving down the mountainside. The weather wasn't too bad, so we were able to cross the valley floor before noontime. While resting at the bottom of our objective, the word was passed to eat some chow and then check our weapons. Among the troops, the mood was dead serious and apprehensive. There was always something foreboding about moving close to the Laotian border.

Due to the rotation of the platoons during a company movement, our platoon had lucked out and was assigned a position behind the lead platoon. The headquarters group, consisting of the Skipper, the XO, their radiomen, and the company gunny, was positioned in front of our platoon. As I looked up at the towering crest, I could hear Zit and M&M bitching about having to climb every damn mountain in this part of the world. Finally, Boyd told them to stow it and keep their eyes open.

As we slowly made our way up towards the summit, our column zigzagged its way up a slope, until we ran into a rocky incline. Since it was too steep to climb, the Skipper ordered the lead platoon to move to the right and climb a fairly large ridgeline (a finger) that led straight up to the top of the mountain. At this point, we were pretty tired and making a lot of noise. I kept thinking to myself that if there were any NVA on the mountain, they sure couldn't have missed hearing our approach.

Once our column had climbed the finger, we began a direct ascent to the top with the lead platoon stopping every few minutes to check out the area. We must have been about halfway up the mountain, when the Skipper ordered a ten-minute break. I was so fatigued that I didn't even bother taking off my backpack. I just flopped down next to a tree stump and lit a cigarette, while the other guys pulled out their canteens for a quick swig. As I watched my cigarette smoke linger above my head, the silence was almost deafening. I couldn't hear any overhead helicopters, planes, or even the sound of birds' chattering. The absence of even a slight breeze made the surrounding jungle as still as a graveyard. Restless, I got up and started looking around the area. On either side of our finger was another ridgeline that also ran up towards the top. Between the three fingers were deep crevices filled with jungle foliage. At that moment I didn't realize it, but those crevices would save a lot of lives.

The company headquarters group was standing right in front of our squad, when I heard the Skipper radio the Battalion Command Center for standby air support. Glancing at Boyd, our eyes rolled in the air, because we both knew that the Skipper suspected something wasn't right. Then after looking at his map, he radioed the platoon commanders to come to his location for a pow-wow. Turning to the other squad members, Boyd ordered them to check their rifles and ammo. A rush of excitement ran up and down the line as each man began preparing for the worst.

Edging closer to the Skipper, I could hear him tell the platoon commanders that he was going to split up the company. Our platoon was to make our way up the mountain, using the finger on the left. A second platoon was to position themselves on the finger to the right, while the lead platoon along with the headquarters group was going to move directly up from the middle finger. Then once everyone was in position, we would approach the summit from three different routes.

Looking straight into the eyes of each lieutenant, the Skipper finally said, "Now, does anyone have any questions?"

Clearing his throat, our platoon commander replied, "What will be your orders if we run into a bunker complex?"

"If that's the case, the NVA will have their mortars pinpointed along the fingers. So if things get hot, keep your platoon together and move them down into the crevices and prepare to attack," the Skipper replied.

At the time, I was so proud of these officers. They really had their shit together. As leaders, I would have followed them anywhere.

It took probably thirty minutes or so, before we were able to move into position through the dense brush. Then once the word was passed, all three columns began moving up towards the top as a well-oiled machine. My squad was positioned immediately behind the lead squad. Red had already informed everyone that if we ran into Mr. Charles, our orders were to move off of the finger and into the crevice to our left as quick as possible.

Then just as we were about to reach what everyone thought was to be the summit, there was a burst of rifle fire to our right. Frozen in our tracks, we stopped for a second and looked at each other in dread. It sounded just like an AK-47. Then suddenly, several M-16s cut loose from about the same location. Frustrated at not being able to see anything, Boyd was about to say something to me, when all hell broke loose.

Up towards the front of the other two fingers, the exchange of gunfire had become so intense that within a matter of seconds it sounded like an ammo dump was going up in flames. In between the crackle of rifle fire and the constant hammering of a machine gun, I could hear several guys yelling out for a corpsman.

"Get our asses off of the pathway," our lieutenant yelled out.

In one quick motion, our platoon leaped from the finger and into the deep crevice. As the firefight was in full swing, our platoon began moving up the steep incline towards the summit. Bullets were zinging through the air and clipping the overhead leaves like a buzz saw. Somewhere among all of the confusion, our squad ended up leading the way. Red was pushing and shoving everyone forward like a man possessed. The lieutenant was right behind him calmly talking on the radio with the Skipper.

Finally working our way to the top, Boyd and I stopped at the rim to check out the situation. And to our immense surprise, we weren't anywhere near the summit as we had thought. We were actually on the edge of a knoll that stuck out from the side of the mountain. Positioned all along the back of the knoll was a camouflaged trench line with several bunkers full of NVA. They were firing like hell at the other two platoons, when Boyd and I began firing into their position. In no time at all, several more Marines came up beside us and began firing.

To our right, we could hear our M-60 machine guns and M-79s blasting away as Red was positioning more and more Marines along the edge of the knoll. Then just when we were beginning to lay down an impressive amount of firepower, the NVA opened up with their deadly fifty-one caliber machine gun. The steel-pointed rounds suddenly ripped across our firing positions, directly in front of us. The impact was so great that it knocked us back down the slope in one big wave of tumbling men and equipment.

After we had recovered from our fall and begun moving back up the slope, Roger began accusing Zit of flinching while under fire.

In an excited voice, Zit responded, "I didn't flinch, asshole. I was trying to keep my frickin' head attached to my shoulders."

In response to the enemy's machine gun, our 60mm mortar crews began pumping their rounds out from the crevices and into the enemy's position. Our lieutenant was sitting on the edge of the rim calling down the adjustments to the crews, when he was almost hit by enemy fire. He had hurled himself down the slope, attempting to avoid the bullets.

Almost as soon we reached the rim, the NVA began dropping their 82mm mortar rounds along the pathways of the fingers. Whistling across the sky, the explosions erupted among the twisted vines and thick underbrush. Just as the Skipper had suspected, they had those pathways on the fingers pinpointed. From the rounds' angle of approach, it appeared as if they were coming from the reverse side of the mountain.

Dropping five or six rounds in succession, they initially hit the finger to the far right.

I could hear Fuzzy's voice shuddering behind me, "Oh, shit."

Then as the NVA shifted their tubes to the middle finger, they began walking their mortar rounds up from the bottom of the finger towards the Skipper's pinned-down platoon.

Again I heard Fuzzy shudder, "Oh, shit."

Shortly thereafter, their rounds began hitting our finger about 100 meters below us. While working their way up the slope in our direction, Fuzzy blurted out with a wild-eyed expression, "Holy shit."

Fortunately, they stopped about thirty meters short of us.

Of course, the mortar rounds didn't hit anything at the time, because we were all in the deep crevices. Temporarily safe for the moment, the impact from their mortars did encourage the platoons in each crevice to move farther up the slopes, thus bunching everyone together. However, everybody knew that it was just a matter of time before they would adjust their mortar rounds into the crevices.

It was at this point that the Skipper made a very wise tactical decision. Instead of ordering us to charge into a hailstorm of AK-47 and machine-gun fire or waiting for their mortars to eventually locate us, the word was passed for every platoon to haul ass back down the crevices as quickly as possible. Profoundly relieved, we grabbed our wounded and scattered equipment and began making our way down the mountainside. Meanwhile, the Skipper called in a flight of F-4 Phantoms to cover our movement. In no time at all, the Marine aircraft were zooming overhead and literally flinging their lethal loads into the enemy's position. Off in the distance, we could see the NVA's anti-aircraft fire blazing away at our diving planes.

I was amazed at the stark courage exhibited by the U.S. Marine pilots that day. It was no easy task for them to face down enemy anti-aircraft fire at such a low altitude and accurately drop their bombs next to a unit of fellow Marines. Even though they had been highly trained and skilled for such a maneuver, they were still incredible to watch. Sometimes, it was almost like a person could reach up and touch their wings, because they were flying so low in order to be accurate.

As several 250-pound bombs were blowing the enemy's position to bits, we moved down onto the valley floor and medevaced our wounded and received several pallets of supplies. Astonishingly, we only had about twenty casualties with five of them in serious condition. But the corpsmen were able to keep them alive long enough to reach a hospital.

Apparently when the Skipper's platoon had reached the knoll, the lead squad was just coming over the top of the rim, when an enemy soldier had panicked and prematurely fired his rifle. Then after our boys had begun to return fire, the rest of the NVA couldn't help themselves. They all started firing their rifles and exposing their positions to us. Under the cover fire of our machine guns, the lead squad was able to make it back to the rim and join their comrades in the crevice.

As darkness began to engulf the western sky, we crossed the valley floor and set up a perimeter on the mountain that our unit had occupied the previous night. Everyone was physically exhausted and emotionally drained. Our officers and NCOs had done a marvelous job, and for the first time, I began to appreciate the U.S. Army's concept of employing their immense firepower instead of blindly charging the enemy. The NVA had set up their position in such a way that it would have been impossible for us to overrun the place without receiving horrendous casualties. For the rest of the night, we lay in our foxholes and watched the burning fires across the valley.

Early the very next morning, we got up to eat breakfast and then prepared ourselves to hump right back up that god-forsaken mountain. Everyone seemed to be in high spirits, yet there was a feeling of foreboding in their gestures. Boyd went around to everyone in the squad and made sure that they had enough ammo and water. As for myself, I tied several strips around my arms and legs that I had made from one of the wounded guy's bloodied shirts to help stop the bleeding if I got wounded. Then I checked my rifle and smoked a quick cigarette. Since our platoon was ordered to lead the way, our squad was selected to go first. For whatever the reasons, Boyd wanted me to take the point. It wasn't the first time that I ended up being the point man for our platoon, so I wasn't new to the job. But it wasn't something that I wanted to do everyday. Usually when one of our units did run into the enemy, more times than not, the point man ended up a casualty.

As we made our way back across the valley floor, the F-4s began heating up the area above us with their deadly canisters of napalm.

None of us were very thrilled about having to go back up there that day, but it was something that had to be done. The Skipper didn't want to ascend the mountain along the same trail that we had used the previous day. So, I led the company up the original trail for a couple of hundred yards and then crossed over a ravine to an area covered in vegetation. Quietly moving through the trees and underbrush, I stopped every few yards to get my bearings and then use my senses to detect the enemy. Since I couldn't see, smell, hear, or feel their presence, we moved up the slope fairly quickly.

As before, each platoon followed a designated finger up to the top of the knoll. Incredibly once we made it back up there, we saw that the enemy's meticulously built trench line and bunkers had been transformed into piles of smoldering ashes and deep craters. There were a few pieces of weapons and equipment scattered around the ground, but that was about all. After the F-4s had showed up the day before, the Skipper believed that the NVA had probably made a beeline back to Laos.

One of the reasons that I survived my year in the bush was because I was lucky enough not to have been caught in the middle of an enemy ambush. Just in terms of the stark numbers, the majority of our infantry casualties in Vietnam would occur from our units' walking into these deathtraps. As a tactic, I can't think of a more deadly way to begin a firefight or a major battle. Concealed in the underbrush and usually hiding in foxholes, the enemy would use the element of surprise to unleash a hailstorm of firepower into a prearranged killing zone. Within a matter of seconds, the entrapped unit would be decimated and the survivors would be pinned down and fighting for their very existence.

In between conducting patrols, cleaning our weapons, and standing watches, grunts have always been bored to tears during the times of inactivity. Since we weren't actually fighting on a twenty-four-hour-a-day basis, there wasn't a hell of a lot to do on a mountaintop. So, we killed the time by either playing poker or talking about everything under the sun.

As for our conversations, it is amazing how philosophical and knowledgeable one gets while living in constant peril. Under normal circumstances, the conversations would start out with a fellow describing his car, his girlfriend, or his plans for the future. Then predictably, they would invariably turn to the subject of religion and the meaning of life. For hours on end, we would argue with each other about our beliefs, as if we were trying to convince the other fellow as much as ourselves. And quite frankly, since I had been raised with two of the most argumentative brothers in the universe, I was pretty good at debating. Some of the black guys even started calling me the "Professor," due to my slippery ways.

Besides religion, the subject of politics also created a lot of disagreements. Profoundly ignorant, everybody had his own theory as to why we were in Vietnam and how we could win the war. Since the idea of stopping the spread of communism ten thousand miles away from home was a pretty weak and vague reason for one to give his life, it became quite common for us to create an assortment of complex and farcical reasons for being there.

For instance, Staff Sergeant Redburn astonishingly believed that we were in Vietnam so that we could control the fertile rice-producing areas in the Mekong Delta and thus starve the other communist countries into submission. Of course, I didn't have the heart to tell him how ridiculous his theory sounded. I figured that he was just searching for something credible to tell his wife and kids. Many of the guys just wanted to nuke the bastards and go home. Not realizing that the Chinese could have easily nuked us in retaliation, the less intelligent fellows thought that it was a practical solution to all of our problems.

Moreover, many of us believed that Vietnam wasn't worth initiating another world war nor was it worth one American life. We unenthusiastically went about our duties, never really knowing the economic reasons behind our intervention. Even though we were young, uneducated, and terribly gullible, it was getting harder by the minute for the higher-ups to justify the strategic value of Southeast Asia without sounding out of touch with reality.

Chapter Twelve

Into the Breech

"The only problem with a nation honoring its war dead is that it
tends to inspire the young to seek out that same honor."

One dismal morning, the helicopters unexpectedly arrived and took
us away in a whirlwind of flying dust and lingering fumes. While
climbing above the clouds, the air was so cold and crisp that we had
to huddle together to keep from shivering. After living in our dirty
foxholes, it had been quite awhile since we had actually seen each
other in a clear and open setting. As a group, we were literally covered in mud and grime, unshaven, and undernourished. Our battle
fatigues were torn to shreds and the equipment we carried was old and
almost useless from the wear and tear. Grinning at each other as if the
governor had just pardoned us, everyone realized that we were flying
in an easterly direction, which could only mean a reprieve of sorts.

Almost immediately, Huff and Fuzzy began taking bets as to our
destination. Personally, I kept hoping that we were headed for LZ
Stud in order to get a few days' rest and some hot chow. Weighing
only about one hundred twenty pounds, I had gook sores running up

and down my arms, swollen feet, and ringworms all over my legs and crotch. Amazingly though, compared to other fellows in my squad, I was somewhat healthy. Several of them were running high fevers and couldn't keep their food down. Poor Roger and Huff had been crapping in their pants for days and Fuzzy had a badly infected leg. Our physical condition was so deplorable that we probably looked like a pack of refugees from Ethiopia.

To my disappointment, we flew beyond LZ Stud and continued towards the coast. Looking down below us, we could see several Army firebases and villages dotting the countryside. This only added to our anxiety, because we didn't want to end up having to patrol some booby-trapped area. Then as our helicopter turned to the south, the scenery quickly began to look very familiar. Stretching for miles on end was the same grassy plain where we had previously stood watch over the Army's artillery base.

Suddenly, everyone became alive again. The prospect of guarding another Army installation was just what we needed. In a moment of exaltation, Roger and M&M began ripping open their backpacks and chucking their C-rations out the window. As we sat there and watched them throwing their food away, the crew chief instantly jumped to his feet and motioned for us to get ready to disembark. In one fell swoop, our helicopter gently landed into a field of golden grass and we were unexpectedly shoved out into the bush again. I don't think that I have ever seen such a group of demoralized people in all my life. Stunned, we just stood there for a second and looked at each other in total disbelief.

Unbeknown to anyone, we were about to conduct a couple of operations that were complete failures from start to finish. Many of the guys blamed the Skipper, but personally, I think that we were all just too physically and mentally exhausted to properly function. Throughout the whole war, our units were constantly being sent from one place to another in an effort to stop the flood. While never having enough grunts in the field, our two-plus Marine divisions were being asked to secure an area which ten American divisions couldn't have realistically covered. But for whatever the reasons, these two operations sure didn't go down in the history books as one of the Marine Corps' finest moments.

As we struggled down a rugged incline and into a small valley, everyone was quiet and lost in his own thoughts. I knew this was a bad sign and that we were being pushed to our limit. Normally, infantrymen are always bitching about something or other. If they aren't complaining about the incessant rain or the nagging insects, they're usually raising hell about the lack of rest or the dreadful tasting water. However, whenever his men quit bitching, a commander should sit up and take notice. It's generally an indication of a company's declining morale.

The Skipper looked down at his map and then he gave directions to the lieutenant of the point platoon. Exhausted and in obvious pain from our afflictions, everybody just went through the motions as if we were walking in our sleep. The guys kept looking around at each other with these cold, blank stares, hoping that we would soon stop and make camp. At this point, the heat had become so intense that I could not have cared less if we had walked into an ambush or into a NVA division. We were so dejected and physically beat, I'm not sure we could have successfully defended ourselves. Then something happened that brought everybody temporarily back to life.

Coming upon a wide stream at the bottom of a gully, our platoon was ordered to wade across and secure the other side. Keeping our intervals of several yards between each other, we reluctantly jumped into the murky water. The stream was waist deep with a surprisingly strong current, thus making the crossing all the more difficult. As we waded through, we discovered the water was somewhat refreshing and a welcome change of pace. It actually washed much of the dirt and sweat off of our bodies. Then once everyone had reached the other side, the Skipper took a few steps and noticed that he had leeches crawling all over his arms. In a fit of anger, he ordered everybody to stop dead in his tracks, strip down, and check each other for parasites.

One of the many myths that came out of World War II was that a person could use a lit cigarette butt to safely remove a leech from his body. From my experience, it only drove the little varmints deeper into one's skin. Thus I learned quite early that the best way to do it was to douse them in insect repellent. Almost immediately, they would curl themselves up into a tight little ball, where they could be easily flicked off. Obviously though, not everyone had gotten the word. While I was in the process of removing my gear, I suddenly heard a blood-curdling scream coming through the tall grass. Reaching for my weapon, I instantly jumped upon a small nearby mound just in time to see a half-naked Fuzzy running around in cycles with his pants wrapped around his ankles. He was cursing to the high heavens and threatening to kill every son-of-a-bitch in the platoon. While he was unintentionally giving our position away to every NVA soldier within a square mile area, the other fellows were trying to keep his rifle away from him so that he wouldn't shoot somebody.

Evidently when Fuzzy pulled his pants down, he had three huge leeches hanging from his genitalia. In a moment of panic, he started pleading for someone to get them off of him. But instead of using his insect propellant, Zit had nonchalantly turned towards him with a lit cigarette in his hand and said, "Just close your eyes, man. I'll take care of this."

Not realizing that leeches can wriggle around on a person's sweaty body, Zit missed his target and accidentally plunged his lit cigarette into Fuzzy's fairly large testicles. There must have been about eighty stripped-down guys standing in the grass having a good laugh at Fuzzy's expense. It was times like these that made Fuzzy an invaluable asset to the unit.

Later that afternoon as we were preparing our positions, I was unexpectedly interrupted from digging my foxhole and told to report to the Skipper. Not knowing if I was in for an ass chewin', I cautiously walked up to him as he was exchanging words with our XO (executive officer). While standing on a small ridgeline next to a grove of trees, they had been trying to establish our predetermined artillery coordinates without much success. Since our regular forward observer was on R&R and they knew that I had previously served as an FO in another unit, they wanted to get my opinion. Thrilled by the chance to show off my skills, I asked them what I could do to help.

"Look, Short," the Skipper said, "The XO and I don't appear to agree as to our exact location." Moving his finger between two sets of coordinates on his map, he continued, "We can't decide whether we are here at this point or at this other set of coordinates."

Having been an ex-forward observer, I knew that map reading could be a very tricky business. Even the most experienced person can become disorientated and lost. Feeling out of place, the last thing I wanted to do was piss off one of these guys. They both had the authority to make my life even more miserable than it already was. So as they were beginning to argue with each other again, I politely interrupted them with a smile and said, "Let's call in a spotter round and see where it lands."

"Good idea," the Skipper snapped, as he grabbed the radio set and began calling in a Willie Peter (smoke) round from a supposedly nearby artillery battery. From the coordinates he had given them, the round should have landed approximately eight hundred meters to our front. But then, the most astonishing thing happened. We not only couldn't hear the gun firing, but furthermore, we didn't see or hear the round land anywhere in our vicinity. In fact, we couldn't see any smoke at all.

After looking at each other with these dumb expressions on our faces, the XO grabbed the radio set from the Skipper and said, "Now, let's try my coordinates." But instead of asking for one round, this time the XO requested that two WP rounds be fired.

It must have taken a few minutes before the artillery battery finally radioed back to us that the rounds were on the way. To our dismay, we still couldn't hear their guns firing nor could we see the smoke from their rounds. Then for the next half-hour or so, the Skipper and the XO continued to yank the radio set from each other and call in their different coordinates. But it was all for naught. I could tell that they were becoming more frustrated by the minute. Their training at Quantico, Virginia, had never prepared them for anything like this. Meanwhile, it suddenly dawned upon me what had happened. I couldn't help it, but I started laughing so hard that my sides began to hurt.

Finally, the Skipper looked over at me and said, "Short, if you have anything intelligent to say just spit it out or keep your mouth shut."

Standing almost at attention and trying to keep a straight face, I replied, "Sir, there can only be one explanation. I don't think our helicopters landed us in the right spot."

I'll never forget the disgusted look on their faces, when they finally realized our predicament. For some reason, the helicopter pilots had gotten confused and had unloaded us quite a few miles away from our intended LZ. It took a little time and a lot of cussing on the part of everyone involved, before the Skipper finally got things squared away.

Later after humping through the countryside for a couple of more days, we finally reached the coordinates where we were supposed to have been originally landed. Since this operation had been a complete bust, it didn't surprise anyone when we were suddenly ordered to move out again. Along the way, everybody seemed to be feeling a little better, because most of us had caught up on our sleep. While operating in a non-threatening terrain like the open grasslands, I doubt if anybody had actually stayed awake and stood their nightly watches. The company lieutenants and sergeants tried their best to keep us awake, but we were just too exhausted.

Without a doubt, the infantry lieutenants in Vietnam had an incredibly tough job. By 1968, the majority of them were fresh out of

OCS (Officer's Candidate School), when they came to Vietnam. Averaging about twenty-four-years-old with four years of college under their belts, their training had been as inadequate as everyone else's. Forced to rely upon their platoon sergeants to pull them through, the more intelligent ones kept their mouths shut for awhile, until they got their feet on the ground. Yet from the very first day, they were expected to lead their platoons into combat situations without any regard for their personal safety. While constantly being pressured by the company commanders to perform their missions, they were expected to accomplish these missions without really knowing the people around them or the layout of the local terrain. Even under the best of circumstances, it must have been an overwhelming experience to find themselves responsible for the lives and welfare of thirty or so kids while in the middle of a no-win situation. Caught between the demands of producing a high body count and the hopes of getting their people home in one piece, they were obligated to make life-and-death decisions, knowing full well that they were liable get everybody killed by making just one little mistake. As forgotten and unsung heroes, they also represented the best that America had to offer.

It must have been around Christmas time when we were loaded onto some trucks and driven next to an area filled with sandy dunes. Dumped out in the middle of nowhere, we spent the rest of the day sitting next to a road and soaking up the sun's rays. What we didn't realize at the time was that it was going to be one of the most grueling and infuriating nights of our military lives.

Just as the sun was beginning to set behind the mountains, we were ordered to saddle up and move out. Forming a line with ten-foot intervals between each other, we began to meander our way through a section of old rice paddies, which led to a vast area filled with sand dunes. It wouldn't have been so bad except for the fact that we had been told that our objective was only a couple of hours away. Thus we went trekking off into hinterlands believing it was going to be an easy hump. And it probably would have been too, if the Skipper hadn't gotten us lost. Somewhere in the darkness, he must have zigged when he should have zagged. Or quite possibly, the trucks had dropped us off at the wrong spot, just like the helicopters did. But whatever the reason, we found ourselves struggling over, through, and around those damn sand dunes from dusk to dawn.

Soaked in sweat and covered in sand, the load on our backs quickly became heavier and heavier as our formation disintegrated into a disorganized mass of highly pissed-off individuals. We couldn't see anything in the darkness, so it was almost impossible for us to stay on our feet. Due to the uneven terrain, everyone was constantly losing his balance and falling to the ground at least every few feet. In fact, there wasn't a rifle or a machine gun among us that could have fired a round, because the chambers were literally packed with sand.

Throughout the ordeal, we just held on to the guy in front of us for dear life. Being so overburdened with equipment, our boots began shifting through the sand like a person trying to walk through loose gravel. With every painful step, the ground would give way to where we had to lengthen our strides just to keep up. For hour after miserable hour, we continued to plunge our way through the night without having any idea as to our destination. Meanwhile, everybody was moaning and cussing so loudly that we could have been heard from miles around. Several of the guys just quit walking altogether when the pain in their legs had become too unbearable. Amid all the confusion and anger, they had to be half-carried by their buddies through what seemed like an endless stretch of sand dunes. Then just when we thought that we had reached our destination, the order was given to get off our asses and move out again.

Looking back, I've walked over every kind of terrain there is in two different continents and in almost every kind of weather. But I have never experienced the physical hardship and mental frustration we endured that night. It was the type of experience that can change a fellow's perception about himself. For when a young infantryman discovers that he has a breaking point and that he is not invincible, he will begin to understand his limitations and those of the men around him. Like it or not, his fearless and confident world will never be the same again.

After reaching the outskirts of a small village, we could see the dawn was just beginning to break over the horizon. Completely exhausted from our ordeal, we didn't even bother digging any foxholes. Everyone just collapsed on the ground like a sack of potatoes. I must have slept for five or six hours straight, before I was finally awakened by voices. Raising myself up to one elbow, I overheard several of the guys tell their squad leader to go screw himself, after he had ordered them to wake up and stand watch. Being a sensible fellow, I guess that he decided not to make an issue of it, because I didn't hear any further discussion. As far as I could tell, everybody in the company had quit the war that day and had decided to get some sleep. Even Red, the hard charging, no-nonsense NCO, was stretched out across the ground and snoring to the high heavens.

Later that evening as one of our M-48 tanks drove up to the perimeter, our lieutenant informed us that we were in the middle of an operation to assist a South Vietnamese Army unit. The plan was actually quite simple. The purpose behind our horrendous night march had been to sneak up and surround this village, which was supposed to be controlled by the VC. Then once we had the villagers completely cut off from the rest of the world, the ARVNs were to enter the hamlet the very next day and flush out the surprised enemy. It was the first and only "Cordon and Search Mission," I would ever have the displeasure of conducting. Anyway, I would have had more faith in the plan, if we hadn't carried out our assignment like a bunch of amateurs. Only a deaf man could have missed our approach that night.

Then as we set up our perimeter around the village, we were given the strangest instructions. Instead of forming a line around an area and defending the inside of the perimeter, we had to alternate our firing positions so that we could defend ourselves in two different directions. As I was watching the area outside of our perimeter and away from the village, the guys in the foxholes on either side of my position were supposed to watch the village itself. From where I was sitting, our perimeter was so thin that the enemy could have overrun a large section of it without any difficulty. Many of the older guys were concerned about this possibility and openly complained to Red, but it didn't bother me. After being in the bush for so long, I understood that the enemy just couldn't attack a position at a moment's notice. Much like every other army in the world, it required some time for them to recon the area, form a plan, and gather their troops before they could make an assault. Thus as long as we were bouncing around from area to area, I felt comfortable about the relative safety of our perimeters. But on the other hand, whenever we spent a week or so in the same spot, the hairs on the back of my head would begin to stand up on end in anticipation of an enemy attack.

Then one bright afternoon as I was talking to Red, M&M, and Huff, the distinctive rip from an AK-47 suddenly rattled from the bushes to our immediate front. As the deadly rounds flew by our heads, we instantly dove into the nearby foxholes. With an M-48 tank positioned to our left, I couldn't figure out why a lone VC would shoot at us with one of our tanks sitting only two hundred feet away. Nevertheless as we began to return fire, I could see the tank's fifty-caliber machine gun erupt into a stream of flying tracers and well-placed lead. Within seconds, the bushes had been blown into twigs as the AK fell silent. After getting to our feet and brushing ourselves off, everybody began joking with each other about how lucky we had been for not being blown away. M&M commented that one of the rounds had come so close to his head that he had actually seen his life flash before his eyes.

Responding with his usual sarcastic wit, Huff replied, "I bet that resembled a cartoon."

It must have been about ten minutes later, when we discovered why this knucklehead had shot at us without any regard for our tank. While we were standing there discussing our good fortune with an ARVN interpreter, an old Vietnamese woman approached our group with a rake in one hand and a blanket in the other. She asked the interpreter in a teary eyed manner, if she could recover the remains of her young grandson. She said that he had disobeyed her wishes and decided to avenge his father's death. Apparently, his father had recently been killed while serving with a VC battalion near Hue. With the Skipper's approval, she slowly walked over to the bushes while wailing in her grief and began to rake what was left of him into the blanket.

The kid was about thirteen years old and way too young to know what he was doing. Similar to Danny (Danh) at Cam Le Bridge, he had jumped into the fray without first learning how to survive. By failing to properly recon the area before he had opened fire, he had unknowingly signed his own death warrant. Of course at this point of the war, I couldn't feel any remorse for the kid. I had seen too many people get themselves killed by doing something stupid. If I had learned anything in Vietnam, it was that the world's dumb-asses were always the first to go.

By the beginning of January of 1969, I had been surviving in the bush in Vietnam for almost a year. I was physically worn down, mentally exhausted, and emotionally drained. As far as I could tell, it was just a matter of time before my number came up. I had been shot at by every weapon in the enemy's arsenal, harassed by countless NCOs, and exposed to every kind of jungle disease known to man. It was at this point that I had decided to do something about my situation. Instead of letting the Marine Corps lead me around by my nose, I made the choice of signing up for another tour of duty. This was not a patriotic act on my part, nor did I believe that my continued presence in Vietnam would bring us victory. On the contrary, it was a calculated act of survival and nothing more.

During my visits to the rear area, I had discovered from the various company clerks that if a fellow re-upped to serve another tour of duty, he would not only receive an extra thirty-day leave, but he could also select his next duty assignment as well. Not being a complete idiot, I knew that meant living in one of the rear areas, where an ex-grunt like me could get three hot meals a day and a cot. After telling the other guys in my squad what I had done, every one of them thought I was crazy. But I knew exactly what I was doing. Besides getting out of the bush a month early, along with going home for a whole month, I figured that I could sign on with some Marine Air Wing unit in the Da Nang area and sit out the war in comfort. And besides, I had already paid my dues.

Before my paperwork was processed, we were choppered back to the Laotian border in preparation for *Operation Dewey Canyon West*, which was conducted from late January to March of 1969. The 9th Marine Regiment had been ordered to clear out the Da Krong Valley in the southwest corner of Quang Tri Province. We were located just north of the A Shau Valley, where the 101st Airborne had been fighting the NVA regulars. It was our Division Commander's intention to build a series of firebases leading into the valley itself. Then once our unit had established itself along the ridgelines, the plan called for another battalion to make a major sweep through the valley floor, while blocking an important enemy infiltration route. Luckily though, I didn't have to participate in this operation, because my orders had come through and I had already been flown back to the rear area. However, before I was sent home, I would spend a couple of harrowing weeks in an area north of the Da Krong Valley.[1]

Descending from the hazy clouds, our helicopter suddenly made a sharp turn in the direction of our LZ. As I gazed out the window, the surrounding terrain looked incredibly thick and foreboding in the morning light. The jungle blanketing the mountain ridges was so dense that it reminded me of the pictures I had seen as a kid of the

African tropical forests. The vegetation extended over the entire rocky area like a thick green rug.

Just as I was checking my rifle, I heard Roger yell out over the whine of the CH-46 rotors, "Damn it to hell, here we go again."

Without any warning, the chopper instantly hit the ground making a loud thud, and knocking us to our knees. Then all of a sudden, the crew chief started screaming at us to stand up and get out the hell of his helicopter. Scrambling towards the end of the ramp, the guys in front of me instantly stopped in their tracks. In his haste, the pilot had apparently landed us short of the LZ. We discovered to our horror that the ramp was extended over a cliff, overlooking an eight-foot drop-off. Knowing we were in a dangerous situation, I yelled for everyone to throw his packs and equipment over the cliff. Then once we had ejected our gear, I sat down on the edge of the ramp and jumped onto the red dirt. With the others following suit, it took a few minutes, but everybody finally made it to the ground.

As we were in the middle of collecting our gear, Red yelled at me to take two of the guys up an adjoining knoll and secure the area. Motioning to Roger and to a black guy named Wills to follow me, I began to lead the way up the incline. Within minutes, we came across several freshly used trails leading up the slope. Since I didn't want to walk into an ambush, I directed everyone to move around the knoll and away from the trails. The idea was to climb the slope and reach the top of the knoll from another direction.

At this point, our helicopters were still landing in the LZ, when we finally reached the crest. To our amazement, the knoll was literally covered with Marine gear from a previous firefight. There were helmets, flak jackets, and old canteens scattered everywhere. Then on one of the trails leading away from the LZ, we discovered something that sent cold shivers up my spine. Propped up on a stick, the enemy had placed one of our flak jackets next to a pathway with a sign on it that read, "Welcome to Death Vally."

Feeling uneasy about our situation, I told Roger and Wills to stay put, while I checked out the surrounding area. Slowly moving across the knoll and down the reverse slope, I came across an old NVA bunker complex. As far as I could tell, it hadn't been occupied in months. Then something happened to me that I had learned to respect and heed over the previous year: the hairs on the back of my head suddenly began to stand up and bristle. Sensing that I had been caught right in the middle of doing something really stupid, I quickly turned around and hauled ass back up to the knoll. Luckily, Roger and Wills were patiently waiting there for me, when I ran up to them and quietly muttered, "Follow me." Not being the type of guys who ignored the obvious, they looked at each other for a second, and then followed me back to the LZ.

Later that night, after we had marched for most of the day and had made camp on another mountaintop, Roger kept asking me what I had seen that morning. I couldn't really explain it to him, because it was more of a feeling than anything I had actually observed. Ever mindful of my surroundings while I was in the bush, I had learned to trust my instincts. Instead of relying upon the intelligence reports or especially what I had been told by my superiors, I approached every assignment as if I could communicate with the jungle. I came to believe that if one actually listened to it and respected its presence, the jungle would tell them everything they needed to know. This was something I couldn't communicate to another person. But I had instinctually known that while I was standing there looking at the old bunker complex, I was being watched and fitted for a body bag.

As a young fighting man, I was never motivated or dedicated enough to lead a charge up a hill or victoriously overcome a stubborn enemy position as my forefathers had done on Iwo Jima or the beaches of Normandy. Slashing my way through a wave of enemy soldiers with a bayonet in my teeth or rushing a machine-gun nest with a grenade in each hand just wasn't my style. In fact, I don't believe it was anyone's style, except maybe in the mind of the Hollywood producers. During my time in Southeast Asia, I had learned fairly quickly that one's aggressiveness could definitely be fatal. The fact that we weren't fighting on American soil also put a damper on any heroic desires that I might have possessed. Whoever said, "The closer to home an army fights, the better they fight," definitely said a mouthful.

Yet when it came to defending myself, I could be extremely deadly. I took it as a personal affront whenever someone tried to kill me. In my mind, I intended to go down swinging and to hell with becoming a POW. On any given day, I was liable to shoot first and ask questions later. If it happened to be at night, it was always wise to avoid my foxhole altogether. On more than one occasion, instead of coming by my hole to see if I was all right, Red would just call out to me in the darkness and then throw some more ammo or food in my direction, much like throwing raw meat to a caged tiger. I was likely to kill the very people who were trying to feed me.

One starry night as I was on watch, I sat in my foxhole listening to the various noises. Sure enough around two o'clock in the morning, I began to hear the distinct sounds of movement to my front. Peering down the slope, I couldn't really see anything until I noticed a shadow gradually moving. Under normal circumstances, I would have thrown a grenade and caught hell the next morning for jumping at shadows. But on this occasion, I wanted to do things differently.

Slowly reaching down, I picked up a rock and hurled it down at them. Within seconds of it hitting the ground, I could see two bushy figures scurrying down the slope because they thought I had thrown a live grenade. I must admit that I was impressed by their ability to get out of the area without making a lot of noise. It seemed as if they glided over the terrain like a pair of graceful deer.

About thirty minutes later, they started working their way up the slope again. Camouflaged with twigs and brush, I was able to observe them this time, because I had been watching the bushes, instead of the exposed areas. Inching their way from tree to tree, they moved ever so slowly. The only sounds I could hear were the occasional cracking of a twig. Then just as they were about fifty feet away from our perimeter, I tossed another rock. Once again, they were forced to scurry down the slope as quietly as possible. Only this time, they made a lot more noise than they did before.

It must have been right before dawn when they made their third and final trip up the slope. As before, they slowly crept their way around the trees and alongside the bushes. Suddenly, my hands began to tremble. In my exhilaration, I sensed that I had these guys right where I wanted them. For most of the night, they had been resolute in their efforts to reach my hole without being seen. Thus I reasoned they weren't about to be put off again by another trick. So instead of throwing another rock at them, I threw a live grenade.

Of course, the blast woke everyone up around the perimeter and Red was mad as hell. But after we had ventured down the slope later that morning and spotted a couple of blood trails, he became almost apologetic. But I really didn't care about what Red thought. I felt good inside. I had beaten the enemy at their own game. It was moments like these that made being a Marine very rewarding. I had outsmarted some of the best soldiers in the world.

Then one unforgettable evening in mid-January as I was adding fresh camouflage around my bunker, I heard a chopper overhead landing in our LZ. I didn't think anything about it, so I continued about my business. Then out of the blue, I suddenly heard Red's voice screaming out my name from atop the hill. Looking up, I couldn't hear him very well above the roar of the helicopter.

Then after he moved farther down the slope, I finally heard him yell out, "Short, your orders for home have come through. If you want to make it back to Quang Tri tonight, you had better hurry. This is the last chopper we'll see for a few days."

For a second, I just stood there completely stunned. His words had echoed in my ears, but I didn't believe what I was hearing. I had dreamed of this moment for almost a year. But I always had my doubts that I would survive long enough to hear them. Then after realizing that I wasn't hallucinating, I decided to act before he changed his mind. In one quick motion, I reached down, grabbed my rifle with the rest of my gear and took off like a streak of lightning.

As I was running up to the LZ, my adrenaline was pumping so hard, it felt as if my heart was about to explode. Regrettably, I didn't get a chance to say goodbye to any of the fellows. Once I had reached the LZ, I was so determined to get out of there that I didn't even stop to shake Red's hand. I just sprinted into the back of the waiting helicopter and stuck my head out the window as it lifted off the ground.

Waving like a maniac, I screamed above the roar of the engines, "Adios, you poor bastards and good luck."

Strangely, I was the only passenger sitting in this huge CH-46 helicopter. There was something symbolic about the whole scene. It was as if I was the only one left from the kids who had initially had come to Vietnam with me the year before. The odds were very high that most of them had gotten either wounded, drenched in Agent Orange, or sent home in a body bag. As I sat there all alone, I was suddenly engulfed in a wave of emotions. The tears ran down my cheeks as I realized my family wouldn't have to bury another son and that I could actually think in terms of a future again. While shivering from the cold air and cradling my rifle on my lap, I just couldn't believe how fortunate I had been during the last year. I had not only survived the bush during the height of the war, but had also not even gotten a scratch. No doubt about it, I had been truly blessed.

As usual, the NCOs were standing in line waiting to make my life as miserable as possible. Within minutes of landing in Quang Tri, this creepy-looking sergeant told me to report to the Battalion Aid Station for duty. He said that they wanted me to haul out a bunch of garbage and mop the floors. But instead of arguing with the guy, I just walked in the front entrance of the hospital and then walked out the back door. I figured what the hell was he going do about it, send me to Vietnam.

Later that night while having a few dozen beers at the club, I overheard someone say that I could catch a vintage World War II Naval LST operating out of the Cua Vet River and sail down to Da Nang. Unknown to me, the U.S. Navy had been routinely transporting supplies up from Da Nang to the DMZ ever since 1966. While sailing in the South China Sea, our ships were able to move up and down the coastline without any fear of being attacked as long as they kept away from the beach. Having a few days to kill before my flight left for Okinawa, I thought that it would be a good opportunity for me to see how the Navy lived.

After I hitchhiked to Dong Ha, I didn't have any problem getting another ride and finding the Navy's launching site located next to the river. To my surprise, there was an LST in the middle of unloading its cargo when I approached an officer and asked him for a ride. I must have been quite a sight being underweight and dressed in extremely worn battle fatigues. Nevertheless, he responded in a friendly manner, "anytime Marine."

From the very instant I walked on board, the crew treated me as if I was one of their own. They went out of their way to make sure that I was given a good meal and a comfortable place to sleep. As a group, they were older than the average grunt and obviously more knowledgeable. Fascinated about the stories they had heard concerning the ground war, several of the crewmembers drilled me with all kinds of questions for least a couple of hours. They kept asking me about living conditions in the bush, the enemy, and the war in general. For me, it was a lot of fun, because I was able to express my opinion to a group of fellows who actually wanted to know something about my experiences.

Yet what I really enjoyed about the trip was when one of the seamen took me up to the ship's helm and let me steer the ship for awhile. Heading in a southerly direction, he showed me how to navigate the ship and use the radar to avoid the other ships in the area. Between the gentle rocking of the waves and the smell of the saltwater, I began to understand why someone would want to sail the seven seas. There was a feeling of unbridled freedom that swept over me as I peered off into the endless horizon. Then all of a sudden, I noticed a huge island off to my left. At the time, I didn't remember there being an island off the coast of Quang Tri Province. So, I asked the seaman, "What's the name of that island?" As he was taking a puff from his cigarette, he responded, "That's the *U.S.S. New Jersey.* The only commissioned battleship in the world today."

Awestruck by its size, I had never seen anything like it. It looked like a floating city surrounded by huge guns, anti-aircraft emplacements, and radio antennas. In my excitement, I asked the seaman if we could change course and get a little closer for a better look. He just smiled and said, "You don't want to be anywhere near that monster when it fires those sixteen-inch guns. The concussion alone could capsize us or at least make us sterile." Needless to say, I didn't argue with the guy.

After arriving in Da Nang, I spent a couple of days hanging around Freedom Hill, and in particular, the infamous beer garden. The sky was clear, the air was cool, and I was on top of the world waiting to go home. Then one afternoon while I was sitting there having a few beers, an incident took place, which was indicative of my attitude and that of the other grunts in Vietnam towards the average South Vietnamese soldier.

Earlier that day, I had run across another buddy from my boot camp days. During his tour of duty, he had been assigned to the Military Police in the Da Nang area. He had spent the previous year manning roadblocks and arresting drunk and disorderly Marines. Anyway, as we were enjoying ourselves exchanging war stories, an ex-South

Vietnamese Army soldier hobbled up to us using a pair of crutches. Not being able to speak our language, he handed us a note in English, which stated that he was a father of five and that he had stepped on a booby trap while serving his country in the Central Highlands. Unable to earn a decent living, his note requested that we make a small contribution towards his family's welfare.

As far as I could tell, it must have been one hell of a booby trap. He had a leg, an arm, and an eye missing, along with four fingers from his remaining hand. Without even blinking, my buddy pulled out a five-dollar bill in government currency from his wallet and then handed it to the guy. Gratefully, the ex-soldier took his money and then looked up at me with an expression of utter humiliation. Clearly, the guy was ashamed of having been reduced to begging for a living. He had a look about him of once being a very capable fellow. But instead of giving him any money, I just stared into his tormented eyes and told him in so many words to go screw himself.

Turning around and hobbling away, he didn't say a word. He just limped down the road with his head low. Then my buddy finally broke the silence by saying, "Man, you're one hard-core son-of-a-bitch."

As I motioned for another beer, I emotionally replied to him, "To hell with these South Vietnamese. If they were worth a damn, we wouldn't even be here."

Chapter Thirteen

Around the World in Thirty Days

"When a nation participates in a war, justified or not, the dissenters will always be looked upon as the enemy."

After taking a couple of boring days to fly across the Pacific Ocean, I finally landed at Love Field in Dallas, Texas. As I unfastened my seat belt, I didn't have any idea who was going to be there to meet me. Deep down inside, I was hoping to see a lot of smiling faces waiting to give me a big hug. I figured between all the people I had grown up with, including my family and our friends, I was expecting quite a crowd. And if they were half as excited as I was about my return, we were going to have one hell of a reunion.

Regrettably though, things didn't work out as I had envisioned. As I walked down the ramp, the only people there to meet me were my mother and an old friend of mine named Rusty Dixon. Mom was grinning from ear to ear while Rusty looked as if he had been up for most of the night. Almost in a state of shock by what I considered a lack of appreciation for my efforts the past year, I gave my mother a big hug and a kiss, and then I feebly shook Rusty's hand.

As we made our way through the bustling crowd to retrieve my luggage, my excitement over being home quickly turned into a mixture of confusion, disappointment, and outright rage. With every step I took, I could feel the anger and resentment swell up within me like a time bomb. I just couldn't believe that all the people I had grown up with hadn't cared enough about me to even show up at the airport. I realized that I had been involved with an increasingly unpopular war, but I couldn't see what that had to do with my coming home. Hell, I was barely nineteen years old. It wasn't as if I knew anything about politics. So I finally broke down and asked my mother why no one else had showed up to greet me. It took a few minutes before she replied in so many words that everybody was either too busy that day or they had something better to do.

Hurt by her paltry reply, I didn't know how to respond. Then while Rusty and I were putting my luggage into the trunk of his car, he whispered something to me that only added to my confusion.

"Greg, you decided to go back to that place. Your family and friends have spent the last year living in constant fear and dread over whether or not you were even going to survive. Then you turn around and decide to put everybody through another year of living hell."

It wasn't until years later that I would come to understand what Rusty was trying to tell me. It had never dawned on me and possibly the other veterans in Vietnam what our presence there was doing to our loved ones back home. We were so engrossed in trying to survive and fight the war that it had never occurred to many of us the level of suffering our loved ones had to endure. On a personal level, I hadn't been able to comprehend the pain and anguish they had been experiencing during my absence. All I could see and feel at the time was a total disregard on their part for the sacrifices I had made for them and for my country.

Before we had even gotten out of the airport parking lot, I was ready to go back to Vietnam. I felt like a fellow who had lost his home and didn't know which way to turn. Although Vietnam was quickly becoming a national tragedy, at the least I felt needed and appreciated there. Looking back, I didn't really understand what was going on around me at home, except that I felt deeply betrayed by my own people.

Over the stretch of time, I have come to believe that the majority of the average citizens were profoundly indifferent about the welfare of the fighting men and women who had served in the Vietnam War. They certainly couldn't have cared less about the hundreds of thousands of innocent civilians who were killed along the way. Unless a family had been directly touched by having a loved one involved, the American people as a whole were more involved with their daily lives, than they were with the death and destruction that was occurring ten thousand miles away.

During World War II there were war taxes, shortages, rationing, and celebrity war bond drives that had helped unite us through our sacrifices and our commitment to victory. However, the war in Vietnam didn't demand any form of personal sacrifice or a commitment to victory on the part of most of the civilian population. Akin our Korean War experience, our government had refused to declare a state of national emergency and put our economy on a wartime footing. Instead, the government chose to borrow the money in the form of a national debt, so that the American public wouldn't have to endure the hardships of paying higher taxes or to suffer the shortages of rationing foodstuffs and gasoline. The result was that as long as our American citizenry didn't have to immediately foot the bill or bear the burden of shortages, they could be expected to turn a blind eye to whatever country our government had decided to militarily control.

In a very real sense, the American people didn't appreciate or recognize the sacrifices made by their country's servicemen and women, because nothing had really changed for them during the war. In their minds, the wars in Vietnam and later in the Middle East were distant, impersonal events that would be eventually paid for by the next generation.

As soon as we got home, I went straight to the bathroom to take a bath. I wanted to soak in some hot water for awhile and then medicate my sores. While I was in the middle of taking off my clothes, my mother suddenly came through the door to bring me a fresh towel and some medication for my ringworms. Since she hadn't seen me for quite a while, she shrieked in disbelief and horror. Apart from being about thirty pounds underweight and looking like a sack of bones, my body was literally covered in gook sores, scabs, abrasions, and ringworm rashes. In fact, I had been living in the filthy jungle for so long, my toenails were completely black from the grime and there were infected lesions all over my scalp. Overcome by my appearance, she gently lay down the towel and began to sob as she left the room. Meanwhile, I remember yelling out to her that it looked a lot worse than it really was.

While I was sitting on the edge of the tub, I began to gingerly smear medicine all around my crotch and up and down my legs. Hesitating for a second, I wondered aloud if this stuff would burn on contact. Then I began to tell her while she stood in the hallway about how the corpsmen in Vietnam had used a form of acid to kill the ringworms, which was not a very pleasant experience. However she assured me that this stuff was different and that she wouldn't do anything in the world to hurt me.

Encouraged by her concern, I continued to put the medicine on my rashes and sores. Then immediately after setting the tube aside, I began to feel an all-too-familiar burning sensation. Within seconds, it felt as if I was being branded by a red-hot iron. While literally taking my breath away, I held onto my knees as the acid in the medicine seared its way down into my pores. Leaping to my feet, I began screaming every curse word in the book as I tried to wipe it off. But instead of removing the medicine, I was actually smearing it deeper into my skin.

In the hallway, Mom was running around in a panic. She didn't know what to do, so she ran to wake up my brother, David. Of course, there wasn't anything he could do about it either.

After getting out of bed, David stuck his head around the bathroom door with a big grin on his face and yelled out, "Hey, welcome home, Greg." Since neither one of them wanted to deal with me at that particular instant, they just stood outside the door and listened to my screams. Then as the pain began to subside, I hollered out to them, "Good gravy, Mom, what are you trying to do, kill me?"

Just like the American Indians' acts of self-mutilation during times of extreme stress and agony, the ensuing pain from the medicine had jolted me back to my senses. Remarkably any emotional distress that I had been feeling was quickly exorcised from my mind. All at once, my anger and confusion had been replaced with a renewed awareness that it was good to be alive, free of pain, and in one piece.

Then just when I thought that there wouldn't be any more surprises, I was blindsided by a succession of shock waves. After spending a few days in my old hangouts and talking with my old friends, it seemed that everything had changed. Sometime during 1968, my hometown had been turned upside down. Instead of the uptight, inflexible society I had come to know and love, I found it had been transformed into something completely different. In my absence, the old neighborhood where I had been raised and the schools that I had once attended had become fully integrated. Blacks were now free to go anywhere they wanted, and under the law, they could patronize and work in the white establishments. For rustic Fort Worth, Texas, this was a welcomed giant step towards civilization.

Moreover the females, God bless them, were walking around braless in their see-through blouses, and wearing mini-skirts. Many of the younger males had grown their hair long and were usually carrying a book around instead of a football. The movies were actually showing women's breasts and the actors were using four-letter-words, while the music was full of political rhetoric and revolution. And instead of passing the time drinking beer and shooting up the countryside with their shotguns, many of my old friends were getting high on marijuana and talking about peace and love.

Now personally, I didn't view any of these changes as earth shattering. Back in the bush, we had heard stories about the free love, the drugs, the flower children, and the college demonstrations. So I wasn't completely ignorant of them. Still and all, I couldn't believe my eyes. Even the old ass-kicking bullies who used to terrorize our neighborhoods were sitting around wearing beads and listening to folk music. The whole atmosphere had mellowed out to where it had become socially acceptable for an individual to be different. Even our ultraconservative barber, Mr. Crowder, had loosened up to the point where he had grown a pair of long sideburns.

Yet the most exciting thing that happened to me during my thirty-day leave was when my brother introduced me to the anti-war movement. At the time, I didn't have an opinion one way or another about the war. I did sense that something was terribly wrong with the conduct of the war, but I continued to believe that our government wouldn't lie to us for the sake of fulfilling their political and economic obligations to various special interests' groups. So I just went along with him in the hopes that I might run into some very appealing and hopefully lustful females.

It must have been shortly after my return, when David loaded up Mom, his wife, Chari, and me into his yellow Chevy and took us to an anti-war demonstration in downtown Fort Worth. The organizers had received a city permit to conduct the demonstration, so I figured it was okay for me to attend. I didn't really know what to expect, but the number and type of people who showed up did surprise me. Instead of a crowd of longhaired freaks looking for trouble, there were probably a couple of thousand people present with the vast majority of them being your typical working folks.

As we began marching down the main street, there were camera crews and reporters everywhere. They seemed intent on taking our pictures and interviewing anyone that would talk to them. Many of the marchers were carrying signs and some of them even began chanting anti-war slogans. While David was running all over the place trying to get the bystanders involved, I kept my mother and Chari within arm's length in case things got crazy. There were a few hecklers along the curb, but I really wasn't concerned about those guys creating a disturbance.

Ironically, I had discovered during this time period that the guys who screamed the loudest about kicking the VC's ass or who liked to proclaim, "America, love it or leave it," were the ones least likely to stand up to defend their country. Even today, the people who speak out the loudest and the most often about sending our troops into combat usually shut up, once I offer to take them to a Marine Corps recruiter.

Yet the ones that concerned me the most were the local police and law enforcement officers that lined the streets. Peering into their hard-set eyes, I could tell that many of them were not at all sympathetic to those in the anti-war movement. I also recognized that most of these guys had already served in the military and that they continued to believe in the war. I figured that if there was going to be any serious trouble, they were ones most likely to furnish it. Luckily though, they behaved as absolute professionals. Unlike what I had seen on television, they treated everyone with respect and went about their jobs like true peace officers. I remember that I was as proud of them as I was of the people who had the courage to march.

As far as I was concerned, the march had been a real learning experience. The energy it produced among the marchers and spectators was electrifying. For the first time, the people in north Texas had become aware of the growing opposition to our government's policies in Southeast Asia. Still in its infancy, the surging anti-war movement hadn't yet been infiltrated by the federal agencies working in Texas, so there weren't any strangers running around committing acts of violence in order to discredit the marchers in front of the national media. Just a few months afterward, David wrote me about several mysterious clean-cut fellows who had joined their little group and were desperately trying to steer the movement towards a violent confrontation with the local authorities. Sensing that something wasn't right, because my brother's group had intentionally formed themselves into a nonviolent movement, they ignored these morons in the hopes that they might go away.

Along with the many other social changes taking place, it had occurred to me that if the other cities in America were doing as well as my hometown, then the war in Vietnam was never going to end. There were just too many people enjoying the benefits of a booming economy. From what I could tell, everybody was on the payroll. The federal government was pouring money into Fort Worth with their huge contracts, which increased employment and helped convince the business community of the righteousness of its cause. The local colleges were brimming with students who were avoiding the draft, and thus there were plenty of jobs for the educators. Then the churches were deeply involved, while they comforted the grieving. Furthermore, the local police departments along with the legal system were having a field day trying to keep up with all the pot smokers, so they had a new lease on life. And finally, the national media had something important to report for a change, besides the never-ending coverage of sporting events, bizarre crimes, and irrelevant celebrities.

During my leave, I did my best to enjoy myself, but it was very difficult. Everything seemed upside down. Most of my old friends were either dodging the draft or they were already in Nam. My brother and his college buddies were trying to save the world from itself without any appreciable support from the average working stiff. Feeling out of place, I even called up and then took out several girls that I had known since high school in an effort to fit in. But it was all a waste of time. They were looking for a permanent relationship, while I was looking for something far less demanding.

Strangely though, Vietnam never left my thoughts. Even when I was having a good time, I would pause and wonder about the guys in the bush. In a way that I can't explain, I missed their comradeship and the struggles we had shared. Because there wasn't anyone that I could share these feelings with, I was forced to keep my thoughts to myself.

Just as I was getting used to being a civilian again, I found myself back on an airplane and headed back to Vietnam. The flight itself wasn't that bad, because I had become accustomed to long overseas trips. However, the plane was full of a group of guys who kept bothering me with their incessant questions about the bush. Knowing that there wasn't much I could tell them, I tried to keep to myself. Mostly, I just sat in my chair and worried about my next duty station. I knew that if I wasn't very careful in my selection, I could end up in another combat assignment. Due to my infantry specialty, there was a real possibility that some clerk would place me in a security outfit, permanently guarding a perimeter somewhere out in the boonies.

Right off the bat, I had already excluded the infantry, artillery, and MP units from my list of prospects. I might have been young and naive, but I wasn't going to stick my head back into the meat grinder again. Thus the only outfit that remained on my list was the 1st Marine Air Wing. They were responsible for maintaining and flying the Corps' helicopters and jet fighters. Yet I still had to be careful. The MAG (Marine Air Group) units were infamous for turning anyone who could pull a trigger into a helicopter door-gunner.

As luck would have it, the fortunes of war shone upon me. While I was in Okinawa, I ran into an old sergeant who had re-upped for the Air Wing. Back in 1966, he had discovered that it was the most laid-back and well-fed outfit that the United States Marine Corps had to offer. In fact, he had it so cushy that he was returning for his fourth tour of duty. Over a couple of beers, he kept telling me in a slurred voice not to forget the unit's designation, MWHG-1.

"That's the ticket, buddy, Marine Wing Headquarters Group One," he kept saying to me. "Even if you get stuck in the Security Platoon, they have the best mess hall and the nicest barracks in Vietnam. Hell, the Enlisted Men's Club is even air-conditioned with a separate room full of slot machines."

At the time, I didn't know how seriously to take this guy. For I all knew, MWHG could have meant, "Mine Warfare and Hand Grenades."

After I landed in Da Nang sometime in early March, I caught a ride to Freedom Hill. Instead of going directly to the transit building, I figured that I had a few hours to kill before I was supposed to report to the officer on duty. Strangely, as I was making my way up to the front gate, I noticed a crippled ex-South Vietnamese soldier was sitting by the side of the road with a set of crutches resting on his lap. I didn't know if he remembered me, but I sure remembered him. Ever since my first encounter with him at the beer garden a month before, when I had refused to give him any money, I had had second thoughts about my actions. Under certain circumstances, I could be a very ruthless and unforgiving fellow, but being cruel to someone was not part of my nature. As a man, I've tried to walk this earth with heart and an appreciation for everyone's suffering. So when I ran into this poor fellow again, I figured that it was God's way of reminding me who I really was as a human being.

To this day, I don't know if he understood my gesture or not. But it really didn't matter. All I knew was that I felt compelled to make amends. As I walked up to him, he suddenly looked up at me with his disfigured face. After reaching down and handing him about thirty bucks, I warmly shook his hand and thanked him for his sacrifices.

After enjoying a good meal and a few beers, I caught a ride heading back towards the airstrip. Along the way, I jumped off the truck on the road leading through the middle of Dog Patch. Lined with small businesses and tin shacks used as homes, I wanted to see if I could purchase a bottle of Jack Daniels from the black market. Normally, I wasn't a whiskey drinker, but I also wanted to check out the Vietnamese marketplace. Of course, the Military Police would have run me off if they had seen me there. But I figured what the hell. I knew that they wouldn't arrest me, unless I was in possession of some dope, which was a prospect that had never entered my mind.

Upon entering one shop, I noticed an old man and his wife sitting behind a small counter. They looked very old and used up. Glancing behind them, I could see their living quarters in the back of the shop. It appeared as if their furniture had been made from American material. Much of the wood was stamped, "U.S. Government Property." Then just as I was about to ask them about buying a bottle of Jack Daniels, a fellow came out of the back room and introduced himself to me as Pham. He was a typical looking middle-aged Vietnamese male, somewhat short in stature, lean, and muscular. However, he did speak excellent English.

"We don't get very many GIs in here. How can I help you?" he said with a broad smile.

"Well, I'm lookin' for a bottle of Jack Daniels. But I can see that you don't have any for sale," I said, after checking out their merchandise.

"Here, follow me to back room," he answered, "and I'll see what I can do for you."

I must have spent a good two hours talking to Pham about everything under the sun. Apparently, he had been raised a Catholic and taught the English language by the local nuns. He said his parents actually owned the shop, but that he still had to support them, because it didn't make them that much money. He also mentioned in a sad way that they had fled from North Vietnam with the rest of the Catholics in the late fifties. And that he had two brothers serving with the ARVNs and ironically a couple of cousins serving with the Viet Cong. From what I had gathered, he was involved in the black market up to his neck. Also I figured that he was probably working both sides of the fence.

Articulate and intelligent, he seemed genuinely interested in my opinions about the Vietnamese people and the war in general. This was a new experience for me, because hardly anyone back home had ever shown any interest in my opinions. Nevertheless, Pham didn't grill me about anything of military importance, as if I actually knew anything of value. On occasion, he would ask me something a little too personal or something about my year in the bush. I would just smile at him and continue the conversation without answering his question. He had a good-natured manner about him and we got along just great. Of course, I didn't trust him any more than he trusted me. But like two strangers wandering in the dark, we found enough common ground between us that it actually illuminated the moment.

Since he didn't have any Jack Daniels on hand, he offered to take me to a place where he could purchase it for me. I told him that sounded great, so he took me outside and we hopped onto his motor bike. While not realizing that I was doing something really stupid, we began motoring our way across Da Nang towards another small residential area near the docks. But along the way, it slowly began to dawn on me that this guy just might be handing me over to the VC for a price.

Here I was without a rifle and driving to God knows where as we careened our way around the maze of traffic. Being extremely pissed off at myself for not thinking very clearly, I removed my K-bar knife from my lower trousers that I had always kept in my boot for situations just like these. While cradling it under my arm, I had decided not to follow this guy any farther. It was my intention to pay for the booze and then get the hell out of Dodge.

After pulling up to the end of an alleyway situated between a row of houses, I suddenly jumped off the bike and told him that I would wait here for him. Appearing not at all suspicious of my behavior, he said, "No problem, I'll be back in a minute."

What neither of us had realized was that we had been followed. Almost immediately after Pham had taken off down the ally, an ARVN jeep with three men riding in it came zooming around the corner and continued to follow him. At the time, I didn't give it much thought. In fact, I was beginning to feel a little bit better about the situation, because he hadn't insisted that I go along with him.

Then as I lit a cigarette, I heard a loud bang from down the alleyway. Moving closer to the edge of the alley, I was almost hit by the ARVN jeep as it roared around the corner and disappeared down the street. Stunned for a minute, I stood there wondering what to do next. There weren't any people around and everything looked normal.

Throwing my cigarette away, I began to creep down the alley with my knife still tucked under my arm. I must have gone about twenty feet, when I came upon Pham's motor bike, parked next to a garage. Then lying only a few feet away in a puddle of blood and hair fragments was Pham. From what I could tell, he had been shot in the back of head at close range.

A sense of terror swept over me as I suddenly realized that I had been right in the middle of an assassination. I didn't know the reasons, but I definitely understood the method. And I had no intention of being a part of it. Quickly looking around to see if I had been observed by anyone, I stuffed my knife back into my trousers and began walking right on through the alleyway. Upon reaching the other end, I suddenly turned right and headed down the street as if nothing had happened. It took a little while, but I finally made my way to a major intersection, where I was able to hitch a ride.

To this day, I have often wondered about Pham and why the ARVNs had decided to do away with him. I have always thought that my first instinct about the guy was probably the correct one. He must have been working both sides of the fence, until someone had made the decision to clear the railing.

Soon afterwards, I showed up at the transit building in order to select my next duty station. Lined all along the wall were the designation symbols for each Marine unit in Vietnam. Then under each designation, an extremely bored-looking clerk was sitting at a table, waiting to process anyone assigned to that particular unit. While completely ignoring the 1st and 3rd Marine Divisions area, I wandered over to the table of the 1st Marine Air Wing. And sure enough, among the list of MAG and fixed-wing units, I spotted the designation MWHG-1. Upon inquiry, the clerk told me that the unit's compound was just down the road from where we were standing and that it was the mother of all rear areas. He also said that the place was full of brass (officers), but the chow was first rate and the living quarters were the best in I Corps.

Well, I didn't need to be struck by lightning to know a good deal when I saw one, so I signed on the dotted line. Within minutes, a skinny little corporal drove up in a jeep to take me to my new duty station. Located just north of the Da Nang airstrip and a mile or so south of Freedom Hill, the square-shaped compound had been built on an old rice paddy that extended out beyond the eastern side of the perimeter. On the western side was a collection of Vietnamese homes that couldn't have been more than ten feet from our barracks. In fact, they were so close to our perimeter that we could literally look over into their living rooms from our windows. Then to the north, a major road ran along the edge of the perimeter with a row of businesses lining the opposite side of the street. I was told that they sold everything from burial candles to Coca-Colas. Like the Marine transit building next to the airstrip, the compound was positioned directly in the line of fire of any incoming enemy rockets that were launched from the VC-infested Happy Valley. If there were any short rounds, the odds were very good that they were going to be landing in our vicinity. But what the hell, I wasn't going to let a few rockets scare me off.

Surrounded by a wall of barbed wire and numerous bunkers, the compound wasn't that large. The adobe-like barracks for the enlisted men formed an arc just inside the fence, thus shielding the commanding general's house and his personal dining hall from any outside onlookers. Adjacent to the Enlisted Men's Club was a group of one-story office buildings that housed the various departments within the Headquarters Group. Then positioned all around a small parade ground in the middle of the compound were an assortment of buildings consisting of medical, accounting, dental, and supply offices. As we drove to the Personnel Building, the first thing I noticed was that everybody was wearing starched uniforms and saluting each other. Oddly enough, they were all decked out in brand-new camouflage utilities and jungle boots, gear that hadn't been available to the grunts in the field. If I hadn't known any better, I would have sworn that I was back in the States. The entire area was covered in palm trees, flower beds, and manicured lawns. In some ways, it reminded me of a middle-class country club.

Undeniably, I didn't feel at all comfortable about my new surroundings. Being a ground-pounder at heart, I just wasn't used to all this spit and polish. Everybody seemed to be more involved with keeping his boots clean and saluting everybody, than with fighting a war. But before I had even gotten out of the jeep, I could tell that these guys operated by a completely different set of rules than I was used to following. The thought of keeping one's rifle clean, constantly changing one's socks, or preparing oneself to move out on a moment's notice was the furthest thing from their minds. Their world was one of exchanging memos, following the proper procedures, impressing the right people, and collecting souvenirs to mail home.

Then just as I was beginning to think that I had made the worst decision of my life, the heavens opened up and threw another piece of good fortune my way. Looking up from his cluttered desk, an over-weight sergeant in the Personnel Office asked me if I knew anything about Special Services.

Thinking that he was referring to a Special Forces unit, I replied, "Are those the guys who wear them funny little hats and think they know everything under the sun?"

The sergeant just grinned at me and with a stroke of a pen, he assigned me to one of the most nonessential outfits in Vietnam. Then after checking in to my assigned barracks and meeting my mama-san, who would clean my clothes, shine my boots, and make my bed on a daily basis for a small monthly fee, I went down to meet the guys in my new unit.

Instead of being a highly trained elite force capable of operating and fighting in any type of terrain, Special Services had been formed in order to provide a variety of entertainment and recreational activities to the guys in the rear areas. As far as contributing to the war effort, it certainly wasn't the most indispensable outfit in Vietnam, but it was one of the choicest. Consisting of four officers, four staff NCOs, and about fifteen enlisted men, we operated out of a large warehouse situated just south of the compound near MAG-11. On a daily basis, everyone would meet there in the mornings for muster and then go to his assigned job.

For those of us working in the warehouse, it was our responsibility to issue an assortment of baseball equipment, basketballs, footballs, volleyballs, table games, and playing cards to whoever filled out the appropriate paperwork. Along with taking the inventory and keeping the place clean, we were also expected to drive civilian bands from club to club during the evenings or help the Officer's Mess throw a party. Then working in the back of the warehouse, during the nights, was an old Korean fellow named Kim, who had been contracted by the U.S. government to repair the servicemen's television sets, radios, recorders, and such. Besides being a really intelligent fellow, the thing that I remember the most about him was his motorcycle. It was a 350cc Honda that looked like it had been juiced up.

All in all, I couldn't have been luckier. Working just eight hours a day, six days a week, it was like a regular job. I didn't have to sweat standing any more of those nightly watches or lying around in the mud on ambushes.

Unbelievably, several of the more fortunate fellows in Special Services had been assigned to manage their own retail stores. Constructed near the warehouse was an air-conditioned building that housed a combination music store, golf shop, and a fishing equipment outlet of all things. Almost exclusively patronized by the wing's officers and staff NCOs, the stores did a brisk business in selling expensive fishing gear, radios, and sets of golf clubs. At the time, I knew that the rear area was a cushy place to work, but I had no idea an outfit like this had even existed. As a person fully aware of the conditions in the field, I was somewhat confused and flabbergasted by all the excess. I could understand the purpose behind having a Special Service unit, but I just couldn't understand why any group of people would want to spend their money on golf clubs. It wasn't as if they could go out and play the back nine at Khe Sanh.

But what really blew me away was when I heard what the rest of the guys in the outfit did for a living. No doubt about it, Chesty Puller would have rolled over in his grave. Apparently, it was the responsibility of several of the guys to take a group of officers or staff NCOs out into the nearby bay and go deep-sea fishing every morning. Referred to as the Rod and Reel Patrol, they had to get up before dawn each morning and pack several ice chests full of beer, gas up two bass boats, and then put together a dozen box lunches. Then once they had everything organized, they would pull their boats down to the landing site and wait for their clientele to arrive.

On any given day, they could be seen taking about six or seven people out into the bay and fishing until mid-afternoon or until they had drunk themselves into oblivion. Since the senior staff NCO in charge had been ordered to avoid the beaches, they usually spent their days fishing between two anchored vessels out in the bay. As far as serving one's country goes, I couldn't think of a better way to do it. From what I could tell, the biggest problem they faced was either running out of beer or getting too sunburned.

For a variety of reasons, my new unit commander, who was a relatively young full bird colonel in the reserves, didn't like grunts. Almost every day, he would have the master sergeant jump down my throat over something trivial. So instead of making matters worse, I did whatever I could to get on his good side. If there was a shit detail to be undertaken, I usually stood up and volunteered without asking any questions.

Fortuitously, I was able to befriend two grunts from the Security Platoon. One of them was a guy from Illinois named Wesley. Tall, slender, and charismatic, he had spent his first tour of duty with the 5th Marines as a machine gunner. After participating in the Battle of Hue, what was left of his unit would spend the next year fighting in and among the coastal villages. From the moment we ran into each other, we got along fabulously. In between guzzling down beers and constantly combing his well-groomed hair, he loved to talk about the women and their mysterious ways. Priding himself on being a ladies' man, he used to say that there wasn't a woman under sixty years old that he couldn't talk out of her underwear.

The other fellow was an aspiring young gangster from New York City named Gino. After being raised in the Bronx and going through boot camp at Parris Island, he ended up serving with the 7th Marines. His outfit had operated in and around the rice paddies until he was about the only one left from his original group. Being of medium height, stocky, and strong as a bull, he was two hundred pounds of muscle. Come to think about it, he looked just like the boxer Rocky Marciano. His dream was to run the rackets in New Jersey one day.

He was forever talking about embezzling someone out of his money or highjacking a load down at the La Guardia or Newark Airports. The thing I remember the most about Gino was that he was one crazy fellow. If he wasn't trying to pick a fight with somebody, he was looking for trouble.

During one unforgettable occasion, Gino was slugging it out with a guy named Frankie behind the Enlisted Men's Club over something profoundly insignificant and stupid. Then all of a sudden, someone came out of the darkness and attempted to break them up. Wesley and I had been sitting next to a garbage can drinking a beer and enjoying the fight, when this stranger leaped in between them and started screaming, "For God's sakes, men, we're in the middle of a war."

With Gino being somewhat intoxicated, he yelled back at the stranger, "no shit, asshole." Then he leaned back and threw a wild punch at Frankie's head. To our surprise, Frankie unexpectedly ducked and Gino's fist came around and knocked the stranger out cold as a cucumber.

Everyone, including Frankie, thought it was funny as hell. After Gino's fist had slammed into the stranger's glass jaw, the poor fellow had dropped to the ground as if he had been shot through the head. Then as we staggered over to take a closer look at this guy sprawled out in the dirt, we couldn't believe our eyes. For several seconds, we just stood there numb and uncertain as to what to do next. The fear was almost paralyzing. Evidently in all of the excitement, Gino had knocked out one of the wing's chaplains. Looking at the possibility of serving several years in the brig for hitting an officer and a gentleman, we hauled ass back to our barracks before the guy could regain consciousness.

The very next day the base commander conducted a lineup for all the enlisted men in the compound. The chaplain and an investigating officer went through every unit looking for the culprits. While the officer was checking for bruised knuckles, the chaplain tried to see if he could identify his assailants. As luck would have it, Gino's knuckles were always covered in calluses and the chaplain couldn't recognize anyone. Nevertheless, as they walked up and down the lines of enlisted men, I could see Gino, Frankie, and Wesley standing on the other side of the parade ground with the Security Platoon. I must say that I have never seen a more pious-looking trio of human beings in my whole life. If I hadn't known any better, I would have thought they were about to be ordained by the Pope himself.

After I had been with Special Services for awhile, I learned how dangerous it could be living in a cushy barracks. One evening, I had spent several hours at the club reminiscing about the bush to whoever was bored enough to listen. When I returned to the barracks, it was quite late and everyone was sound asleep. So I stripped down to my underwear and went straight to bed. Then around three o'clock in the morning, I was suddenly awakened by the shrieking sound of a salvo of 122mm rockets roaring directly over our compound. In a drunken stupor, I instantly rolled to my left onto the cement floor and propelled myself under my bed.

At that very instant, a stream of electricity from an exposed fan wire went through me like a bolt of lightning. As I was screaming above the sounds of the exploding rockets, the current from the electricity began bouncing my body between the springs of the bed and the hard floor like a basketball. It was so powerful that I could feel the current rush down my spine and into my toes. I must have flopped around for several excruciating seconds before I was finally able to separate myself from the hot wire. Quickly jumping to my feet, I looked through the shadows in embarrassment to see if any of the other fellows had been watching my circus act. Incredibly though, everybody in the barracks was still asleep. They were snoring away as if they were dead to the world.

It must have been some time in the latter part of March, when the young brash colonel and the master sergeant rotated back home. I couldn't have been happier. In fact, I even helped them load their gear into the jeep and patted them on their backs with a fond farewell. Due to the fact that both of them had gone out of their way to make my life as miserable as possible, I was looking forward to a change of command. I figured the odds were extremely slim that I would have to endure the likes of them again.

Chapter Fourteen

In-A-Gadda-Da-Vida

"The only war I ever approved of was the Trojan War.
It was fought over a woman and the men actually knew
what they were fighting for."
William L. Phelps (1933)

Our new commander was an older colonel named Woodson, who had worked his way up from the ranks. Stoic, distant, and hard as nails, he was a no-nonsense type of officer, but I had no complaints. He was a fair man who just wanted to get the job done and go back home to his ailing wife. The new top sergeant was a master sergeant named Venables. Always the consummate bureaucrat, he eventually gained my respect and admiration. As a young boy of seventeen, he had joined the Corps in order to go fight the Japanese during World War II. After serving with the 1st Marines at Guadalcanal, he was wounded at Bougainville. With a little over twenty-eight years in the Corps, he had seen it all. There was no way anyone could feed him a line without a big smile forming across his tight lips. He would just stand there and nod his head for awhile, until he had heard enough. Then he would gently put his arm on your shoulder and say, "Son, if you are going to try to bullshit somebody, you need to show at least a little sincerity. For heaven sakes, lad, didn't your mother teach you anything?"

Up to this point, I had always worked in the warehouse, while the other guys either worked in their own air-conditioned shops or went fishing. However, Master Sergeant Venables had a couple of surprises for me. First, he informed me that I had been promoted to the rank of corporal, which was a pleasant surprise. In a span of fourteen months, I had gone from being a private to a full-blown NCO. Then he told me that I would be temporarily assigned to mess duty. The only problem I had with this assignment was that I would be working from six in the evening to six in the morning for thirty days straight. This not only meant that I wouldn't to be able to see Wesley and Gino for awhile, but also, I wasn't going to be able to show off my new stripes down at the warehouse.

If I had known that mess duty was going to be an ordeal unto itself, I would have gone into hiding. To this day, I still get sick to my stomach whenever I smell the sickening aroma of fried bologna and onions. Every evening like clockwork, I would show up to work with an overweight lance corporal named Eddy and we would begin to make three hundred god-forsaken sandwiches for the various units in the area. As one of us would lay out three hundred slices of bread on a huge counter and cover each slice with a glob of greasy butter, the other guy would pull out a twenty-five-pound loaf of frozen bologna from the freezer and begin cutting it with a machine into thick slabs. Once everything was ready, we would place a frozen slab of bologna on each slice of buttered bread and then cover it with a slice of old, green-looking cheese. Then after covering the pile with another piece of bread, we would individually wrap the sandwiches in cellophane and stuff them into a brown paper bag for delivery. On a good night, it could take us anywhere from three to four hours to prepare the sandwiches, depending upon how hung-over we were.

Immediately after making the sandwiches, the two of us were expected to help prepare the midnight meal (mid-rats), which consisted of one serving of meat and potatoes along with two vegetables and a roll. The idea was to provide a decent meal for the guys in the compound working the night shift. Then afterward, Eddy and I were expected to wash the dishes and clean up the dining area from top to bottom. Normally, we were able to finish this task just in time to help begin to prepare the breakfast. Besides working my butt off for twelve hours straight, I quickly discovered that it was almost impossible to get any sleep during the day. The heat was stifling and the Vietnamese cleaning ladies that worked in the barracks were always keeping me awake with their constant jabbering. It didn't take long before Eddy and I were walking around completely exhausted.

A skinny white sergeant named Willard and an old Hawaiian pastry cook named Tu Tu supervised our shift. Because neither one of them had much of an education, it was difficult to have a conversation with them that didn't revolve around the art of slopping food onto a metal tray. Both of them were around forty years old and had been in the Corps for almost twenty years. Not being the most ambitious guys in the world, they were completely content spending their lives making spaghetti and hamburgers. However, they were both decent hard-working men without a chip on their shoulders, so we got along just great.

During the month of April, the enemy began pounding the airstrip on a regular basis. It seemed that every two or three nights, the rockets would come screaming over the mess hall towards the airstrip. Of course, the idea of getting blown away while I was in the middle of serving a midnight meal had very little appeal. So instead of just standing there and listening to the explosions, I ran through one of the mess hall doors and into the nearest bunker. Since Eddy didn't know what was going on, he figured it was a good idea to follow the guy with the longest time in country. Meanwhile, Willard and Tu Tu would just stand there at their post and watch us in amazement run through the mess hall like a couple of Olympic sprinters.

During one memorable attack, Eddy and I were in the middle of peeling potatoes when a rocket fell short of the airstrip and landed just a couple of hundred yards away from the mess hall. Caught by surprise, we began to run down a hallway towards the bakery where Tu Tu was working. As we turned into the bakery, I caught a glance of Tu Tu standing there with flour all over his apron. With an innocent look on his face, he pleaded with us, "Why are you boys running around like maniacs? There's nothing to be afraid of here." While totally ignoring his plea, Eddy and I ran up to the bakery's side entrance and grabbed the wooden two-by-four that was used to secure the door and flung it behind us without even looking where it went. Then after kicking the door wide open, we made our way to the nearest bunker as the rockets continued to hit the airstrip.

The attack must have lasted a good ten minutes before the all-clear signal was finally given. Brushing ourselves off, we slowly walked back to the bakery congratulating each other for another job well done. Then entering the doorway, we spotted an unconscious Tu Tu lying in the middle of the floor. Besides having a large dent across his forehead, there was a familiar-looking two-by-four lying across his flour-covered chest. Abruptly stopping at his up-turned feet, Eddy leaned towards me and muttered, "Jesus Christ, I think Tu Tu had a heart attack."

"Ah damn it to hell," I said to him, "He just doesn't know when to duck."

Shortly afterwards, Sergeant Willard sat us down and tried to explain the facts of life to us. He said if your number is up, there is nothing you can do about it. Therefore, it was kind of stupid for a person to drop everything and race out to the bunker every time a rocket came flying overhead. Then he reminded us of our responsibility to stay at our post under any circumstances in order to get the job done. He was very sincere in his efforts to assure us that a person just can't run away from his own fate, and that a Marine must face his fears and carry on with the mission at hand.

Eddy and I just sat there for awhile and listened to his impeccable logic. Of course, Eddy couldn't respond to him, because he was just a supply clerk on mess duty. But as I sat there and listened to Willard, I kept wondering if he or Tu Tu had ever seen what a 122mm rocket could do to a human body. And as for staying at our post, it wasn't as if our jobs were all that important. I mean, if we had been radiomen for an artillery unit or an FO looking for the rocket batteries, then that would have been a completely different story altogether.

At that point, I gazed up at Willard and asked, "Then what you're trying to tell us is that if a person's number is up, no matter what he is doing, nothing in the world can save him? And that we need to have a little faith in our leaders and in ourselves."

"That's about the size of it, fellows," Willard replied with a satisfied grin stretched on his face.

"Well Sarge," I said to him, "I know your intentions are good and that you mean well. But when my number is up, it's going to come up while I'm hauling ass towards the nearest bunker."

Then to my immediate left, I could hear Eddy's voice echoing through the mess hall, "roger that bubba."

Tragically only a few nights later, a 122mm rocket went through the roof of a small building that quartered the general's cooks. None of the four guys who were peacefully sleeping in their bunks at the time knew what hit them. Willard and Tu Tu had personally known all of them, so they took it very hard, especially after personally viewing their shattered remains. However, Eddy and I never heard any more nonsense about staying at our post during a rocket attack. From then on, the race was on as to who was going to beat Willard and Tu Tu to the bunkers.

On the morning of April 27, 1969, as I was lying in my bunk trying to get some sleep, a crackle of small-arms fire suddenly erupted in the distance. Exhausted from working all night, I didn't think anything about it, so I just stuffed my head deeper into my pillow. At the time, it sounded as if it was several miles away. But to my uneasiness, it didn't stop. It just kept crackling away.

Then about an hour later, Eddy ran into my barracks in a near panic and woke me up.

"Do you hear that? I think we're under attack," he yelled in excitement.

Rubbing the sleep from my eyes, I slowly raised myself from the bed and said, "No way, man, it sounds like it's on the other side of Freedom Hill. So why don't you go back to your barracks and try to get some sleep."

Strangely though, it didn't sound like a firefight. The discharges of the rounds were just too continuous and intense to be an infantry engagement.

Thus in an effort to ease Eddy's discomfort, I told him that it was probably some engineers setting off a load of old rounds and that there was nothing to worry about.

"Until it gets a helluva lot closer," I reassured him from under my bed sheet, "I ain't gettin' out of this frickin' bed."

Then suddenly, a shock wave from a massive explosion hit the barracks as if we were in the killing zone of an atomic bomb. It seemed like the whole room was lifted into the air. As Eddy and I were being hurled up towards the ceiling, every bunk bed and locker in the barracks began crashing into each other and into the walls. The only thing I remember hearing was the sound of shattering windows.

Amid the swirling dust and rubble, I looked around to see if Eddy was all right, but he was nowhere to be seen. Stunned, I yelled out his name as loudly as I could in desperation. Then I heard his voice from across the room, coming out from underneath a locker.

"Is that close enough for you?" he bellowed.

Leaping to my feet, I quickly put on my fatigues and began looking for my rifle and gear. Once I had found everything, I nervously
put on my helmet and flak jacket. Then just I was beginning to load
my rifle, another tremendous shock wave hit the barracks. This time,
it just moved the rubble from one end of the room to the other as it
shifted the building off of its foundation. Still not knowing what the
hell was going on, I instructed Eddy to go back to his unit and check
in with his sergeant.

"Back to the mess hall?" he asked.

"Hell no," I replied, "go back to your supply unit, the mess hall is
probably gone by now."

As we emerged from the wrecked barracks, I looked off into the
distance and saw the most amazing and frightening sight. Extending
up to a thousand feet in the air was a mushroom cloud from the last
explosion. Similar to an atom bomb detonation, the energy from
the blast was moving through a long, vertical stem and expanding
into a mushroom-like cloud. Suddenly, a cold chill ran through my
body and settled into my intestines. As far as I could tell, it looked
as if the Soviets or the Chinese had finally nuked us. While running
to the warehouse, I honestly thought that this was the beginning of
World War III.

When I finally reached the warehouse, everything was in a sham-
bles. The huge garage-like doors had been blown completely off of
their hinges and part of the roof was gone. The furniture inside the
offices, along with the supplies on the main floor, had all been lifted
up into the air and thrown in every direction. Since the building was
in danger of collapsing, our commander had ordered everyone outside
into the parking lot. It was there MSgt. Venables informed us that the
bomb dump on the other side of Freedom Hill had caught fire and that
what we were witnessing was the individual bunkers igniting into one
massive explosion. He also said the bunkers were filled with I Corps'
yearly supply of artillery rounds and aircraft bombs. Thus unless our

firemen were able to put out the fire, all of the reserve ammo in that part of Vietnam was going to go up in flames.

Then just as he was about to finish his pep talk, I looked over and saw the eruption from another explosion. All at once, a huge cloud began to swell high into the air as the shock wave from the explosion rippled towards us. After turning our backs and placing our fingers in our ears, we felt the shock wave suddenly roll over us like a wall of water. The impact was so forceful that it literally knocked us around like rag dolls. Among the dust, the smoke, and the debris-filled air, we could hardly breathe, much less talk. The explosions were sucking the oxygen right out of the atmosphere.

For the rest of the day, the explosions continued to erupt into the sky about every thirty minutes or so. At the time, we had no idea how many bunkers were in the ammo dump, but there must have been a lot of them. With each new explosion, we just stood there mesmerized and watched this rippling shock wave come towards us. Then at the last second, we would jump behind the warehouse and cover our ears. The terrific roar that accompanied each wave was truly deafening. I had never heard anything like it. Not even an arc light made that much noise. From what I understood afterward, our boys at Chu Lai could actually hear the explosions from over thirty miles away. Due to the obvious danger, the Da Nang airstrip had been temporarily closed down and everything around us was at a standstill. I kept thinking to myself that the enemy must have been having a big laugh over this one.

In between the explosions, we could see fire engine after fire engine racing down the road towards the ammo dump. I just couldn't imagine anyone facing those exploding bunkers with nothing but a water hose. Then just as I was about to say something to Venables, another huge explosion thundered high into the air and formed an enormous black cloud. But before I could move behind the warehouse again, a second bunker suddenly erupted into the black cloud. Filled with white phosphorus rounds, the combination of explosions helped create an unbelievable light show. As a black cloud from the first explosion was expanding into the heavens, the second explosion literally shot hundreds of illuminated phosphorus rounds through the dark cloud in every direction leaving a trail of white smoke in their wake. The scene was right out of a Jackson Pollock painting. Amid the awesome display of churning black gases, exploding colors, and spiraling arcs of white smoke, I was overwhelmed with a feeling of complete helplessness and wonder.

Since the devastation had been substantial, it was decided by our commander that everyone in Special Services was to be moved to the other side of the airstrip. Looking at each other, we became extremely excited about the prospects of getting away from the explosions and the general mayhem. Then amid all the confusion, the word was passed that our intelligence people were expecting a VC attack and that the Military Police had reported widespread looting.

Turning to Captain Hensen, Colonel Woodson suddenly ordered him and another captain to remain behind in the warehouse and protect our supplies, until it was safe for everyone to return. Glancing at each other in bewilderment, the captains turned and asked the colonel if a couple of enlisted men could stay behind with them in case there was any trouble. The colonel looked at the ground for a second and then said to them, "You can have one."

"Okay then, we'll take Short," they replied in unison.

I was already sitting in the bus and eagerly waiting to go with the rest of the fellows, when Venables stuck his head into the doorway and yelled for me to disembark. After slowly getting off the bus, he took me to one side and said, "The captains have selected you to stay behind with them to help guard the area tonight."

Sensing my disappointment, he said in a fatherly manner, "Apparently, you're the only one in this outfit that they can trust with a rifle. So while we're gone, I don't want you shooting up the place unless you have to."

Grinning from ear to ear, I replied to him, "No sweat, Top, we'll be here when you get back."

I must admit, it was a very proud moment. They could have chosen anybody, but they wanted me. Up to that point, I hadn't gained much respect from the other guys in the unit, because I was an outsider. Many of them regarded me as just a dumb grunt with little or no skills. But after the captains had personally selected me to stay behind and help defend our area, the other fellows began to treat me as one of their own.

That night, I doubt if any of us got any sleep. The bomb dump continued to periodically explode, while one of us had to constantly stand watch outside the warehouse. However, I did get a chance to get to know the captains on a personal level. Like me, they were both in the middle of their second tours of duty and questioning the sanity of the war. Because they had been trained as pilots, neither of them knew a heck of a lot about using a rifle. So I went out of my way to show them how to properly aim and use the weapon in the dark. Then I showed them a few other tricks about using one's ears in the darkness and staying in the shadows. It didn't take long before they realized that they had selected the right fellow. For a short period of time, it felt as if I was back in the bush and I must admit that I loved every minute of it.

That was the strangest part about my second tour of duty in Vietnam. Almost every day, I would look off into the distant mountains and yearn to return to the bush. Whether it was from survivor's guilt or a need to be with my fellow grunts, I had no idea. But as long as our troops were still in the field fighting and dying, I felt that I was betraying them in some way. In spite of the fact that I knew the war was a lost cause and that we probably never had a chance of winning it anyway, something in the countryside kept calling out to me. Much like a beautiful temptress, I could hear her seductive voice echoing in the wind and through the palm trees. On more than one occasion,

I entertained the thought of re-upping for another tour in the bush. With my experience and rank, I figured that I could make a positive contribution as a squad leader. But whenever I shared such thoughts with Gino and Wesley, they just burst out laughing and accused me of having a death wish.

By the next day, over 40,000 tons of explosives had gone up in smoke. I never did hear how many people were either killed or wounded by the calamity or how it actually happened. The official line was that a grass fire had ignited the bunkers, which I found hard to believe. It had been a common practice for our engineers to remove the grass and anything else that might burn from around a new ammo site. Thus I figured the enemy probably put a rocket into one of the bunkers or some bald-headed guy named Curly had screwed up in the dark and lit a match as he was looking for his buddies, Larry and Moe. However, I do remember one report stating that over seventy individual explosions occurred during a thirty-six hour period. Now, this figure I did believe. I hadn't seen that many explosions since I was at Khe Sanh.

Nevertheless, there was one good thing that did occur during all of the commotion. When we returned to the mess hall, much of it had been reduced to a pile of rubble. Therefore Eddy and I were relieved of our duties and told to report to our original units.

In the surreal ceremony that followed, I warmly grasped Willard's hand and apologized to Tu Tu for almost killing him with a two-by-four. Then I turned around, shook Eddy's hand, and tried to kiss him on the cheek like a French officer. Overwhelmed with a sense of insincere camaraderie and down-right relief, I began to make a speech about how proud we should be about our accomplishments.

"Considering the remarkable standards we had achieved in the mess hall," I said with mock satisfaction, "the bologna industry back home might have gone completely under."

Of course, I wasn't the only one whose life was about to change because of the bomb dump accident. Everyone in the compound was greatly distressed the day we exchanged our goodbyes at the mess hall. In fact, when I had heard the terrible news, I was almost overcome with grief and sense of personal loss. Not knowing what the future might hold, I didn't know where to turn or how to cope. Many of us just stood around the barracks deep in our own bewildered thoughts. We had lost an old friend and much of the meaning that life had to offer. For some, the sun's majestic rays would never rise again over the compound. Totally devastated, we just couldn't believe that a large section of the Enlisted Men's Club had been blown somewhere out into the South China Sea.

After returning to the warehouse, I began to look for another job. All the good jobs had been taken before I had joined the unit, so it didn't look too promising. But I was determined not to be the only guy in Special Services who actually worked for a living.

Then one fine day in early May, a fellow in the warehouse named Pope went on R&R and left his responsibilities to me. Previously, I had noticed that for two or three days out of the week, he would spend his time in the air-conditioned film room located in the back of the warehouse. One of his many duties was to repair and then schedule the 16mm movies shown throughout the Da Nang area. Then once they had been repaired, he was supposed to make sure that they were sent to the correct units for viewing. During all this time, he was also responsible for maintaining and checking out a variety of film projectors to anybody who wanted to see the newest movies from Hollywood.

I wasn't consciously aware that I was trying to steal the guy's job. But I must have had something in mind, because when the opportunity arose, I went into the film room and began organizing it into a full-time occupation. Besides regularly repairing the films, I began keeping a log of the films' condition and their suitability for viewing. Then I began making a monthly schedule of where the films would be shown and at what time. Later, I would begin to personally drive the repaired films to their next destination, instead of dropping them off in the base mail. In this manner, the other units stopped complaining to our commander about any late or non-arriving movies.

In order to maintain the projectors, I spent my spare time studying the repair manual. Thus in no time at all, I began to repair them whenever the need arose. I also created a simple manual for the operators, so that they would quit tearing up the films and destroying the projectors. Then along with taking charge of the film room itself, I also took it upon myself to pick up and deliver the weekly *Star & Stripes* newspaper.

Needless to say, when Pope returned from his R&R, he was somewhat irritated about losing his job. Venables was so impressed with my ability to organize the area that he made me the official Special Services' "Film Coordinator and *Stars & Stripes* Manager," a pretty heady title for a kid with a ninth-grade education.

It took awhile, but a bunch of us finally got together and helped the engineers rebuild the club. Sadly though, we weren't able to completely repair the roof. So Wesley, Gino, and I would spend our evenings sitting in the club and drinking our beer while we looked up at the stars. It was during one of these muggy evenings that we were introduced to a couple of new fellows assigned to the Security Platoon. Both of them were corporals and had been together since they had met each other at boot camp. Stationed at the Marine Barracks in Washington, D.C. for the last three years, they had been part of an elite unit called "Eighth" and "I." Composed of several companies of Marines, it was their unit's responsibility to stand guard over the president and his family at Camp David, to ensure the security of the U.S. Naval Academy at Annapolis, and to guard the home of the Marine Corps' commandant.

Everybody called these two guys Mutt and Jeff, because they were as thick as thieves. As a twosome, they did everything together. In fact, their wives had also become best of friends and adoring neighbors back in the States. None of this made an impression on me, because I had seen a lot of close friendships in Vietnam. However, what I couldn't understand was how these two guys ended up in the Air Wing together. They had been trained as infantrymen, so somebody back in Washington must have pulled a few strings in order to keep them out of the bush. But I must say that as spit and polish Marines, they had few equals. When it came to passing inspections, doing the manual of arms, or cleaning a rifle, Wesley said, they were the best.

Yet there was something about Mutt and Jeff that didn't seem right. They didn't talk, walk, or act like any grunts I had ever known. They could quote the Marine Corps field manual word for word, but they didn't seem to understand that the manual didn't apply in Vietnam. They had been so busy performing honor guards and endless ceremonies back in Washington that they had never known what the real Corps was all about.

Of course, Gino wouldn't have anything to do with them. He thought they were a couple of candy store jarheads. I'll never forget what Gino said to me after I had been introduced to them that night. "Greg, I bet you a dollar that they'll end up doing something really stupid."

I just turned to him in amazement and said, "That's crazy, these guys have had almost four years of training. They are probably the most highly trained guys in the Marine Corps."

"Well then," Gino responded, "Is it a bet?"

"You're on buddy," I said to him with supreme confidence.

May 19, 1969, started out for me much like any other day in Vietnam. I got up from my civilian-like bed to shower and shave, before the barracks mama-sans arrived to clean up the joint. Overall, I was expecting a very long day of having to drive all over the Da Nang area, passing out films and transporting recreation supplies to the different American units. But I was also expecting a very long and trying night as well. Being Ho Chi Minh's birthday, it didn't take a genius to figure out that the enemy was going to hit the airstrip and the surrounding compounds as their way of celebrating the event. It had become a Vietnamese tradition in honoring the father of their revolution. Although our intelligence officer had passed the word that there was a 90 percent chance of enemy activity that night, he wasn't telling me anything that I didn't already know.

So as I left the barracks that morning, I made sure that our little bunker was in good shape. I stashed several beers and some canned food under the sandbags so that we would have some refreshments and a snack during the upcoming light show. I also placed my helmet and flak jacket in there, so that they would be readily available. During the rocket or mortar attacks, it was always a pain in the ass to try to find my gear in the dark, when everyone was running around the barracks half-naked and screaming at each other. A large number of the rear area guys just never got the hang of the art of avoiding incoming in both style and comfort.

In my own way, I also wanted to celebrate Ho Chi Minh's birthday. So I decided to go have a few beers with Wesley and Gino. Not surprisingly, they also had spent the previous May 19 on their bellies, dodging a hell of a lot of bullets. Thus in a strange way, they also wanted to celebrate it, too.

And sure enough, they were waiting there for me with a big surprise.

It seemed that someone had scheduled a Filipino band to play at our club. So when I finally arrived, Wesley and Gino already had taken possession of a table right in front of the bandstand. It wasn't the first time that we had been treated with a musical performance. But that night was special to all three of us. We kept laughing to each other about what kind of well-meaning fool back in headquarters would schedule an entertainment event on the evening of a major attack.

Looking back, I guess things started going haywire when the band showed up late. By that time, the place had been packed with wall to wall people for about two solid hours as we waited for them to arrive.

Since the air-conditioning unit was never replaced after the bomb dump explosions back in April, everyone was extremely hot, irritated, and somewhat intoxicated.

It was during these types of events that Wesley, Gino, and I had developed a very bad habit. Instead of getting up very thirty minutes or so, and fighting the crowd in order to go to the restroom, we would just lean forward at the table and piss into an empty beer can. Then once we had finished the dirty deed, we would gently place it underneath the table. Since everyone was sitting almost elbow to elbow and intently watching the band's performance, nobody around us ever noticed. Of course, this would have thoroughly outraged the likes of Emily Post or Helen Gurley Brown, but as infantrymen, we had been taught to adapt and improvise in any given situation. And by golly, we didn't want to miss any of the show, fighting our way back and forth to the crowded john.

Oddly enough, this particular band was really good. They had a young kid as a lead singer who sounded just like Ray Charles. In fact, when I closed my eyes, I couldn't tell the difference. While he was singing, "I've Got a Woman," "Georgia on My Mind," or "I Can't Stop Loving you," the whole place rocked with screaming enthusiasm.

In between guzzling down the ten-cent beers and listening to this incredible music, a bunch of fellows suddenly jumped up and began dancing with each other in the aisles. In one quick motion, several of the bouncers attempted to break them up, when suddenly, a big fight broke out between them. Just like in the old western movies, most people started running for the doors, including the band, as about twenty guys were slugging it out on the beer-stained floor. Tables were being knocked over, chairs were flying through the air, and people were yelling bloody murder at each other, as Gino, Wesley, and I just apathetically sat at our table, too drunk to even move.

Amusingly, when our table was finally knocked over in the scuffle, there must have been over forty beer cans full of urine, neatly stacked together in one big pile.

Then right in the middle of all this commotion, one of the bouncers named Hinton was having a great time beating up the drunken kids. Being an older sergeant and a martial arts expert, he was infamous throughout our compound for having earned a Brown Belt in karate. Almost everyday, he could be seen practicing karate in a small gym with several of the officers. The rear area Marines were scared to death of him, because he definitely had a cruel streak about him. He was very abusive and physically intimidating to anyone who didn't out rank him. But Wesley, Gino, and I weren't all that impressed with the guy. Not being a ground-pounder, he was just another rear area commando to us who enjoyed mistreating the younger Marines.

While Hinton was in the middle of knocking around this defenseless kid, Gino unexpectedly yelled at him to lay off the kid. And what happened next was simply unbelievable. Suddenly, everyone in the club could hear a pin drop as Hinton slowly turned towards Gino and waved at him to get out of his chair.

Wesley and I immediately staggered to our feet and basically told Hinton, "We'll take a piece of that buddy."

Nudging us aside, Gino uttered, "I'll take care of this."

The surrounding crowd became silent in anticipation. Half of them wanted to see these two tough guys have it out, while the other half just wanted to see Hinton get what was finally coming to him.

As Gino put up his fists in the style of a boxer, Hinton began doing his Bruce Lee imitation by waving his arms around in the air and making these weird grunting sounds. It was kind of impressive, watching him contort his body into several different positions, while he thrust his fists outward and kicked his feet high up into the air.

Then while they began circling each other, several of the guys in the crowd started egging them on as the excitement mounted. At that moment, Wesley and I were eyeballing everybody in the club to make sure it was a fair fight. Then Gino quickly leaned in towards Hinton and threw a left jab. In an air of supreme confidence, Hinton easily blocked the punch as if he was swapping away a fly. However and unfortunately for him, he was completely unprepared for the right cross that followed. To his total surprise, Gino's fist had hit him so hard that it could be heard all across the crowded room. Poor Hinton must have slid about ten feet along the floor before his limp body finally crashed into about forty beer cans full of true-blue grunt piss.

As Hinton's buddies were in the process of waking him up, we made our way to the door, laughing and patting Gino on the back. We couldn't have walked but about fifty feet, when several 122mm rockets came soaring overhead and landed just outside our compound. In one huge flash, we hit the dirt as the sky suddenly lit up into an assortment of fiery colors. Struggling to our feet, we had no idea what could have made such a big explosion. Wesley thought that one of the rockets must have hit a fully loaded F-4 Phantom. But whatever it hit, it was definitely combustible.

Running to the southern side of perimeter to see if there had been any casualties from the blast, we came upon a most awesome sight. Located next to the airstrip were several huge petroleum tanks about the size of a two-story building. After being hit by a deadly rocket, one of them was engulfed in flames and discharging a funnel of black smoke high up into the air. Unable to help, we just stood there captivated by the sight.

Realizing that this was the beginning of a long night ahead of us, I went with Gino and Wesley to the Security Platoon's Headquarters to report for duty. The platoon lieutenant didn't know me from Adam, but he was glad to see me just the same. Right before we were hit by another rocket attack, he instructed us to go get our rifles and report to bunker number six, which overlooked the main road on the northern side of the perimeter.

Luckily, there wasn't any chance of a major ground attack swelling up from the surrounding suburbs and overrunning our compound. We were situated too far within the main perimeters of Da Nang for that to have occurred. So we took turns standing watch as the rockets and mortars periodically hit the airstrip. Off in the distance, the huge petroleum tank was still burning away as the military firemen were doing their best to put it out.

In an effort to uplift everyone's sagging morale, Colonel Woodson and MSgt. Venables had decided to throw the unit a little party. After bringing over a pile of steaks and lobsters from the general's mess, Venables opened the beer locker in the warehouse and began passing out several cases of Pabst Blue Ribbon. At this point, I really didn't appreciate their efforts. The colonel was an impersonal, reserved fellow, while Venables had a way of making a person feel comfortable, right before he sent him up the river without a paddle. Leery of Greeks bearing gifts, I figured that they were just showing us a good time, before they dropped the hammer. However, I was completely wrong. They were honestly trying to express their appreciation for our efforts. Most of the guys in Special Services didn't like them, but I came to admire their style.

After the party was over, Venables did something truly remarkable. He crammed about ten of us into a van and took us into Da Nang to visit an old French buddy of his. Of course, we had no idea as to what was in store for us. Many of the fellows thought he was probably taking us to some boring USO show. It had never dawned on any of them that he might actually have been young once himself.

To everyone's surprise, he drove us to a huge French mansion located in one of the suburbs. I didn't know houses like this even existed in Vietnam. Built like an old southern plantation house, it was two stories high with a large porch in the front that was supported by Doric styled columns. Surrounded by a picturesque garden and white fences, we walked up the steps to the mansion and were met by a very round and heavyset French fellow named Jacques. With a wide grin on his face, he introduced himself and then took us into a spacious living room, where there must have been at least twenty young ladies waiting for us. Completely stunned, everyone stood there for a second in complete silence. Then I noticed a real cutie was standing behind the bar giving me the eye. As I began to walk towards her, I suddenly spread my arms out as wide as I could and yelled out, "come to papa."

While Jacques and Venables sat around and talked to each other and drank their coffee, we were free to meet the ladies and then take them upstairs for a roll in the hay. Since there were twenty of them and only ten of us, a couple of the more ambitious fellows began taking two at a time. It was like a fellow walking into Eden, Valhalla, and Disney Land all rolled up into one. Several of the guys were so stunned, they just wandered around the room as if they were in some kind of a trance.

In all the excitement, I grabbed the cutie from behind the bar and we made our way up the stairs. In no time at all, we were unclothed and in a teenage embrace. Incredibly though, there must have been about three or four other couples in the room with us. Using separate beds, none of us acted self conscious, because the sensation was more like a bunch of young kids exploring each other than an intense sexual experience. Then after we were all finished, everybody began running around the room half-naked, slinging pillows at each other in one big pillow fight. We were all laughing and giggling as if there was no such thing as a war going on.

Comparable to a feeding frenzy of a school of fishes, several of the guys returned to the living room, picked out another young lady and then went back upstairs. As for myself, I sat down with Jacques and Venables and enjoyed the show. Meanwhile, an old-looking mama-san was sitting in a corner and marking down how many times a guy went upstairs with a lady. What many of them didn't realize until it was too late was that we were being charged five bucks a pop for every jaunt upstairs. Of course, Venables was nice enough to cover the cost for those who were dead broke, which they gladly repaid him on the very next payday.

The thing that I remember the most was the melody of this one particular song that Jacques kept playing on his cheap record player. For at least three hours straight, he played it over and over again, until it became embedded in my brain. To this day, whenever I hear, "In-A-Gadda-Da-Vida," by the Iron Butterfly, I instinctively reach for my wallet.

Then one hot night in June, Gino walked into the club and informed me that I owed him a dollar from the bet we had previously made concerning Mutt and Jeff. Thinking that they had probably been caught sleeping while on watch or that they had gotten lost on some patrol, I handed him a dollar bill and asked him what had happened.

Evidently, Mutt and Jeff had been playing around in the barracks after evening chow, when Mutt pointed a shotgun at Jeff in jest and threatened to blow his balls off. As they both stood there laughing at each other in their underwear, Jeff called his bluff and told him to go right ahead if he had the nerve. From what Gino said, the ensuing shotgun blast almost cut Jeff in half, when it had unexpectedly discharged in Mutt's hands.

All of a sudden, I felt completely drained and emotionally exhausted. Here we were in one of the most easygoing outfits in Southeast Asia and these two guys decided to play a game with a supposedly unloaded shotgun. I just sat in my chair in disbelief. How in the world could two highly trained individuals break the first rule in handling weapons? Even as a young kid back in Texas, I knew that there is no such thing as an unloaded gun.

That night, I kept wondering how Mutt was going to be able to live with himself. Something that tragic just doesn't evaporate from a person's psyche. Later, we were informed that the naval corpsmen had had to take Mutt to the hospital in a straitjacket. In his agony, all Mutt wanted to do was make amends for the tragedy by killing himself.

At this point of the war, I was beginning to have my first problems with depression. Besides the thought of losing the war, it seemed that every other week or so, somebody in the compound was getting needlessly killed. The longer I stayed in country, the stranger these deaths were becoming. One poor fellow was run over by a truck while he was jogging down the road and another guy was accidentally crushed to death by a forklift. Yet what got to me the most was this nagging feeling that I was wasting my time in Vietnam. I knew that there was a future out there for me somewhere. I just wasn't sure that I would be able to find it back home. The States had changed so much in my absence and I was so confused about my future goals that I really didn't have a burning desire to return.

By the middle of July, I had become an expert on repairing films and projectors and delivering the *Stars & Stripes*. On occasion, Captain Henson would use my dubious talents to help him drive the civilian bands around to the various clubs. Most of the time, it was a real bore. But then sometimes, I actually ran across some very attractive females. Besides having to drive the bus, I was also expected to protect the band, so I would take my rifle along for security reasons.

One evening after their fine performance, Captain Henson and I escorted a band back to their hotel in downtown Da Nang. The band consisted of four hot-looking Australian ladies from Sydney. When the captain wasn't looking, I asked each of them for their autographs and their room numbers in the hopes that one of them might be interested. To my surprise, one of them did actually slip me her room number with a sly wink. She was a blonde-haired temptress with beautiful blue eyes and golden colored skin. Consequently after dropping the captain off at the compound and promising him that I would behave myself, I turned the bus around and headed straight back to the hotel.

It must have been around four o'clock in the morning when I finally pulled up. Unfortunately by this time, I had become severely intoxicated from all of the beer I had drunk. I knew that I was at the right hotel, but I'll be damned if I could remember the lady's name or her room number. So without even thinking of the consequences, I began banging on the doors and yelling for Blondie with a hot beer in one hand and a loaded rifle in the other. The more that I thought about the warmth of this lady's arms wrapped around my semi-broad shoulders, the harder I kicked. Then after waking up a dozen people or so, one of them finally threatened to call the MPs. In no time at all, I jumped back into the bus and hauled ass back to the warehouse.

When I eventually pulled into the parking lot, everyone in my unit was standing in morning formation ready to go to work. Embarrassed, I comically stumbled out of the bus and staggered over to the front of the formation. The other guys started giggling as I half saluted the colonel and requested permission to go to sick bay. After being awake for the past twenty-four hours and drinking heavily for eight of those hours, I figured that I probably did look a little sick.

Yet what really started the guys laughing was when Venables came up to me and demanded to know if I was drunk.

Standing at attention, I replied in an offhand manner, "Yessir-re-Bob." Then he demanded to know if I had stolen the bus that night.

"Yesss sir, I think did," I replied, after trying to hold back a burp.

Then he asked me, if getting laid was worth all this?

"Well sir, it would have been," I said in discouraging disappointment, "if I could have found the gal."

It would be an understatement to say that Captain Henson and Master Sergeant Venables were not very pleased about my behavior. And I did feel terrible about letting them down. However, in my defense, I told them that I hadn't been with a real Caucasian woman since leaving the States, which was an exaggeration. And that by God, I just couldn't control myself after seeing all those beautiful white women with their pink nipples pointing towards the sky.

"Hell, Captain," I cried, "I was a victim of circumstance."

It was during times like these that I came to truly love the Marine Corps and the men who served in it. Instead of flipping out and assigning me to some shit detail for the rest of my life, Captain Henson and Venables had a chat with the colonel in his office. Amid the sounds of laughter behind the close door, I had a feeling that they were rather amused by the sight of me staggering off the bus and looking like a caveman. Realizing that I was just a grunt in a strange outfit and any form of punishment would have been a waste of time, they decided to take the novel approach.

After I was called into the colonel's office and I personally apologized to everyone, Venables informed me that the Security Platoon needed a man from Special Services for thirty days of temporary duty and that I had been elected.

When I walked into the Security Platoon's barracks, it was like a family reunion. Wesley and Gino introduced me to the rest of the fellows as they showed me the ropes. Most of the guys had been ex-grunts with a lot of bush time under their belts, so I felt right at home. For the rest of the afternoon, we laughed and lied to each other about our days in the field. We talked about how the difference between life and death was such a fragile thing, and about how we had survived the numerous close calls, only to be left alone with our dreaded memories. Bonded together by blood and fire, we didn't speak of the dead or of the wounded, but rather of the good times we had shared with our comrades-in-arms. Although none of us wanted to admit it; there was a deep sadness in our voices and a room full of regrets. Unfortunately, it was the last time that I would ever get a chance to visit with a bunch of real infantrymen.

I quickly discovered that serving with the Security Platoon was a piece of cake. After standing watch in a bunker for eight hours, I didn't have to return to work until the next day. Occasionally, I did go out on patrol with a squad into the surrounding suburbs, but I didn't view that as anything but a walk in the park. Normally, Gino, Wesley, and I would spend our time together either at the club, playing baseball, or leaping over the fence to visit the cat-houses. Before I even realized it, my thirty-day assignment was almost up and it was the early part of September.

One Saturday evening after coming back from watching a movie at the chapel the barracks was near empty, so I went straight to bed. About an hour later, the platoon sergeant woke me up and said that I was needed to stand watch at one of the bunkers. One of guys had become sick and the sergeant needed a replacement. Instead of arguing with the guy, I just told him, "no sweat." I didn't really mind, because I was looking forward to Sunday, which was always a special day at MWHG-1. In addition to the manager opening up the Enlisted Men's Club early for the guys to quench their thirst, the mess hall would lay out a nice spread. Instead of serving a regular meal, the cooks would prepare charcoal-broiled steaks, baked potatoes, and salad. Naturally, the steaks weren't of the best quality, but it was still a welcome meal.

After the platoon sergeant left, I got up from my bed and went to the restroom. Standing in the semi-darkness, I was just about to finish, when suddenly I heard several booming sounds off in the distance. As I dove onto the floor, three or four artillery rounds came roaring overhead and hit the airstrip. Strangely enough, those were artillery rounds. In fact, 122mm rockets did not make a booming sound when they were fired nor did they travel faster than the speed of sound. And as far as I knew, the NVA and the VC didn't have any artillery that far south. Jumping to my feet, I turned on the lights and began getting everybody up and out into the bunker. Most of the guys were very angry about being woken up and didn't understand the urgency of the situation. And to tell the truth, I didn't quite understand what was happening either.

Luckily, we were only hit by that one salvo. For the rest of the night and into the next day, I kept telling everyone that would listen that we had been hit by artillery. And if the enemy had artillery around Da Nang then we had better look out and begin digging some real bunkers. Of course, nobody believed me because none of them had ever experienced an artillery barrage. Even Wesley and Gino thought that I was nuts. But what did they know? They had never operated in the DMZ.

It was only a few days later when I finally realized what had happened. Since there was just no way the NVA could have moved and then supplied their artillery pieces that close to an American airstrip without being discovered, the rounds must have been fired from our own guns. Mistakes like that happened all the time in Vietnam. Whether it was a South Vietnamese battery or one of our own, coordinates get misunderstood, maps aren't properly read, and people get confused. I'm sure that when the battery commander discovered that one of his gun crews had fired a mission into our own airstrip, he must have crapped all over himself.

Up to this point, I was still considering re-upping for the bush. The rear area was an enjoyable place to serve one's country, but I never felt at home. There were just too many uptight officers and staff NCOs around with too little to do except give us noncoms a hard time. Then something happened that ended any thoughts that I may have harbored about signing up again. It was the type of thing that stays with a fellow for a long time.

A few days before I was to report back to the warehouse, I went on one last patrol. Led by a young sergeant, who had aspirations of becoming a young staff sergeant, the patrol was made up of seven guys. Gino and I were the only fellows in the squad who had any bush experience. The sergeant had made his stripes back in the States and the other guys were just cherries. Being short-timers, Gino and I covered each other's back and tried to keep everyone else out of trouble. Walking from hamlet to hamlet, I knew that there was very little chance of us running into the enemy. The area was within earshot of the Da Nang airstrip and had been under our control for years.

It must have been in the early afternoon, when we began to head back to the compound. Suddenly, as we turned a corner on a trail next to a group of hamlets, we came upon four other Marines. At least, I thought that they were Marines. Half dressed in civilian clothing, they were armed with an assortment of American and Chinese weapons. Suspicious, we stopped and confronted each other on this narrow trail.

As our young sergeant began questioning them, it became obvious to me that these guys were deserters and renegades of a sort. Completely perplexed by their presence, I had an uneasy feeling. They were armed to the teeth and pretty much telling our sergeant to go screw himself, after he had suggested that they follow us back to the compound. Gino and I kept looking at each other in apprehension as we tightly gripped our rifles. We had heard stories about Marine and U.S. Army renegades roaming the cities and countryside, but we didn't believe any of it. The idea of turning one's back on his own country and trying to exist among the Vietnamese was completely alien to us. In our minds, only a complete moron would attempt to play bandit in this crazy environment.

Once our sergeant realized that these guys weren't going to cooperate, he told them that everything was cool and that they could go their own way. Agreeing to his proposition, they slowly turned around and began moving back down the trail. Then without warning, the sergeant inexplicably pulled out his pistol and began shooting at them. In one quick motion, they turned around and started pumping lead at us. As the rest of the guys in our squad began running in every different direction, Gino and I instinctively hit the dirt and returned fire. Within seconds, it was all over except the screaming. While two of the deserters lay on the ground wounded, the other two had disappeared into the nearby hamlets.

Personally, I thought what the sergeant did was an extremely chick-en-shit thing to do and I told him so to his face. Those deserters would have eventually returned to their units just out of necessity. I didn't see any need to start a firefight over a bunch of guys playing cowboy. They may have been breaking the law, but we were all from the same country. Of course, the sergeant didn't hear a word I was saying to him. All he wanted was another stripe and he didn't care how he got it. Afterward, it began to dawn on me that if the Marine Corps expected me to shoot down other Americans while in the line of duty, it was time for me to go home and become a civilian again.

For the next few weeks, things settled down into a monotonous routine. Every morning I reported to work and repaired the films and projectors. Then during the evenings, I would hang out at the club with my friends. Many of the guys in Special Services were beginning to rotate back home, so there was a constant influx of new people into the unit. It was at this point that I began to notice a change in Colonel Woodson and Venables' behavior. All of a sudden, we were required to stand weekly inspections and sign in and out every day from our post. I'm sure they thought that we were in need of a little discipline. Yet I viewed it as another reason to move on. If they wanted to tighten the screws on the new guys, that was find with me, but I didn't want any part of it. If I was going to have to stand inspections, I might as well stand them back in the States.

When I flew home in late October of 1969, I had decided to get out of the Marine Corps when my enlistment was up and then go to college. I had developed a burning desire to further my education. There had to be some sane reason for our being in Vietnam and I was determined to find it. Everything our government had been telling us just didn't ring true any longer. In my confusion, I wanted to find a shred of purpose behind the whole tragic affair, so that I could find some semblance of emotional peace. After serving in Vietnam for nineteen months, I had lost all faith in my country's leadership and my fellow citizens who had blindly followed them. In essence, I wanted to become knowledgeable enough to know the difference between a legitimate reason for going to war and a contrived scan.

After flying into Love Field in Dallas, I was met by three happy faces. My mother was filled with joy, as my brother David and his wife, Chari, stood next to her. While I was away this second time around, David had grown his hair down to his shoulders and wore a long, ragged beard. He and Chari had obviously crossed the line into what would become quaintly known as America's counterculture.

It was a very awkward moment for all of us. As I was trying to reassure Mom that I was still in one piece, David and Chari kept running around the airport terminal freaking everybody out. Whenever they came across a colorful picture on the wall or a glittering light, they would rave about it as if it was the most beautiful thing in the world. Then they would suddenly turn to me and yell, "Now, that's far out." At the time, I didn't know how to react. Since they had both been in college the last couple of years, I figured they had attended one too many art classes.

As we drove up to David and Chari's house, I noticed about thirty of my friends and relatives standing out in the front yard waiting for us. Unknown to me, Mom had organized a welcome home party for me. To my surprise, I was sincerely moved and caught off-guard by the gesture. After I got out of the car, everybody came up and gave me a big hug. The lump in my throat was so big that I had a hard time just thanking them. For the rest of the evening, we had to actually reintroduce ourselves to each other, because everyone had changed so much. David was much more educated and mature than the last time I had seen him. And as for Mom, God love her, she looked a lot older and worn.

During the party, everybody had a great time listening to the music and enjoying the food. Mom and Chari had really gone out of their way to make it a memorable experience. They had even hired some fellow to play his guitar for us. Even though he looked like he was stoned to the gills, he had a wonderful voice and sang some great songs.

And yet, the funny thing about the whole experience was that I really wasn't there with them. Sure, I sat around and conversed with everybody as if everything was back to normal. And I even shared a few laughs with some of my old friends. But in a very real sense, I hadn't come home at all. And come to think of it, I probably never will. To this day, my heart and soul are still lurking in the jungles of Vietnam with the haunting spirits of the men and women that we laid to rest there.

Notes

CHAPTER TWO

1. James P. Coan, *Con Thien: The Hill of Angels* (Tuscaloosa: University of Alabama Press, 2004), 71–72.

2. Ibid., 86–87.

3. Ibid., 101–5.

4. Gary L. Telfer, Lane Rogers, and V. Keith Flaming, *U.S. Marines in Vietnam: Fighting the Vietnamese, 1967* (Washington, D.C.: History and Museums Division, Headquarters, U.S. Marine Corps, 1984), 96–100. http://www.marines.mil/news/publications/Documents/U.S.%20Marines%20in%20Vietnam%20Fighting%20the%20North%20Vietnamese%201967%20%20PCN%2019000309000_1.pdf

5. Keith Nolan, *Operation Buffalo* (Novato, CA: Presidio Press, 1991), 68.

6. Coan, 114.

7. Ibid., 129.

8. Ibid., 134–36.

9. Telfer, Rogers, and Flaming, 125–35.

10. Coan, 175–76.

11. Jack Shulimson, Leonard A. Blasiol, Charles R. Smith, and David A. Dawson, *U.S. Marines in Vietnam: The Defining Year, 1968* (Washington, D.C: History and Museums Division, Headquarters, U.S. Marine Corps, 1997), 126–27. http://www.marines.mil/news/publications/Documents/US%20Marines%20In%20Vietnam%20The%20Defining%20Year%201968%20%20PCN%2019000313800_1.pdf

CHAPTER THREE

1. Robert Pisor, *The End of the Line: The Siege of Khe Sanh* (New York: W. W. Norton & Co., 1982), 235.

CHAPTER FOUR

1. Pisor, 34–36.
2. Edward Murphy, *Semper Fi, Vietnam* (New York: Ballantine Books, 1997), 3–5.
3. Loren Baritz, *Backfire* (Baltimore: Johns Hopkins University Press, 1985), 165.
4. Pisor, 134.
5. Stanley Karnow, *Vietnam: A History* (New York: Penguin Books, 1997), 536–40.
6. Ibid., 549.
7. Coan, 307.
8. Baritz, 184–85.
9. Neil Sheehan, *A Bright Shining Lie* (New York: Vintage Books, 1988), 717–20.
10. Pisor, 117.
11. Samuel Zaffiri, *Hamburger Hill* (Novato, CA: Presidio Press, 1988), 271–72.

CHAPTER FIVE

1. Pisor, 50.

CHAPTER SIX

1. Edward F. Murphy. *The Hill Fights: The First Battle of Khe Sanh* (New York: Ballantine Books, 2003), 8–9.

2. Shulimson, Blasiol, Smith, and Dawson, 60.

3. Prados and Stubbe, 63; Murphy, *The Hill Fights*, 205–6.

4. Jack Shulimson, *U.S. Marines in Vietnam: the Expanding War, 1967* (Washington, D.C.: History and Museums Division, Headquarters, U.S. Marine Corps, 1982), 11–14. http://www.marines.mil/news/publications/Documents/US%20Marines%20in%20Vietnam%20An%20Expanding%20War%201966%20%20PCN%2019000308600_1.pdf

5. Murphy, *Semper Fi, Vietnam*, 93–95.

6. Pisor, 18–20.

7. Murphy, *The Hill Fights*, 246–52.

8. Ibid., 179.

9. Ibid., 230.

10. Karnow, 554.

11. Prados and Stubbe, 336–38.

12. Pisor, 226.

13. Ibid., 213.

14. Ibid., 218.

CHAPTER SEVEN

1. Shulimson, Blasiol, Smith, and Dawson, 318.

2. Ibid., 313–15.

CHAPTER EIGHT

1. Allen, 246–49. One of the biggest misconceptions of the war was the Pentagon's implementation and eventual obsession with a body count system that kept tabs on the number of enemy soldiers we had killed. Used by McNamara and Westmoreland as a measurement of our success on the battlefield, every U.S. unit was expected

to meticulously count the enemy's dead after each engagement. But in reality, all it revealed was the deepening level of our failure.

CHAPTER NINE

1. Shulimson, Blasiol, Smith, and Dawson, 378–80.

CHAPTER TEN

1. Baritz, 284–86.

CHAPTER TWELVE

1. Charles R. Smith, *U.S. Marines in Vietnam: High Mobility and Stand-Down, 1969* (Washington, D.C: History and Museums Division, Headquarters, U.S. Marine Corps, 1988), 27. http://www.marines.mil/news/publications/Documents/U.S.%20Marines%20in%20Vietnam%20High%20Mobility%20and%20Standown%201969_%20PCN%2019000310300_1.pdf

Glossary and Abbreviations

AO Aerial observer.

AK-47 Soviet designed, Chinese-built assault rifle.

Arc Light Concentrated B-52 strike.

Artillery 75mm U.S. made, sold to the Chinese and then used by the NVA.

Artillery 100mm Soviet, towed light gun.

Artillery 105mm U.S. towed gun.

Artillery 130mm Soviet, long range gun.

Artillery 152mm Soviet, towed gun.

Artillery 155mm U.S. towed, self-propelled gun.

Artillery 175mm U.S. long-range, self-propelled gun.

Artillery 8" U.S. heavy, self-propelled gun.

ARVN Army of the Republic of South Vietnam.

B-40 Rocket-propelled grenade, anti-armor weapon.

B-52 U.S. Strategic Bomber.

BAS Battalion Aid Station.

Blooper M-79, U.S. 40mm, grenade launcher.

Booby Traps Viet Cong handmade bombs.

Bush U.S. infantryman's term for the countryside.

C-123 U.S. cargo plane.

C-130 U.S. cargo plane.

CH-46 Marine troop-carrying and medium transport helicopter.

CH-53 Marine troop-carrying and heavy transport helicopter.

CDC Fire Direction Center for directing U.S mortar gun crews.

Chicom Chinese hand grenade.

Chinook U.S. Army transport helicopter.

Claymore U.S. anti-personnel mine.

CO Commanding Officer.

Cobra U.S. attack helicopter.

Cordon & Search Missions To surround a village and then search for the enemy.

Corpsman U.S. Navy medical personnel attached to the U.S. Marine Corps units.

DMZ Demilitarized Zone dividing North and South Vietnam.

Dy-bunker Huge bunker, which can house up to fifteen Marines.

E-Tool U.S. infantryman's portable shovel.

F-4 Phantom U.S. fighter jet used for ground support.

FO U.S. forward observer of either mortars or artillery.

Friendly Fire Friendly incoming fire.

Gook U.S. derogatory term for any Vietnamese.

Gunny USMC gunnery sergeant (E-7).

Grunt Slang for a U.S. infantryman.

H & I Harassing and interdiction fire.

HE High explosive rounds.

Huey U.S. light attack and transport helicopter.

Hump To carry full combat gear while on patrols or operations.

KIA Killed in action.

L-19-01 Bird Dog, U.S. observation aircraft.

LST Landing ship tank.

M3-A1 "Grease gun," U.S. 45 caliber submachine gun.

M-16 U.S. infantryman's rifle.

M-42 "Duster" Antipersonnel tank.

M-48 U.S. tank.

M-60 U.S. machine gun.

M-79 U.S. grenade launcher.

M-1939 Russian 37mm anti-aircraft gun.

MACV The U.S. Military Assistance Command in Vietnam.

MAG Marine Aircraft Group.

Medevac U.S. term for transporting casualties to a medical facility.

MIA Missing in action.

Mortar M2, 60mm Small size, U.S. high-projectile weapon.

Mortar M1, 81mm Medium size, U.S. high-projectile weapon.

Mortar Type 67, 82mm Chinese built, high-projectile weapon.

Mortar M30, 107mm (4.2 inch) Large size, U.S. high-projectile
weapon.

MOS Military Occupation Specialties.

Mule U.S. four-wheeled, small cargo vehicle.

Napalm Gelled gasoline.

Nation Building U.S. program to establish a democracy in third
world countries.

NCO Noncommissioned officer.

NLF Communists' National Liberation Movement in South Vietnam.

NVA North Vietnamese Army.

OP Observation post

Pacification Programs U.S. civil programs within the South Vietnamese villages.

Pistol U.S. 45 caliber hand gun.

PRC 25s & 77s U.S. field radios.

Puff gunship AC-47 mini-gun, armed aircraft.

Quad-fifty U.S. Army, four 50 caliber, anti-aircraft, machine guns.

R&R Rest and Relaxation.

Recoilless rifle U.S. 106mm anti-tank weapon.

Rocket 122mm Soviet, medium-range rocket.

RPG Soviet, rocket-propelled grenade.

Sappers Highly trained NVA engineers for breaching U.S. perimeters.

Search and Destroy Missions To actively seek out the enemy and destroy them.

Skipper USMC, company commander.

Starlight Light-gathering scope for night vision.

Stars & Stripes U.S. military newspaper.

III MAF Third Marine Amphibious Force.

Top USMC, First Sergeant (E-8).

Trace A bulldozed 600-meter strip from Con Thien to Gio Linh.

UH-34 Marine troop-carrying helicopter.

USA United States Army.

USAF United Sates Air Force.

USMC United States Marine Corps.

USN United Sates Navy.

VC Viet Cong, enemy civilian soldier.

WIA Wounded in action.

WP White phosphorus.

XO Executive officer.

Zippo M-67 U.S. flame-throwing tank.

Bibliography

Allen, George. *None So Blind: A Personal Account of the Intelligence Failure in Vietnam.* Chicago: Ivan R. Lee, 2001.

Baritz, Loren. *Backfire.* Baltimore: Johns Hopkins University Press, 1985.

Coan, James P. *Con Thien: The Hill of Angels.* Tuscaloosa: University of Alabama Press, 2004.

Collins, John, M. *OPLAN: The Military Geography for Professionls and the Public.* Washington D.C.: NDU Press, 1998.

Karnow, Stanley. *Vietnam: A History.* New York: Penguin Books, 1997.

Murphy, Edward. *The Hill Fights: The First Battle of Khe Sanh.* New York: Ballantine Books, 2003.

———. *Semper Fi, Vietnam.* New York: Ballantine Books, 1997.

Nolan, Keith. *Operation Buffalo.* Novato, CA: Presidio Press, 1991.

Pisor, Robert. *The End of the Line: The Siege of Khe Sanh.* New York: W. W. Norton & Co., 1982.

Prados, John. *The Blood Road: The Ho Chi Minh Trail and the Vietnam War.* New York: John Wiley & Sons, 1998.

———. "The Navy's Biggest Betrayal." *Naval History Magazine* 24, no. 3 (June 2010).

Prados, John, and Ray W. Stubbe. *Valley of Decision: The Siege of Khe Sanh.* New York: Dell Publishing, 1991.

Sheehan, Neil. *A Bright Shining Lie.* New York: Vintage Books, 1988.

Shulimson, Jack. *U.S. Marines in Vietnam: The Expanding War, 1967.* Washington, D.C: History and Museums Division, Headquarters, U.S. Marine Corps, 1982.

Shulimson, Jack, Leonard A. Blasiol, Charles R. Smith, and David A. Dawson. *U.S. Marines in Vietnam: The Defining Year, 1968.* Washington, D.C.: History and Museums Division, Headquarters, U.S. Marine Corps, 1997.

Smith, Charles, R. *U.S. Marines in Vietnam: High Mobility and Stand-Down, 1969.* Washington, D.C: History and Museums Division, Headquarters, U.S. Marine Corps, 1988.

Stanton, Shelby. *The Rise and Fall of an American Army.* Novato, CA: Presidio Press, 1985.

Telfer, Gary L., Lane Rogers, and V. Keith Flaming. *U.S. Marines in Vietnam: Fighting the Vietnamese, 1967.* Washington, D.C: History and Museums Division, Headquarters, U.S. Marine Corps, 1984.

Zaffiri, Samuel. *Hamburger Hill.* Novato, CA: Presidio Press, 1988.

Index